The Himmler Brothers

Katrin Himmler

The
Himmler Brothers

A German Family History

Translated by Michael Mitchell

MACMILLAN

First published 2007 by Macmillan
an imprint of Pan Macmillan Ltd
Pan Macmillan, 20 New Wharf Road, London N1 9RR
Basingstoke and Oxford
Associated companies throughout the world
www.panmacmillan.com

ISBN 978-0-230-52907-6

1 3 5 7 9 8 6 4 2

A CIP catalogue record for this book is available from
the British Library.

Typeset by SetSystems Ltd, Saffron Walden, Essex
Printed and bound in Great Britain by
Mackays of Chatham, Chatham, Kent

Visit www.panmacmillan.com to read more about all our books
and to buy them. You will also find features, author interviews and
news of any author events, and you can sign up for e-newsletters
so that you're always first to hear about our new releases.

For my son

Contents

'If we had been in their shoes, we might have done the same'

Tzvetan Todorov 'On Human Diversity'

Prologue: The Old Stories

When I was fifteen, one of my classmates suddenly asked during a history lesson whether I was related to *the* Himmler'. I managed to stammer a 'Yes'. There was a deathly hush in the classroom. Everyone was tense and on the alert. But the teacher lost her nerve and went on as if nothing had happened. She missed the opportunity of getting us to see what connection, if any, there still was between us, the new generation, and those 'old stories'.

It was a question I avoided myself for a long time. I knew about Heinrich Himmler, my great-uncle. I knew about the 'greatest murderer of the century', who was responsible for the extermination of the European Jews and the murder of millions of others. My parents had provided me with books about the Nazi period from an early age. Shaken and tearful, I had read about the failed uprising of the people in the Warsaw ghetto, about the experiences of refugees and the survival attempts of children who were kept in hiding. I identified with the victims, felt ashamed of my name and, in some inexplicable yet distressing way I often felt guilty. Later, when I studied political science, the German past was a key topic for me.

{1}

But at the same time I always shied away from looking at the history of my own family. The impetus to do so came only later, and more by chance. My father asked me to search the Federal Archives in Berlin for files about his father. Until then my grandfather, Ernst, whom I had never known, had for me been simply the younger brother of Heinrich Himmler, a technologist, an engineer, Chief Engineer of the Reich Broadcasting Company in Berlin – a fairly unpolitical person, from everything that was said. Until then there had been nothing about him to arouse my curiosity.

At my very first perusal of the material I made the unsettling discovery that most of the stories I'd heard about him at home did not correspond to what was contained in the thin files. From very early on, it appeared, Ernst Himmler had been a convinced Nazi who, in return for a helping hand in his career from his brother Heinrich, the Reichsführer SS, carried out dubious tasks for him. I also gradually discovered that Gebhard, the oldest of the three brothers, was an ambitious careerist and a convinced Nazi from the earliest days of the Party. In 1923 he had taken part in the Hitler, or Beer Hall, Putsch with his brother Heinrich; later he had made a successful career as head of department in the Reich Ministry of Education. I was forced to conclude that both brothers had willingly put their expertise in the service of a conviction they shared with Heinrich and other relatives, and with colleagues and neighbours.

This was also true of the brothers' parents. Before 1933 Gebhard Himmler senior, head of a secondary school, and his wife Anna had regarded their second son and his apparent lack of ambition with a certain scepticism and disapproval. Later, however, as their letters to Heinrich show, they became enthusiastic Nazis. They, too, enjoyed advantages and privileges that Heinrich was able to procure for them thanks to his position at the centre of power in the Third Reich.

In the years that followed I was mostly occupied with other things than my family history. At the same time I felt drawn to countries such as Poland and Israel, whose histories had such a close and disastrous connection with the history of Germany and also with that of my own family. Poland was not only the country where Heinrich Himmler had organized the Nazis' merciless campaign of extermination against the Jewish and Slav 'subhumans'. In 1939 his brother Gebhard had taken part, as a company commander, in the invasion of Poland, which long after the war he was still describing as a 'daredevil' adventure pursued 'at breakneck speed'. Gebhard's brother-in-law Richard Wendler had been the Governor of Cracow when the city's Jews were deported. And it was in the Warthegau, as the Germans called the part of Poland incorporated into the Reich in October 1939, that my grandmother and her children had lived after they had been evacuated from Berlin during the war, on an estate from which the Polish owners had previously been expelled. I kept coming across traces of my family. But the overwhelming guilt of Heinrich Himmler seems to have led his brothers' families largely to exonerate their own fathers, despite vague if persistent fears that their involvement might have been greater than they liked to think.

I shared those fears. But, unbelievable as it may sound, it was a full five years after I began my researches that I came across significant documents, certificates, letters and address books in my parents' house. I knew that, as far as possible, in the Himmler family every scrap of written material, from electricity bills to drafts of letters to official documents and photos, was kept, but until then I had never specifically asked or looked for them. Here was a folder in which my grandmother, whom I had known and admired, had kept a variety of things. The belated realization that even many years after 1945 she had still been part of a network of old Nazis who gave each other support, had been particularly painful for me.

When pursuing research into one's own family, it is difficult to overcome blind spots and no-go areas created by the closeness to one's subject. It remains a painful process, and one constantly jeopardized by fears of what one might lose.

It took me three years after I first found material about my grandfather in the files before I could accept that I was going to have to see this family history through to the end. In the meantime I had become the mother of a son who would have to bear the burden not only of my own family's legacy: his father comes from a Jewish family that was persecuted by the underlings of my great-uncle Heinrich and whose members to this day remain profoundly traumatized by the murder of many of their relatives. It became clear to me that I must give my child a family history that did not perpetuate the legends current in the family.

That this intention resulted in a book is due to the many who have contributed to it. I would like to thank them here.

It was my father who provided the first impulse to my

researches. It was Professor Wolff-Dieter Narr and the seminar group studying 'The Generation of the Grandchildren of Active National Socialists' at the Free University of Berlin who turned it into a concrete research project. I would also like to thank all the members of my family who have put documents at my disposal and endured my repeated interviews with patience.

My extensive researches have been supported by the employees of numerous institutions. I would particularly like to thank Herr Pickro of the Federal Archives in Koblenz, who was extremely helpful and always ready to make time for me. I was also assisted by many at the Federal Archives in Berlin-Lichterfelde, the archives of the Technical University in Munich, the Main State Archives in Düsseldorf, the Berlin regional archives and the Kontakte (Contacts) organization in Berlin.

I am particularly indebted to Michael Wildt of the Institute for Social Research in Hamburg. He was the first specialist historian to read the draft version of the manuscript. My work could not have continued without his encouragement, advice and practical assistance.

Heinz Höhne put material from his private archive at my disposal; Anne Prior was kind enough to provide me with information on the Dinslaken side of my family. Andreas Sander of the Stiftung Topographie des Terrors (Topography of Terror Foundation) helped me with important information, as did Peter Witte.

I would like to offer my special thanks to Ingke Brodersen, who not only found a publisher for my manuscript but edited it with a critical eye and accompanied it on its way. She was always there for me; to collaborate with her was in every way a piece of good fortune.

My husband helped me with countless discussions; from the very beginning he and my parents-in-law encouraged me to write this book. Friends listened patiently, discussed the project, read parts of the text and put me up on my travels.

Finally, I would like to thank my parents, who have supported me and helped me bear the burden through all these years. Without them this book would never have been written.

1

I never called him 'Grandfather':
The Telephone Call

Ernst Himmler had already been dead a long time when I was born. For my generation that is nothing unusual. Many husbands, fathers and grandfathers never came back from the war. The unusual thing about my grandfather is not his death, but the fact that he was the younger brother of the Reichsführer SS, Heinrich Himmler, who organized the systematic murder of millions during the Third Reich.

I had always known about this, even as a child. But I had never wondered about my unknown grandfather's personal and political attitude to his brother. That did not change until the telephone rang one morning in the spring of 1997. My father. Could I submit a request for him to the Federal Archives to see if they held any files on his father? They had been opened to the public, he told me, since the Americans had handed them over to the Germans. And I could get there more easily than he could.

Yes, it was easier for me to follow up such a request, as my parents lived a long way from Berlin. After reunification, the German Federal Archives took over the files held in the former Berlin Document Center and released most of the extensive holdings of personal material on Party officials, SS leaders and people guilty of Nazi crimes. But why did my father think there might be something on his father, Ernst Himmler, in those archives?

I requested sight of the files. At that time demand was still great and I had to wait months for an appointment. I was relieved at the delay; it gave me time to think about a man who until then had played no part in my life. Only once, as a child, had I asked my grandmother Paula, Ernst Himmler's wife, long since dead, about the rather stiff-looking young man in the black suit whose framed photograph hung on her living-room wall. I can well remember the tears that suddenly appeared in her eyes and the fright they gave me. I can no longer remember what she told me about him. She never mentioned him of her own accord, and I never asked her about him again. My father, too, had been sparing with information. 'He was an engineer with the Deutscher Rundfunk in Berlin and I suppose he was also in the Party,' was one of these vague pieces of information, which was always accompanied by the rider: 'But then they all were.' He presumed, he said, that his brother Heinrich had had to persuade him to join the Party, since 'Ernst didn't have much to do with politics.' And presumably, my father went on, he 'didn't want to spoil his career prospects'. Heinrich had probably got him the post with the Reich Radio. 'Heinrich always felt responsible for his younger brother. But the two didn't see each other very often.'

Up to this point such remarks about my grandfather had always sounded plausible. I had never questioned anything. There was nothing about him to arouse my curiosity, nothing I found disturbing. That changed only after my father's request to look for files on his father in the Federal Archives. I began to ask myself what I knew about my grandfather. Not very much – and fairly trivial stuff, at that. The kind of facts you might find laid out in tabular form in a CV: born Munich, 1905, grew up in a respectable middle-class family, radio engineer, from 1933 onwards employed by the Deutscher Rundfunk, around the same time married Paula, subsequently father of three daughters and one son – my father. The family lived in a semi-detached house with a garden in the Berlin suburb of Ruhleben. During the last years of the war Ernst Himmler was promoted to Chief Engineer and Deputy Technical Director; shortly before the end, he was called up into the *Volkssturm*, a German version of the Home Guard. He died at the beginning of May 1945, circumstances unknown.

I knew nothing about this man who was my grandfather: how he grew up, how he behaved towards his wife and children, what he was interested in apart from his work, what his attitude to the Nazis was – or to his brother Heinrich. Up to this point Ernst Himmler had seemed a thoroughly average, unexceptional person. The repeated insistence that the two brothers didn't have much contact with each other merely seemed to confirm the image of an engineer with little interest in politics. It suggested there was an ideological gap between the two, as did the assumption that Ernst had to be persuaded by his brother to overcome his reluctance or indifference and 'join in'. Had the younger sibling simply yielded to the authority of the older one, the man with political influence, but kept his distance from him politically? But what then had been Heinrich's motivation in supporting Ernst in his career? Did they really see each other as rarely as was claimed? And if so, why? Because Ernst was uninterested in what his brother was doing, or because Heinrich, head of the SS and later Minister of the Interior, was so completely taken up with the immense task of purging Germany and the neighbouring occupied countries of the 'enemies of the German people'? What had my grandfather Ernst and my grandmother Paula known about what Heinrich was doing? Perhaps his father had known something, my father always said, but definitely not his mother, who was 'politically very naive'.

I was starting to wonder both at the assurance with which he said this and at my lack of scepticism. Anyone who was as close to the head of the SS as my grandmother must have had to make great efforts not to know anything about the arrests of political dissidents, about the way the German Jews had been deprived of their rights and had 'disappeared' in the concentration camps.

I found it impossible to get the picture of Ernst into sharper focus. Suddenly I felt ashamed of my lack of knowledge, of my naive ignorance of my family history. Although I knew my grandfather had been close to Heinrich Himmler, I had always drawn a clear line separating 'Heinrich the Terrible' from 'Ernst the Unpolitical'. And this, I realized to my amazement, was despite the fact that I had studied National Socialism intensively for years and had a particular interest in the fluid boundaries between active Nazis, those who knew what was going on, those who profited from it and those who simply went along with it – but I had not applied it to my own family.

In June 1997 I was given an appointment at the

Federal Archives. I drove out to Lichterfelde, and even as I entered the huge grounds of the former barracks I had the feeling I was travelling back in time. The first thing you see through the fence is the old, shiny red-brick buildings from the time of Wilhelm II, built at the end of the nineteenth century for the Prussian Military Academy and used for that purpose until the First World War. By the entrance were a number of buildings from the Nazi period – grey, monumental monstrosities with colonnades and sculptures of athletic Nordic figures. During the Third Reich they housed Hitler's Bodyguard Regiment, the *Leibstandarte-SS Adolf Hitler* under its commander Sepp Dietrich, which, having taken a personal oath of loyalty to the Führer, saw itself as the 'elite within the elite'. After 1945 the compound was taken over by American troops, who replaced the buildings, which had largely been destroyed, with accommodation and administration blocks, known as the Andrews Barracks. Today the Federal Archives are housed in one of these buildings.

In the reading room I was handed a few thin files on Ernst Himmler together with a long list of references for further research. It was with mixed feelings that I took the documents. First of all there was the shock of finding that there was actually something on him, but there was curiosity as well; relief that the dossier was thin, but also fear of what it might contain.

In the personal folder there were just a few photocopied sheets: a Party membership card with a photograph, a curriculum vitae and a few official papers. I had a closer look at the membership card and saw the date he joined: 1 November 1931. Strange. Why 1931, more than a year before the Nazis assumed power? How did that fit in with the claim that Ernst had to be persuaded by Heinrich to join the Party? I read on, and discovered among the documents one that stated that he had become a member of the SS with effect from 1 June 1933. That was the day on which he had taken up his post with the Reich Radio. The SS? That had never been mentioned! The SS was Heinrich's organization, and the striking fact that Ernst's joining coincided with his starting work with the Broadcasting Company fitted in with my father's assumption that Heinrich had assisted Ernst in his career. I sat looking at the documents, which suddenly made the past seem more tangible. After all the speculation and muddled thoughts of the past few weeks, their matter-of-factness was a relief. I kept on looking at the photo, a plain passport photo in which Ernst looked so young and so correct. In that moment he seemed more alien to me than ever before. What concern of mine was this man who had already been dead for twenty-two years when I was born?

Among the papers I found a reference to a loan Ernst received in autumn 1937 for the purchase of the house in the Ruhleben district of Berlin, which he had bought together with a Dr Behrends. The loan came from the Personal Staff of the Reichsführer SS – his brother Heinrich. The papers also included a typewritten letter of May 1944 from Ernst to Heinrich which shows that there were clearly occasions when he could be of service to his more powerful brother. In this particular case he responded to the latter's request for an expert appraisal of the deputy managing director of a Berlin firm called C. Lorenz.

At the time both the occasion and the significance of this letter were unclear to me. But it made me uneasy.

Perhaps it was the language. While Ernst stuck to the sober style of an official report, his long-winded sentences were peppered with ideologically loaded expressions such as 'ideological standing' and 'the perspective of aryanization'. The letter demonstrated his evident overzealousness in carrying out a commission from Heinrich, but also seemed to express interests of his own which were unclear to me. Besides the appraisal, the letter mentioned a long conversation with Walter Schellenberg, the head of the foreign section of the Security Service (*Sicherheitsdienst*, SD). I had no idea what my grandfather, who was supposed to be interested only in technology and not in politics, could have had to discuss with the head of the foreign section of the SD, nor what Schellenberg could have had to do with the matter in hand. Perhaps Ernst just wanted to show off, to take advantage of the opportunity for a chat with such a major Nazi figure. The whole affair was a mystery to me.

I continued to work my way through the files. I came across various awards: the 'SA [*Sturmabteilung*] Sports Badge', the 'Olympic Badge of Honour', but also the 'Military Distinguished Service Cross, Second and First Class'. As a senior SS officer, Ernst was initially assigned to the SS Personnel Department, later to the staff of the head of telecommunications. The assignment seemed to be purely formal – I could find no indication that he had ever seen active service as an SS officer. His last promotion, to *Sturmbannführer* (major), came in 1939, ten days after the invasion of Poland. But why had he been awarded the Military Distinguished Service Cross? After all, he'd never been involved in front-line action.

From a statistical report on the Party of summer 1939,

I learnt that Ernst, though a Party member, hardly belonged to any of the numerous affiliated organizations of the Nazi Party (the NSDAP, the National Socialist German Workers' Party) apart from the German Labour Front, of which almost all 'producers of labour', from blue- and white-collar workers to their employers, were members, and the National Socialist People's Welfare Organization.

Everything, I was relieved to establish, seemed to point to the fact that Ernst had not been a particularly committed Nazi. No senior activity in the Party or in any of the affiliated professional associations, scarcely any record of special distinctions on his SS index card, and *Sturmbannführer* was not exactly a rank demonstrating great ambition in that feared organization. Obviously his main interest was in radio technology, perhaps in his own career, but politically he kept his distance. However, I was still not entirely convinced. There was the early date of his Party membership that I found disturbing; his conversation with Schellenberg; and the fact that during the war he was was declared 'indispensable', that is, unavailable to the Army. He was called up in 1942 – to the replacement battalion of the *Leibstandarte-SS Adolf Hitler*. He presumably never entered the Lichterfelde barracks, since he was not required for military service until shortly before the end of the war, because as 'senior manager and Chief Engineer with the Reich Broadcasting Company's Central Technical Section' he was 'indispensable and irreplaceable'. But it was not clear to me what tasks 'essential to the war effort' he was involved in.

Both my father and his only sister who was still alive were astonished at the early date of his Party membership.

When I asked my father what his mother had told him, he replied that her response to his questions had been silence and tears. Afterwards she had not spoken to him for days.

Why had my grandmother found it so difficult to talk about the past? Perhaps there was something to hide, as my father had suspected when he was young. But perhaps her silence was simply a defiant reaction to the lack of understanding shown by the younger generation. Compared with the hard life she had had after 1945 as a widow bringing up four children on her own, the Nazi period must have been, for her personally, the happiest days of her life.

My father and my aunt were grateful to me for my researches. However, after the second consignment of documents from the archives that I sent, my aunt declared that the important thing for her had been 'to see everything in black and white' but now we should 'leave it be'. I found it exasperating that neither of them had any questions to ask about all the incomprehensible hints in the documents. Even they had been able to form only a hazy picture of their father from the little – and that contradictory – they had been able to squeeze out of Paula, their mother. At best, with the regular repetition of the same stories, it had taken on firmer contours. Or did the two of them know more than I did?

Originally I had searched the archives only at the request of my father and with the approval of his sister. But what I found there had touched a chord in me and I was disappointed at the lack of response from the two of them. I wanted to talk to them about things that were unclear, pursue conjectures. It was not yet clear to me whether my curiosity was simply the thrill of the chase, aroused by the bare facts that concealed more than they revealed, or whether I was suddenly interested in this man who was my grandfather.

After my first discoveries I felt disorientated. In my imagination I played out all sorts of scenarios about what my grandfather might have done and thought between 1933 and 1945. I tormented myself with reproaches for my lack of interest over all the years. I was furious with my father, who avoided direct confrontation with the documents, leaving that to me instead – though he could have had no more idea than I did of how devastated I would be by what my researches threw up. I had obviously completely misjudged my detachment, my ability to remain unscathed by my grandparents' past. I battled with persistent health problems. I was struck by fits of panic about the future. I was stuck.

Then, in the autumn of 1997 I had the opportunity to have a long talk with my father about the things I had found in the archives. While he made it clear that he regarded the past as 'over and done with', he was prepared to talk, and patiently answered all my questions about his family. We spent a long day together, walking through small towns of half-timbered houses and climbing up into the vineyards in the mild October sun. As we looked down over the vines to the plain, I asked him for the first time what memories he himself had of his father and was astonished at his vehement reaction: 'What do you imagine I think of a father I can only remember punishing and beating me?!'

Paula, he said, had had a fairly liberal attitude to bringing up children, but she had still held their father up to them as a shining example – above all to him, the son, until there came a time when he 'just couldn't listen to that stuff any longer', especially as he was having increasing doubts about the spotless image of his father she was presenting. He knew from his two elder sisters that Ernst could also be a loving father, so he must have found it particularly distressing that his own sparse memories were so negative. My questions seemed to have stirred it all up again – contrary to his repeated assurance that 'all that' was no longer important to him. During our conversations I kept coming up against barriers I could neither see nor understand.

Almost casually, my father mentioned a chest containing family photographs I might have a look at. There must also be a folder with documents belonging to his mother, he went on, though he had no idea whether it would contain anything of interest. My curiosity aroused, I opened the green folder and quickly realized that here was a wealth of information complementing the bare facts of the documents in the archives. Among papers relating to my grandmother's housekeeping during her final years, I found a curriculum vitae for my grandfather from 1931, which for the first time provided information on the time before he started working for the Reich Radio. I found personal letters from Ernst, as well as various attestations regarding his employment with the Broadcasting Company, which my grandmother had obtained from former colleagues of her husband during the seventies. She had probably needed them to support her claim for a pension.

In September 1948 a chief engineer had declared, 'at the request of Frau Paula Himmler', that Ernst had been called up to the Volkssturm in April 1945 and 'had been detailed, along with a number of other members of the radio staff, to defend the broadcasting building in Charlottenburg [a district of Berlin] . . . I last saw Himmler on the evening of 30 April or 1 May in the courtyard of the building. Since I was taken prisoner by the Russians soon after that, I cannot say what happened to him later.'

I tried to imagine what it must have been like for technical staff, news readers and other employees to 'defend' the building where they worked against the advancing Red Army, all of them civilians with no military training or experience, men like my grandfather, who, at the last moment, when the war was already lost, were sent to the slaughter in the Volkssturm.

Less than a year later, in August 1949, Ernst Himmler was officially declared dead; the document attesting that was also in the folder. Years later, at some point during the seventies, Paula must have made a further request for a search to the missing-persons service of the Red Cross in Munich. It was not until October 1983, two years before her death, that the reply came that 'it is highly likely that Ernst Himmler fell in the course of the fighting in the Berlin area in April 1945'.

Despite this, my grandfather's death remained a mystery. A few years after the end of the war, according to my father, a man came to see them claiming he had been with Ernst 'right to the end' and had been there when he had bitten on a poison capsule. It was an end I found difficult to accept. I asked myself what the effect on my grandmother must have been to learn that her husband might have committed suicide, leaving her with four children to look after.

My grandmother's photograph chest was in a hopeless mess. I was familiar with most of the pictures, above all the early family portraits of my Himmler great-grandparents with their sons Gebhard, Heinrich and Ernst. My great-grandmother, who came from Munich, had been a pretty young woman and, later on, a picture-book granny with her kindly smile, white hair that was always slightly tousled and round spectacles on the end of her nose. My great-grandfather, head of a secondary school and bearing the title *Geheimrat* (privy councillor), looked similarly disciplined and dignified, whatever his age. They were both said to have had reservations about National Socialism. To their children, as the photos make clear, they were strict but loving parents. Even as a seven-year-old Gebhard, the eldest, has a self-assured, confident look. Ernst, the youngest, was obviously the spoilt baby of the family. It was only the pictures of Heinrich that had aroused a feeling of disgust in me every time I saw them, not only because I knew what had later become of this harmless-looking boy from a respectable family, but also simply because he was there, among all the others in the chest; they were my family, and he was an inescapable part of it.

However, after my first researches I started to see these photographs with a different eye. My grandparents' romantic wedding photos, which I used to admire so much, had lost their innocence. Only now did I notice the Party badge on Ernst's lapel. Heinrich, his best man, posed outside the registry office with the happy couple. He was wearing his SS uniform with its swastika armband, right hand on hip, chest thrown out and a smile on his face. As well as those, I found other pictures which had clearly been taken or cut out of albums. One of them showed my grandfather; beside him someone had been cut away, presumably by Paula.

My father was obviously genuinely surprised at the things I had found in his house. He had kept them after his mother's death but, he said, had never looked at them. At my expression of surprise and disbelief he said, somewhat brusquely, that I was well aware of his 'dislike of any kind of paperwork'. Several times it was on the tip of my tongue to ask him why, then, he had sent me to look in the Federal Archives. What had he expected my researches, which he had requested, to turn up? I never managed to bring myself to ask the question. Perhaps because by this time I had the feeling that there were two sides to it that were inseparable: the desire to find out and the fear of what might come to light.

2

A Perfectly Ordinary Family:
Gebhard, Anna and Their Sons

Many years ago my father recommended a book, which I only glanced through: Alfred Andersch's autobiographical story *The Father of a Murderer*. As a secondary pupil Andersch attended the Wittelsbacher Gymnasium in Munich of which Gebhard Himmler, the father of the three brothers, was headmaster. The story is about him. It takes place a few years before the beginning of the Third Reich, one day in May 1928 when Himmler senior made a surprise inspection of Franz Kien's (Andersch's) class, in order to test the pupils' knowledge of Greek, but above all to improve their discipline. 'I hope that one day each of you will have to serve in the armed forces,' he told the class. 'I hope the Reich will soon be strong enough again,' for in the Army, he warned a recalcitrant boy, 'they would certainly teach you the meaning of discipline'.

In the course of the lesson Franz remembers that the day he started secondary school his father had warned him about this man, about whom everything was so 'pale, smooth, unctuous, as immaculate as his white shirt'. 'Old Himmler' was dangerous, his father had said, 'Catholic to the core', and a careerist who aspired to belong 'to the

cream of Munich society'. Old Himmler, he had concluded, was a man to beware of.

It was a memorable lesson, in the course of which the
headmaster mercilessly made Franz Kien look a fool in
front of the whole class; Kien's inadequate knowledge of
Greek grammar was only the pretext. The head mocked
him as a lazy, petty-bourgeois failure. The end of the
lesson was also the end of the school career of Franz Kien
alias Alfred Andersch. Andersch was expelled from the
school.

When my father first read the book in 1980, he was
deeply disturbed by the character of his grandfather, who
appeared in Andersch's story as an autocrat proud of his
classical education, self-righteous and authoritarian, mili-
taristic and nationalistic. He immediately rang up his
cousin in Munich, the daughter of his grandfather's eldest
son Gebhard, who tried to reassure him. Andersch's
portrait, she said, 'had nothing to do with the truth' but
was a slander on their grandfather. She sent him an article
from the *Süddeutsche Zeitung* by a lawyer, one Dr Otto
Gritschneder, who had been a pupil at the same school
and who went to some lengths to make good the damage
to the reputation of Geheimrat Himmler. Many years
later I, too, was sent the article by Gebhard's daughter.
Her grandfather had certainly been strict, she told me,
but also kind. She herself had only known 'his most light-
hearted side'; when they went for walks he often used to
give her 'a sweetie'.

When it appeared in 1980, shortly after Andersch died,
the book set off a heated debate. It was above all former
pupils of the Wittelsbacher Gymnasium, some of them
classmates of Alfred Andersch, who argued in the letters

to the editor of the *Süddeutsche Zeitung* about what their
former headmaster had really been like. He was, according to some, 'an energetic person, highly cultured and
intelligent, who commanded respect', and who had been
'equally feared, revered and admired by teachers and
pupils alike'. To others he had been notorious for his
'overriding desire to get on in the world, one of those
types who crawl to those above them and take it out
on those below'. The tireless Dr Gritschneder sent off
another salvo in 2001: everything in the book was 'a pack
of lies', it was nothing but a 'piece of character assassination', 'a slander on the memory of people now dead'.

Twenty years after its publication I read this story
again and I was just as disturbed by it as my father had
been when he read it. But more deeply disturbing to me
than the rather unsympathetic characterization of the
school's headmaster is the question the author raises in
his afterword. There he points out that Heinrich Himmler, 'the greatest destroyer of human life that has ever
existed', did not 'grow up in the lumpen proletariat'
but 'in an old middle-class family, well educated in the
humanities'. And, despairing, he asks, 'Can the humanities not protect us from anything?' Some of Heinrich
Himmler's biographers make his father's strictness and
pedantry partly responsible for the son's later horrendous
career. Strictness, discipline, respectability – the Germans'
key secondary virtues – had, they claim, played an all-too-
important part in the upbringing of the three Himmler
sons.

In the old photos he looks stiff, dignified and imposing,
his wife beside him tiny and delicate. To her grandchildren she was 'darling Granny'. There are many photos

showing the two of them amid the solid, good-quality furnishings of a turn-of-the-century drawing-room, surrounded by numerous portrait photos of their forebears. They both look as if they have lived up to their expected roles: necessary paternal strictness on the one side, compensatory maternal kindness on the other. Naturally there are also photographs in which the family poses stiffly in the photographer's studio, just as there are other, carefree ones from the summer holidays in which it can be seen that parents and children are attached to each other. All in all, and taking the period and social background into account, the Himmlers seem to me to have been a perfectly ordinary family.

But who *was* Gebhard Himmler? How had he got to know his wife, Anna? What was the world from which the two of them came?

Joseph Gebhard Himmler, my great-grandfather, born in 1865 in Lindau on Lake Constance, had grown up in modest circumstances. His father, Johann Himmler, was a trained weaver, but had quickly sought his fortune as a soldier in the Royal Bavarian Regiment. There, however, he was not particularly remarkable for his devotion to duty, rather for his brawling and 'immoral behaviour with a low woman', which presumably meant that he went with prostitutes and made no attempt to conceal the fact. His trail vanishes for five years, until he reappears in Munich in 1844 as a member of the Royal Police Company. At that time he was living with, though not married to, a cottager called Katharina Schmid. In 1847 they had a son, Konrad, who later acquired the right to call himself Himmler. When Konrad was fifteen, his father abandoned the family and took up a position as a customs official in Lindau on Lake Constance where, a few months later, he married Agathe Kien, the daughter of an official from Bregenz and twenty-four years younger than her husband.

It was only many years later that the family's relationship to Konrad Himmler came out. The discovery was triggered by the fever of genealogical research that Heinrich Himmler had made obligatory for the SS. Heinrich was pleased at this unexpected addition to the family and furthered the career of Konrad Himmler's grandson Hans in the SS. In *The Theory and Practice of Hell: The German Concentration Camps and the System behind Them* Eugen Kogon, who was a prisoner in Buchenwald from 1939 to 1945, claims that Heinrich Himmler 'had his own nephew, who whilst drunk had artlessly tattled secrets, demoted and sentenced to death, a sentence from which he was paroled to the front as a parachutist. Young Himmler was subsequently again incarcerated for having made certain derogatory remarks and finally "liquidated" at the Dachau concentration camp as a homosexual.'

That it was so long before the Himmler family became aware of this unexpected relationship does not necessarily mean that Johann Himmler had kept his illegitimate son secret from his wife. He probably regarded his other son, Gebhard, as too young to be told of the existence of his half-brother. He had only just turned eight when his father died, at the age of sixty-three. His widow would have had other things to worry about than the past life of her late husband. His customs official's pension does not seem to have been that generous, and it was only with difficulty that his widow managed to provide for herself and her son. The harsh material circumstances in which he grew up were something my great-grandfather never forgot.

As a good pupil who was without means because he had lost his father, Gebhard received financial support at primary school, and a scholarship allowed him to attend the classical Gymnasium in Neuburg an der Donau as a boarder at the Royal Seminary there. Gebhard was such an outstanding pupil that he was proposed for a scholarship to the Maximilianeum in Munich, a highly regarded educational foundation that covered all its students' expenses. In return, they had to sit regular rigorous examinations to prove they were progressing in their studies. In October 1884, at the age of nineteen, Gebhard enrolled at the Royal Bavarian Maximilian University in Munich.

He registered for philosophy. At the time, along with theology, it was the preferred subject area for less well-off students because it was the one in which the most scholarships were on offer. Gebhard's main focus was on the Classics – Greek and Latin; he also took some unusual subsidiary courses such as 'Anthropology combined with the ethnography of primitive tribes'. He learnt shorthand as well, and used it throughout his life for making notes. He also gave his sons lessons in it; all three mastered the skill and used it as adults.

In his first semester there Gebhard became a member of the Apollo student fraternity, to which his son, Heinrich, was later also to belong. Unlike the liberal *Burschenschaften* of the early nineteenth century, the German student fraternities of the imperial years were decidedly conservative and nationalistic. The most exclusive ones were the duelling fraternities, the so-called *Corps*, in which mainly rich young men disported themselves. Here, contacts were established that would be useful for a student's later career, and lifelong friendships formed, but above all the fraternities saw their task as rounding out the university's scientific and professional training by moulding the character. This included submission to the authoritarian hierarchical structure of the fraternity ('You serve voluntarily in order to be able to rule in future'), the obligation to keep pace at the official drinking sessions, and the formal duels with swords, in which the *Corps* student had to show not only courage and self-discipline, but also that he was able and prepared to give satisfaction and defend his 'honour' against insults. Given his extreme short-sightedness, my great-grandfather must have found the unflinching resolution the latter demanded difficult. In 1885 he was declared permanently unfit for military service because of this defect. How must he have felt later on, then, when many men from the same conservative nationalist background were rushing to enlist at the start of the First World War?

Despite this, Gebhard seems to have been well liked in those circles. In an obituary of December 1936 we read that the late member of the fraternity had been 'a pillar supporting the fine edifice that once was the Apollo fraternity'. For him membership was above all an opportunity to get on socially. And that was very important to him. While a student he was already working as a private tutor, sometimes for several families at once. One of his employers was Geheimrat von Bacyen; another, Freiherr (Baron) von Bassus-Sanderdorf. Another student to whom he was giving private tuition in Latin and Greek in 1887 was Ernst Fischer, the son of a professor at the Polytechnic who was later to be a fellow member of the Apollo fraternity and my grandfather's godfather.

Despite his many activities, Gebhard gained his degree in Classics with distinction, in August 1888, at the same time also being awarded his first teacher training certificate. In the autumn of that year he went to St Petersburg, where, from November 1888 to Easter 1890, he was tutor to the two sons, Albrecht and Ferdinand, of the honorary consul Freiherr von Lamezan. This is not entirely surprising, given his previous employment as private tutor by upper-class families. And yet I am astonished that he went so far away from home, though at the time there were many Germans living in St Petersburg: scientists, doctors, pharmacists, merchants and craftsmen who had been recruited as foreign specialists since the founding of the city by the Czar. St Petersburg was intended as a 'window on Europe' for the Russian Empire, through which Peter the Great hoped to catch up with developments in the West. The German community there had its own schools, newspapers, theatres and clubs; culturally and economically the nineteenth century was the heyday of the German diaspora there. This made it extremely attractive to potential immigrants from the German Empire. Decades later even Heinrich Himmler was toying with the idea of emigrating to Russia.

After Germany's defeat of France in the Franco-Prussian War of 1870–1, relations between Germany and Russia rapidly cooled, despite all the efforts made by Bismarck, who tried to cement the friendship with Russia for strategic reasons. During the second half of the century Germany had become a booming economic power and the German middle classes were making ever louder demands for equivalent status in the political order of things. The increasingly charged nationalist mood also had colonial goals in its sights, and was already flirting with the idea of new *Lebensraum* in the east. In 1888 Wilhelm II became emperor. He was not much taken with Bismarck's 'diplomacy with a sense of proportion', instead regarding imperialist expansion as an absolute necessity for Germany if it was to hold its own in the concert of world powers.

It was in this tense climate that my grandfather took up his post as tutor in the house of the German consul in St Petersburg. His key consideration was probably that he saw the position as a great opportunity for social advancement. A position with an honorary consul would not only bring good references – an employer such as Freiherr von Lamezan would also offer an ambitious young man from a modest background excellent opportunities to meet important people from the upper middle classes and the nobility. Lamezan was a friend of the Bavarian prince regent, Luitpold, and through him my great-grandfather made contact with the Bavarian royal family, the Wittelsbachs – a connection that was to remain important to him for the rest of his life. Gebhard Himmler must have made an impression on the Lamezan family; as late as 1936 a friend of the family recalled in a provincial Bavarian newspaper how much he was respected as a teacher by Lamezan's two sons. Among other things, his task in St Petersburg had been 'as a German tutor to implant German character and German culture more firmly in the hearts of his charges'.

When Gebhard returned to Munich at Easter 1890 he

took up an appointment as assistant teacher at the Lud-wigsgymnasium. But he wanted to get on. Three years later – doubtless because of his excellent references, but presumably also through Lamezan's contacts with the royal family – he became, in addition, tutor to Prince Heinrich von Wittelsbach, a post he filled for four years. The father of Gebhard's pupil was Prince Arnulf, the third son of Prince Regent Luitpold. His appointment to a permanent post as teacher at the Wilhelmsgymna-sium, after he had finished his term as private tutor, was probably largely due to the influence of his royal employer.

By this time Gebhard was thirty-two, his personal situation was secure, and so he took the next step: in that same year he married Anna Maria Heyder, who was one year younger than him and came from a family of wealthy merchants. Her father's first wife had been a widow, eighteen years his senior, who had left him a considerable fortune. Like Gebhard, Anna had lost her father when she was eight.

At the time of the marriage my great-grandmother Anna was already thirty-one, well on the way to becom-ing what in those days was considered an 'old maid' and well over the ideal marrying age. Since his appointment at the Wilhelmsgymnasium Gebhard was well situated financially and had good connections and the prospect of advancement both professionally and socially. For her part, Anna Heyder brought 300,000 gold marks to the marriage.

They were married on 22 July 1897 in the Catholic church of St Anna in the centre of Munich. The wedding breakfast was held in the Silver Room of the elegant Café

Luitpold in Briennerstrasse – a street where Heinrich Himmler later lived as a student and later still set up the SS's own prison, where political opponents of the Nazi regime were interrogated. Members of the Bavarian royal family were invited to the wedding breakfast, and the menu – in French, following the custom of the German aristocracy at the time – was a reflection of the meals Gebhard had become familiar with during his years as private tutor to a prince, with a multitude of courses and wines.

At first the young couple lived in Anna's apartment in the central district of Munich, 13 Sternstrasse, but soon moved to a larger apartment in the same area, 6 Hilde-gardstrasse. Two months later, on 29 July 1898, their son Gebhard Ludwig was born (his second name was a mark of respect to the Bavarian crown prince). Their second son, Heinrich Luitpold, was born two years later, on 7 October 1900. Both of his names came from princes, and Prince Heinrich was his godfather.

On 17 June 1901 Gebhard Himmler was invited to an 'Absolutorial Dinner': the prince had passed his school-leaving examination, which at the time was called the *Absolutorium*. It must have been a memorable occasion for my great-grandfather – a banquet with eight courses of choice dishes and wines; the dessert was a *charlotte à la Prince Henri*; he kept the invitation his whole life long, together with a short newspaper report of the event. The relationship between Gebhard Himmler and Prince Hein-rich was cordial. The teacher addressed his many letters to his former pupil 'Dearest Prince Heinrich', while the prince, who often replied in shorthand and took a keen interest in all matters concerning the Himmler family, would sign off with 'Yours with sincere affection, Heinrich'.

Sometimes members of the Bavarian royal family visited the Himmlers during their summer holidays in the mountains, and every year they came at Christmas. 'A traditional part of our Christmas,' Gebhard junior wrote later in his 'Reminiscences', was a visit from Prince Arnulf's wife and her son, Prince Heinrich von Bayern. On those days they had to be 'especially well behaved', even though the two royals 'never brought the least little present' for them.

That these princely visits involved a certain amount of expense, but were also of great importance for Gebhard senior, can be seen from a piece of paper dated April 1914, on which he noted down the details of one such meal: a traditional Sunday lunch with all the trimmings, including wine, coffee, liqueurs and cigars. The next day he proudly cut out reports from two local newspapers which announced that on Sunday 26 April the prince and his mother had 'travelled by automobile from Altötting to Landsberg', where they had visited 'the prince's former tutor, the deputy head of the Gymnasium', and taken lunch in his house. The prince died young, but his mother continued to visit the Himmlers. Gebhard's eldest daughter once told me with a laugh of her encounter with the princess: 'I was *so* disappointed. A doddery old lady, dressed all in black, covered in wrinkles – and that was supposed to be the princess?!'

In the summer of 1902 the family moved to Passau, where Gebhard had been appointed 'professor' (a title for senior secondary school teachers) at the Gymnasium. They were happy there – there were friends and relatives living in the town. Six months later, however, young Heinrich fell dangerously ill – even in Munich his health had been delicate. The two doctors treating him, a Passau doctor and their family doctor from Munich who was also consulted, could not agree whether it was tuberculosis or recurrent pneumonia; both, though, urgently advised a permanent change of air. Consequently, in the spring of 1904 the family returned to Munich, taking an apartment at 68 Amalienstrasse. Heinrich recovered, though for the rest of his life he had a weak constitution and was prone to illness, which was a constant worry for his mother, who as a child had lost her father through typhoid and her brother through diphtheria.

Gebhard junior started school after their return to Munich, in September 1904. At first he too fell ill so often and had so many days' absence that his parents spent the summer holidays after his first year at school nursing him back to health and teaching him themselves; by the time the second year started, he had caught up with the rest of the class.

Anna Himmler became pregnant once more and on 23 December 1905 their youngest son, Ernst Hermann, my grandfather, was born in Munich. A late addition to the family, five and seven years younger than his brothers, he was the spoilt darling, the 'little ray of sunshine' of his parents, who were both over forty when he was born.

The apartment in Amalienstrasse was very spacious. The children had a bright, pleasant nursery with wooden Anker construction sets, a clockwork railway and a steam engine. In the guest room at the back, looking out on to the courtyard, Gebhard, the eldest, spent many hours at fretwork and other handicrafts. Next to it, the nanny, Thilde, had another small room, with a splendid zinc bathtub, at that time a rarity in Munich households. While Gebhard's main interest was in the steam engine and the technical constructions such as the suspension railways he built himself, 'Heini', as he was called by family and close friends, showed from his earliest years a definite preference for tin soldiers. His greatest pleasure on Sunday afternoons was to assemble the wooden castle on the expanding table in the living-room as the setting for a great battle with Gebhard. They had toy cannons they could load with caps and rubber shells or peas.

At the front of the apartment was their father's study with its heavy oak furniture in the neo-Gothic style and the steadily growing library. At Christmas it was transformed for the children into the mysterious 'Christ-child room', where the presents were spread out on the sofa. Until the children were finally allowed in, they would spend a lot of time on their swing in the hall, swinging up high to get a forbidden glimpse through the little window over the locked door.

In one corner of the drawing-room, which was furnished in red velvet and brocade and where visitors were received, stood a gilded baroque easel with a portrait of the young Prince Heinrich. Here, too, the photos and relics of the family forebears were kept, to which, in the course of time, were added presents and souvenirs from relatives and close friends. Gebhard Himmler senior collected stamps, coins and documents relating to German history; everything was meticulously catalogued on index cards.

The family would spend the evenings together, their mother occupied with sewing, their father reading from one of the books in his extensive library. These seem often to have been works on German history; at least, his sons knew the names and dates of all important historical battles by the age of ten.

3

'Bring up the Children to be German-minded':
Childhood in the German Empire

Every morning the two elder brothers set off for the Cathedral School, accompanied by their father, whose Gymnasium was next door to it. Gebhard Himmler senior used these morning walks to talk to his sons. Their education was important to him and Gebhard and Heinrich were good pupils. It was only in sport that Heinrich had problems, for which he tried to compensate by showing particular keenness. Year in, year out, their father meticulously recorded their marks and made notes on their teachers, their classmates and their classmates' fathers. On the basis of the latters' professions he decided which of their fellow pupils it would be appropriate or advantageous for his sons to associate with.

After school the two brothers played together and cooked up various pranks, for which they were 'liberally rewarded' by their parents, as Gebhard ironically described the punishments meted out, which will have included regular doses of corporal punishment. Ernst, the baby of the family, who was still under the watchful eye of his mother, the nanny and the housekeeper, could not, as Gebhard recalled, really join in their games.

Gebhard and Heinrich were allowed to go by themselves to a nearby shop selling handicraft materials and model-railway parts, where they were regular visitors and occasional customers. On the way there, at the corner of Amalienstrasse and Theresienstrasse, as Gebhard was to recall in his 'Reminiscences', 'we sometimes looked in through the windows of Café Stefanie, called "Café Megalomania" because of the artists from the Schwabing district who went there, and watched the chess players making their moves with earnest expressions on their faces, often with a glass of water before them and a toothpick between their teeth'. A few years later both brothers had mastered the game and Gebhard, like the artists he admired as a child, was to display musical and artistic talents too. And yet the Schwabing bohemians and the two boys from a sheltered background who watched them through the window with such fascination were worlds apart. The café was the meeting place of the city's intellectual set whom Gebhard, a few years later, during the anarchic weeks of the so-called November Revolution, was to see as a criminal 'clique of scribblers' from whom Munich had the good fortune to be 'liberated' by Heinrich and other members of the *Freikorps* (right-wing paramilitary units).

Every summer the family spent their holidays in the mountains south of Munich. In 1910 they were in the village of Lenggries on the edge of the Alps. The parents took the children on many excursions: to marvel at the tightrope-walkers in the village square, for example, or to visit a wood-pulp factory. The two elder sons would often walk with their father to somewhere close by, while their mother and Ernst followed by train. As the youngest, he could not keep up with the others and their mother was not much of a walker.

It must have been a glorious summer; by the time they left on 2 September, Heinrich noted in his diary that they had gone swimming forty times. It was during those weeks that the nine-year-old learnt to keep a diary. It would certainly not have been his own idea – he would have been required to do so by his father, who wrote the first entry to show his son how a proper diary was to be kept. For years Heinrich recorded everything to do with the family: the weather, meals, excursions, piano lessons, swimming trips. His entries are prosaic, matter-of-fact, without any of a child's imaginative touches. Nor were these desired, for his father checked the diary regularly, occasionally inserting additions or corrections, mostly relating to the proper way to recount experiences, often the exact form of people's titles. His father also censured his son's poor handwriting, though this clearly made little impression on Heinrich, as he continued to write in the same slovenly manner. This suggests that, initially at least, writing up his diary was a tedious duty rather than the matter of course it later became.

From the third week of the holidays onwards, Heinrich had a daily quota of schoolwork to get through, since the entrance examination for the Gymnasium was imminent. It was an important juncture in his life and he was to be well prepared for it, especially since his father would not be there for the beginning of the new school year. At the end of these holidays Gebhard Himmler senior would be travelling to Greece, 'the only long voyage he ever made', his eldest granddaughter recalled. And he made thorough preparations – in case he did not return alive.

He had arranged everything months before his departure; three weeks before he left he wrote long letters of farewell to every member of the family, larded with all kinds of instructions for their future lives. In the letter to his wife he explained the financial safeguards in the case of his death, told her which were the friends to turn to for advice on various matters, reflected on the way a smaller household might be managed, laid down the amounts by which the servants' wages were to rise, went into detail about what was to be done with his books, letters and notebooks, and stipulated who would be acceptable as sponsors for the children at confirmation.

His letter to Gebhard, who at the time was twelve, testifies to their affectionate relationship, to his respect for his son: 'You have brought me much joy, my dear Gebhard, and I thank you most warmly for that.' This, however, is immediately followed by exhortations and instructions to his eldest son. If his father were not to return, Gebhard was to anticipate his mother's 'every wish, gladden her heart with his *industry*, *devotion to duty*, *moral purity* [underlining in the original. K.H.], and, as eldest, quickly become a support to her, esp. in the upbringing of your brothers'. But above all: 'Become a hardworking, religious and *German*-minded man.' What can he have meant by that?

Unfortunately, the farewell letter to Heinrich has not been preserved; the one to four-and-a-half-year-old Ernst has, however:

My sweet, darling Ernstimändi,
My heart breaks at the mere thought that I might
never cuddle you again, never look into your sweet,

{ 39 }

*dark little peepers again, and I've already had a quiet
cry; my eyes are all red from the tears. With your
sunny smile you are and always have been Mummy
and Daddy's little ray of sunshine.*

But despite the affectionate start, even the youngest was
not spared his father's instructions:

*You must be nice and obedient and always love
Mummy and your brothers and do everything your
teachers tell you, so that they will like you and you
will bring good marks home, like your brother Beda
[Gebhard, K.H.]. And then when you grow up, you
can be a nice doctor or build ships, engines, houses or
some other fine things. Only don't become a
schoolteacher, like your father; there's no pleasing
anyone when you're a schoolteacher. But even when
you're a big, strong man you must still love your little
Mummy and look after her with your brothers and be
a joy to her as long as she lives.*

Industry, devotion to duty, pure morals and obedience:
these were the supreme ideals of Professor Himmler. He
seems to have regarded his wife as so weak and helpless
('your little Mummy') that he made it his sons' duty to
support her, even though they were still children. This
responsibility for their mother, which he imposed on his
sons, was something he displayed towards his own
mother to a limited degree only. In his farewell letter to
his wife he suggests that they had done a lot for his
mother over the last few years; but the tension between
them had in the meantime become so great that Anna, he
emphasized, was 'under no circumstances' to take her

mother-in-law into her own house but, if necessary, to find a nursing home – 'the best' – for her.

He even had thoughts about his sons' possible university studies: from the very beginning they were 'to pursue their studies according to a well thought-out plan and aim at a doctorate'. He himself had not achieved a doctorate, and nor did his three sons later on. However, they were to be allowed to choose their own profession: 'They do not necessarily have to become state officials.' But the fierceness of the conflict within Gebhard senior between indulgence and strictness, between his liberal and his authoritarian side, can be seen in the fact that he was only prepared to let them choose for themselves within certain limitations: 'It will be better if they don't become Classical scholars or officers, and, I beg you, don't let them study theology,' he instructed his wife. In questions of religion my great-grandparents do not always seem to have seen eye to eye. Anna Himmler was a pious Catholic and the religious upbringing of their sons was her responsibility, but her husband clearly sometimes stepped in if he felt the piousness was going too far. In this letter, too, Gebhard reminded his wife, 'do not allow Christian influence too much scope'.

At the appropriate time, when they were older and more mature, they were to be 'gently told the facts of life' by the family doctor; and, finally, he asked his wife 'to seek to guide the choice for life they will make in love, but not to determine it. Make them aware of the ideal, but prevent them, in making this decision, from plunging materially into the depths of a life of hardship, which can stifle all initiative and out of which I had to pull myself.' Even though Gebhard Himmler always took great care not to spoil his children, he was even more concerned to spare them the bitter experience of material privation he had been through himself. A general education was important to him: 'Any sacrifice is worth making for a *good* and *all-round* education for the children.' For him this included, besides what they learnt at the classical Gymnasium, 'modern languages (pract. instruction), music, drawing, shorthand'; but also, that they should continue to have a 'small but select' circle of friends.

It must have been important for him to have his sons grow up to be 'German-minded men': 'As we have done so far, continue to bring up my d[ear]. children according to our way of thinking, strictly, but with love, with religion, but not to excess, to be really *German*-minded men.' The upbringing he gave them followed political ideals that all three sons were to take up later in life; Heinrich, the first to do so, took them to the most radical extreme. But despite all the strictness, relationships among the Himmlers were warm-hearted and affectionate. The older the children became, however, the greater the expectations and demands for discipline the parents attached to their affection. And the three brothers clearly made great efforts to satisfy them. All were outstanding pupils throughout their school careers, displaying that exemplary discipline their father, both as a teacher and later as a headmaster, demanded 'with kindly strictness' of his pupils.

On 31 August 1910, Gebhard Himmler set off light of heart after he had made dispositions for all eventualities.

In September Heinrich entered the Wilhelmsgymnasium in Munich, which his brother Gebhard was already attending. At times both were taught by a colleague of their father's called Hudezeck. Their friendship with him lasted for many years of mutual assistance: Heinrich helped Hudezeck in his later career and Hudezeck helped Gebhard junior during denazification proceedings after the war.

Ernst started school in September 1911. He was only five, but cheerful and self-assured. He learnt his lessons effortlessly and, like his brothers, was always one of the best in the class. The only problems he had, like Heinrich, were in sport, since he was very short-sighted and therefore somewhat uncoordinated physically.

Two years later his father was appointed deputy head at the Gymnasium in Landshut, north-east of Munich. After a long search, the family found a romantic old house with a garden which Gebhard junior still recalled enthusiastically many years later: 'For the first time we had a garden, a real delight for us boys.' Here, too, the two elder boys attended the school where their father taught, he took Gebhard for German and History. 'I very quickly got used to it – there were no problems, at most I had to do a little more than if there had been someone else at the teacher's desk.' The deputy headmaster's sons got no special treatment.

All in all these years were happy ones for the three brothers. Their parents made every effort to see that they had a sheltered but at the same time a stimulating childhood. They also took care to ensure their children were suitably prepared for their future professional and social positions, and this demanded not only an all-round education in the humanities, which was chiefly their father's responsibility, but also the secondary virtues that were so highly valued in those days. As in most respectable middle-class families of the time, particularly as his sons grew older, it seems to have been their father who assumed the strict role of disciplinarian, while their mother's sphere continued to be that of more emotional support. She was still providing it many years later, after her sons had left home, in the form of comforting letters and parcels of treats for which Heinrich especially had an insatiable appetite. She also tried to interest her sons in the hobby she herself had had as a girl, drying plants and flowers and arranging them in a collection. Heinrich, at least, responded with enthusiasm; even as a boy he had an extensive collection.

In July 1914 the family spent their holiday with some old friends, the Lindners, in Tittmoning, close to the Austrian border. As always, their holiday programme included walks, visits to churches and boat trips. Heinrich kept his holiday diary and the three boys played with the two daughters of the house: Heinrich's photograph album shows the five of them outside the holiday house, the boys in lederhosen. A few days after Gebhard's sixteenth birthday the summer idyll was rudely interrupted: on 1 August, Germany declared war on Russia's ally Serbia, then on France, forcing the Himmler family to break off their holiday. On the platform, while they waited for the train to Landshut, the boys amused themselves playing at soldiers, marching up and down and practising drill.

The outbreak of war came as no surprise; it had long been in the offing. Under Wilhelm II the German Empire had built up its armaments and the other European powers had followed suit. Everyone seemed to assume war was inevitable – many even looked forward to it. Thus in 1914 the entry into the war met with overwhelming assent, above all from the middle classes and intellectuals, who saw it as Germany's chance finally to win the place they deserved among the world powers. There were only a few who, like the leader of the German Social Democrats, August Bebel, realized that the approaching war would herald the 'twilight of the gods of the bourgeois world'.

But the initial enthusiasm gradually gave way to a rather apathetic determination to see it through. After the intoxicating speed of the early victories, the front soon became bogged down in attritional trench warfare, incurring heavy losses. Faced with these losses, as well as the shortages that were increasingly making themselves felt on the home front, the Empire attempted to combat the growing discontent with glossed-over reports from the battlefield, but also by applying permanent pressure on the people at home – for example, through action programmes in the name of national solidarity. Collections were constantly being held, and my maternal grandmother, born in 1901, vividly remembers her whole class committing themselves to knitting socks for the soldiers and preparing lint for dressings, which gave them blisters on the tips of their fingers. As the eldest of four children, at fifteen she had to contribute to providing for the family by giving private lessons, which at least put some bread on the table.

Initially Gebhard and Heinrich, although older than she was, were able to continue their normal lives. 'Almost every late afternoon we met up with our classmates to stroll round the old town. And our garden was ideal for us boys.' There the two elder brothers fought 'battles with rotten apples', which regularly led to scoldings for their dirty clothes. And they still enjoyed playing with their tin soldiers and guns and homemade ammunition. 'At the time,' Gebhard said, 'it was still a harmless game during which neither of us thought of the deadly seriousness of real warfare.' In Landshut, Gebhard later recalled, there was very little to remind them of the war apart from troop transports passing through the town, along with a 30cm Skoda mortar from Austria, a gun that aroused keen interest in the boys. Heinrich noted in his diary that his parents often went to the station with supplies for wounded soldiers. In contrast to others, they made no distinction between the German and the French wounded; for them, providing care was a natural human gesture. Otherwise the war had little impact on them, 'apart from the occasional person being called up'.

The brothers had to work hard at school, especially in the subjects their father taught them. After afternoon classes they had to stay in until five o'clock doing their homework, so that during the week there was little time left for their friends or leisure activities. Despite that, in his 'Reminiscences' Gebhard talks of enjoyable late after-noons spent skating on frozen flooded meadows in winter or, when they were given bicycles one summer, cycling in the environs of Landshut. As with all sporting activities, Gebhard found it easier than Heinrich, who often lost control of his bicycle and would jump off at the last moment, letting his bike crash into his brother's or a friend's.

Gebhard liked to go to concerts, or in the evenings he would play on the new organ in the local Church of the Dominicans; Heinrich and his friend Falk Zipperer often went to listen. He also became interested in watercolours, encouraged by a keen art teacher at school. Gebhard's first, impressive sketches of the old parts of Landshut date back to 1915. Heinrich, on the other hand, often went to church in the mornings, occupied himself with his stamp and coin collections, and met up with his friend Falk almost every day. The two of them dreamt of being able to take part in the war, the great adventure that was going on so far from their serene everyday lives: 'Most of all, Falk and I would like to join in the scrap.' Heinrich got annoyed at the lack of enthusiasm the people of Landshut showed for the war. He himself followed the news from the battlefields intently, wrote out pages of reports from the newspapers and rejoiced in his diary at the early victories. 'Now we're advancing magnificently. I am as delighted at these things as the French & especially the English will be annoyed.' In September 1914 he noted the rising number of Russian prisoners-of-war: 'The number of Russians captured in East Prussia is not 70,000 but 90,000 (they must breed like vermin).'

The image of Eastern Europe as filthy and primitive had arisen at the end of the nineteenth century as a reaction to the sight of poverty-stricken Jewish immigrants from the east fleeing the Czar's pogroms. Between 1881 and 1914 more than two million East European Jews left their homes for the west, most hoping to go to America. Many got no further than Germany. Influenced by the growing anti-Semitism of the time, people saw them as backward, destitute, dirty and alien. The war confirmed the image of Eastern Europe as 'filthy, in need of cleansing, expansionist, threatening, a region that could be and should be subjugated', as Sarah Jansen put it in her historical survey *Schädlinge. Geschichte eines*

wissenschaftlichen und politischen Konstrukts 1840–1920.
It was above all doctors and specialists in public health
who propagated this image on the home front, promoting
the idea of 'ethnic cleansing' in the occupied zones. From
1915 onwards a campaign of memoranda submitted to
the government by the Five Economic Associations put
forward the idea that regions to be annexed should be
taken over without their populations, which became a
matter of increasing public debate; the question of what
was to be done with the people there who were 'surplus
to requirements' was left open.

Perhaps the fourteen-year-old Heinrich had picked up
something of the debate on the supposed 'primitive
nature' of the Eastern European nations at school, in the
newspaper or even at home. At the time he made the
entry in his diary he could naturally not have suspected
that years later, in the next war started by Germany, it
would be he who, as Reichsführer SS and Reich Commissioner for the Occupied Eastern Territories, would try
to make the dream of the German colonization of the east
a most cruel reality. However, a few years after this diary
entry, while he was a student, he was already developing
the concept of a 'mission to the barbaric east' – initially
as a romantic idea of settling as a farmer in Eastern
Europe, which was 'uncultivated' and therefore simply
waiting for civilized conquerors.

4

'Just One Shell Hole after Another':
The Collapse of the Old World

While my maternal grandmother spent her summer holidays during the First World War gleaning ears of corn left in the fields to mill grain for soup and often, especially during the 'Turnip Winter' of 1916–17, 'was so hungry she couldn't get to sleep', the Himmlers continued to go away for the summer. And on 5 August 1915, as good patriotic Germans, they celebrated the capture of Warsaw with fireworks in Burghausen, not far from Tittmoning, where they had spent the previous summer.

But after the initial victorious battles, the German advance soon ground to a halt. Soldiers died in their thousands in the murderous trench warfare in Flanders and in the Ardennes. Germany urgently needed new reserves of young men ready to sacrifice themselves 'for the Fatherland'. Increasingly, schoolboys were not just brought in to help with the harvest and collections for the soldiers at the front, but were given premilitary training in preparation for active service. Since the 1890s there had been *Jugendwehren* (cadet corps), organized on strict military lines under the command of officers as sections of various patriotic and nationalist associations. Their

goal was to inculcate in the following generations 'obedience to father, mother, teachers and instructors', to turn
them into 'citizens loyal to the King, rejoicing in and
proud of their Fatherland' and, last but not least, to
encourage them to cultivate a 'warlike spirit'. Such
notions were widely accepted among the conservative
German middle classes.

From the beginning of 1915 Gebhard and Heinrich
too were members of the voluntary *Jugendwehr* of Landshut. There, along with other senior pupils, they received
training in the use of firearms and in close combat; took
part, under the direction of officers, in mini-exercises; and
paraded at the Gymnasium on the occasion of national
celebrations. However, as Heinrich noted in his diary, the
two of them quickly found the whole affair too much
'fun', not military enough.

What were these years like for my grandfather Ernst?
The family papers tell us little. From very early on, like
his eldest brother, he was interested in technical toys such
as railways and steam engines. At the beginning of the
war he was eight and a half, at the end almost thirteen.
After the summer holidays of 1915 he followed Gebhard
and Heinrich to the Gymnasium. He, too, was a model
pupil, whose behaviour and, even more, whose marks left
nothing to be desired. At this time, as Heinrich noted in
his diary, Ernst also started to learn to play the piano; he
was, however, as unmusical as his brother Heinrich.
Sometimes his brothers took him with them – for
instance, when they were invited to their friends the
Zipperers. Falk Zipperer, Heinrich's best friend, had a
younger sister whom Ernst enjoyed playing with, which
left the older boys in peace. He still could not join in their

more exciting activities, and even at the end of the war he was too young for the *Jugendwehr*. But presumably he dreamt as much of heroic deeds of arms as his brothers.

Sebastian Haffner, two years younger than my grandfather and from a similarly worthy middle-class, conservative family, has described how boys who were left at the 'home front' regarded war as a game 'in which, according to certain mysterious rules, the numbers of prisoners taken, miles advanced, fortifications seized and ships sunk, played almost the same role as goals in football and points in boxing'. This war, Haffner goes on, gave a whole generation of German schoolboys 'far more profound excitement and emotional satisfaction than anything peace could offer'. The experience, Haffner claims, was later to become one of the roots of Nazism – indeed, it was 'the underlying vision of Nazism', which had its origin 'in the experience of war – not by German soldiers at the front, but by German schoolboys at home'. It was from this generation that National Socialism was to recruit its keenest and most ambitious adherents.

On 29 July 1915, on his seventeenth birthday, Gebhard joined the *Landsturm*, the reserve army. He was tired of the mock heroics of military games and could hardly wait to take part in a real battle. Heinrich, though only fifteen, sighed enviously, 'Oh, if only I were that old too, I'd have been out there ages ago.'

The writer Carl Zuckmayer, who volunteered at the outbreak of the war, also shared this thirst for action that sent the young men of the time marching off enthusiastically to war. On the side of the railway vans taking the soldiers to the front was chalked the inscription, 'Free excursion to Paris!' For the young men it was not simply patriotic fervour, Zuckmayer says, but the sense of suddenly being grown up, of being taken seriously. At the same time, he claims, there was 'a kind of death wish, a mystical yearning for blood sacrifice', and not only among the Germans. They sang fervently of their longing to die on the field of battle, until they lost their taste for singing. For in the war, Zuckmayer goes on, they learnt 'the hardest thing, the immense boredom, the prosaic, unheroic nature of warfare, which includes horror, terror, dying'.

As a rule those at home heard little of this disillusionment. Officially there were no defeats. And men on leave or returning from the front mostly found it impossible to describe the real horror of war to those at home. In his novel *All Quiet on the Western Front*, probably the best-known description of the First World War, Erich Maria Remarque has his hero say, 'It would be dangerous for me to try and put it all into words, I'm worried that it might get out of hand and I couldn't control it any more. Where would we be if everybody knew exactly what was going on out there at the front?'

In 1916 Gebhard's age group became liable for conscription. At first it was announced that the whole year was to be called up, but then the call-up was deferred for those who, like Gebhard, were to be allowed to take their *Abitur* (the school-leaving examination that brought entry to university) first. After he had taken his oral, which had been brought forward to March 1917, he had the choice of going directly to the front or first completing officer training. For months Gebhard had been discussing this question with his brother and with friends, and certainly with his parents too. Finally he came to a decision: he wanted to train as a regular officer. At the beginning of May he was assigned as ensign, the usual rank for officer cadets, to the reserve battalion of the 16th Bavarian Infantry Regiment in Passau. The quarters allocated to his unit were already full, so the young soldiers were allowed to find lodgings in the town. Gebhard found accommodation with a former colleague of his father's, where he was very comfortably situated. Things only started to get tougher when he was sent on an officer cadet course at Grafenwöhr in north Bavaria in the summer, followed by a machine-gun course at Lechfeld Camp near Landsberg, about twenty miles (30 km) south of Augsburg. From there he sent keen and cheerful letters home.

Shortly afterwards Falk Zipperer volunteered and Heinrich started to get more and more restless. Entries in his diary reveal his great impatience finally to be able to 'prove himself' in battle. He longed to leave school early in order to train as an officer like Gebhard. His father called on all his contacts – including those with the royal family – in an effort to fulfil Heinrich's wish, even though his son's intention did not exactly fill him with enthusiasm. The war and the associated patriotic fever seem to have swept away his earlier misgivings about a military career for his sons, but he would have preferred Heinrich to finish school first.

Initially, all his father's efforts were in vain, but eventually, on 23 December 1917, Ernst's twelfth birthday, Heinrich received his call-up papers, and on 1 January – fired with enthusiasm, as he wrote to friends and relatives – he went to Regensburg for officer training. Unlike Gebhard, however, he did not enjoy the harsh drill and suffered greatly from homesickness. He wrote home almost daily and, despite the frequent replies, constantly moaned about the lack of letters from his parents, as for example: 'At last I've got something from you. I've been through agonies waiting for it.' His letters show how torn he was between making such complaints and the pride he felt at finally being a soldier. One letter in January he signed '*Miles* Heinrich', Latin for Heinrich the soldier, and gave detailed descriptions of military rituals. He regularly asked for provisions to be sent from home because of the poor food, and for other items to be sent or favours done, even though after the first month he was given passes that allowed him to go home almost every weekend. His mother tried to alleviate the rigours of military life with regular parcels of apfelstrudel ('truly excellent'). His assessments of the canteen food ('quite good, but overcooked and cold') and of the roast pork on offer in the beer garden ('excellent, though not so tender as yesterday') were as appreciative or critical as during normal times.

Soon, however, he grew accustomed to his new life and his letters became both more confident and less frequent. He now described his daily routine in great detail in order to make it clear to his parents that he 'really did not have a minute to spare' for writing letters, immediately assuring them, 'despite that, I like it here because it is an important military organization'.

On 9 April 1918, after an accelerated training course that had lasted just one year, Gebhard was posted to the western front. En route from Passau to Lorraine, his regiment stopped in Regensburg, where Heinrich fell over himself to find lodgings and food supplies for Gebhard's unit. Heinrich was a very talented organizer, but he also enjoyed giving presents to people close to him, doing favours and giving them practical help or support.

At first Gebhard's regiment was deployed in Lorraine, but then it spent a long time in the front line, at Château-Thierry, north-east of Paris. He recorded later in his 'Reminiscences':

> They were very eventful [sic!] times, the bombard-ment by heavy artillery constantly increasing until the American/French counter-offensive forced us to retreat. We were right at the front of the huge German breach in the enemy lines, which we could not exploit because of a lack of reserves and material. Carrying messages to and from the battalion and the regiment, every day I passed a milestone with '65 km to Paris' on it!

Gebhard, too, would presumably have liked to take the 'free excursion to Paris'; even many years later one can still sense in his memoirs the magical attraction the city exerted. In the peace years he never managed to get to Paris.

According to Gebhard, they emerged from this rear-guard action 'with all of thirty men left in the battalion'. Apart from a burn on his hand from a shell splinter, he was unscathed. The figure varied, but a battalion gener-ally consisted of three to five companies with four hun-dred to eight hundred men in total. That would mean that less than 10 per cent of Gebhard's unit survived.

In *All Quiet on the Western Front* a company suffers similar losses to Gebhard's battalion. But Remarque, unlike Gebhard, tells in uncompromising detail how the almost total annihilation came about, describes the horrendous slaughter, the mutilation, the agonies of a death that takes days. While the older soldiers, according to Remarque, are mentally better equipped to survive the war, since for them it is merely an interruption to their lives, the twenty-year-olds were 'swept away' by it, 'in some strange and melancholic way [they] have become hardened'. Even after only a few months at the front their own youth seems infinitely far away: 'We are old now.'

After the enforced retreat, Gebhard's unit was sent to recuperate in Flanders near the Belgian town of Ypres, which had been completely destroyed in the months of trench warfare that had transformed the surrounding area into a lunar landscape. On 4 September 1918, shortly before the end of the war, he wrote a letter from there to his brother, who was still stuck impatiently at the barracks. Gebhard had just been promoted to lance corporal and awarded the Iron Cross, 2nd Class. He was fine, he said, apart from all the lice in the dugout they had taken over from the English. The scenery was 'very Flanders, not an undamaged tree or bush in sight, just one shell hole after another', that was all.

He was worried how his younger brother would get through his forthcoming machine-gun course, in which the officer cadets in particular were given a hard time. He was even more worried, though, that Heinrich might be sent to join a regiment 'that is still stuck in a real mess – that wouldn't be the place to get used to it'. By a 'real mess' he was presumably referring to the savage artillery duels accompanied by huge losses of life that he must have been through himself, even though neither his letters nor what he later wrote about his wartime experiences mention them.

His daughter, however, recalled her father telling her how he was so exhausted that he fell asleep in a crater and slept so soundly he was not even woken by a shell that missed him by a hair's breadth. She showed me a sketchbook from that last summer of the war in which he had sketched churches, landscapes, villages and towns, some of them in watercolours. Amid the devastation, in which he himself had had a part, Gebhard painted idyllic scenes. Only one of his sketches shows shattered trees and shell holes after a battle; another is a night scene on the very front line, illuminated by the guns' firework display. Perhaps this was his way of surviving the war emotionally, of fighting against his own hardness of heart.

In *I Was a German* Ernst Toller wrote of battles in which, surrounded by filth, mud and corpses, men no longer knew who they were fighting against or what they were fighting for; battles in which everything was reduced to the question of their ever more unlikely survival, until eventually even that became irrelevant. Zuckmayer and Remarque saw this war as the 'suicide of a world', the self-chosen destruction of the future by obliterating almost a whole generation. The experience made Toller into a pacifist and a left-wing revolutionary. Not long afterwards he played an important role in the short-lived Bavarian *Räterepublik* (the revolutionary Soviet-style republic) – while Gebhard and Heinrich were on the opposing side as members of the Freikorps fighting against the republic.

On 23 September 1918 Gebhard was leading a raiding party when they came across a few English artillery observers and took them prisoner. For that he was given the Iron Cross, 1st Class. A few days later the last battle of Flanders began, in which the Germans had no choice but to retreat in the face of the enemy's superior strength.

For many Germans the end of the war, with Germany's offer of an armistice on 3 October, the abdication and flight of the Kaiser and the proclamation of the republic on 9 November, came as a complete surprise. Years of propaganda, with the frequent announcement of victories, had left them living in an unreal world; now they were suddenly and rudely woken from their dreams of world power and hopes of victory. Germany had not been directly affected by the devastation caused by the war, since it had taken place on the territory of neighbouring countries, but there had been an immense number of Germans killed and maimed. Furthermore, its economy was almost bankrupt and the victorious powers left no doubt that they were not interested in seeing Germany return to its former strength.

The military – first and foremost the powerful General Ludendorff, the bemedalled hero of the battle of Tannenberg in East Prussia who had had the decisive voice in determining German strategy during the last two years and who had thwarted all steps towards a negotiated peace – found it easy to lay the blame for the defeat and its catastrophic consequences on those who, after the short-lived postwar revolution, were attempting to create the first democratic order in Germany. A myth was propagated according to which the Social Democrats and the Communists had long prepared a revolution in Germany and, as traitors to the Fatherland, had 'stabbed in the back' the soldiers fighting for their country. This myth enjoyed immense popularity among conservative circles, especially after the harsh conditions set by the victorious powers and the astronomical reparations agreed at the Treaty of Versailles.

The Himmler family's world collapsed. Like many others, they had taken out war loans. If family tradition is to be believed, they had even invested a considerable part of their wealth in them. Given their usual thrift and their safety-first attitude in money matters, they must have been firmly convinced Germany would win. Not only did the defeat destroy all their hopes for Germany's future role as a world power, the end of the monarchy also destroyed once and for all their network of influential contacts with the royal family, which they had put such effort into building up and which they had always been able to rely on, even though it had been weakened by the death of Prince Heinrich, fatally wounded in Romania in November 1916.

The death of the thirty-two-year-old prince was a heavy blow for the Himmler family; even then they must have felt the first tremors of fear of a possible loss of social status. As loyal supporters of the monarchy they had always striven to be as close to the aristocracy as was possible for a middle-class family that was rising in the world. They would, therefore, hardly have been in favour of the political changes that were beginning to take place. 'In November 1918,' Gebhard junior lamented in his 'Reminiscences', 'the revolution swept away the German monarchies. Ludwig III, the last king of the house of Wittelsbach, which had nothing at all of the arrogance of the Prussian monarchy, had fled by night without any of the numerous soldiers with a cushy home posting in Munich lifting a finger to help him.'

After the November armistice Gebhard marched back,

in daily 'portions' of thirty to forty kilometres (18–24 miles), from Flanders to Aachen, a distance of some four hundred and fifty kilometres (280 miles). His unit was briefly posted as guard on the bridge over the Rhine at Duisburg; then – by this time it was the middle of December – they were finally given transport back to the garrison in Passau, where Heinrich was overjoyed to see his brother again. They both managed to be back home in Landshut in time for Christmas Eve. Gebhard enjoyed 'the marvellous feeling of being back home and of having emerged unscathed from the terrible experiences of a brutal war fought with heavy munitions'.

How did a young man of twenty come to terms with such experiences, especially having had such a sheltered upbringing? Even Heinrich could hardly have been the right kind of person with whom to talk about what he had been through, since as a soldier he had never left the garrison. For Heinrich, the hero manqué, the lack of any opportunity to prove himself in battle was not only a great disappointment, it probably remained with him as a stigma for the rest of his life. Not only did he have to renounce his dream of a career as an officer, he was without a school-leaving certificate. While Gebhard had come home from the war battle-hardened, decorated and, as if by a miracle, unharmed, and could start at university immediately after his return from France, Heinrich had to return, extremely reluctantly, to the classroom. What his experience, or lack of it, did mean, though, was that he could hold on to his longing for heroic deeds; his romantic, mystical vision of the soldier's life could remain intact.

Heinrich's diary makes clear the mixture of admiration and envy he always felt towards his elder brother, despite his attachment to him. It was not simply a matter of Gebhard being older, he was also Heinrich's superior in many respects. Even as a child Heinrich made great efforts, if often clumsy and unsuccessful, to learn everything Gebhard clearly mastered with ease. But he could not compete with Gebhard's effortless mastery. For years his self-assurance, such as it was, derived from his sense of superiority vis-à-vis Ernst. He was doubtless very fond of his little brother, whom he called 'Ernsti' or 'Ernstl', 'Bubi' or 'Mizzi' like everyone else, and Ernst was pleased that Heinrich, in contrast to Gebhard, took an interest in him. Until the end of his schooldays it was not least Heinrich's worrying state of health that secured him his portion of his parents' care and attention. His constant complaints in his letters about his poor health would promptly increase the attention he enjoyed, especially on the part of his mother; on the other hand, his role as the family weakling made it difficult for him to stand on his own two feet. The homesickness from which he suffered in Regensburg shows that.

Once he had left home, to gain the family's recognition Heinrich threw himself with dogged determination into a new role: that of the organizer who was ready to see to everything, who made himself indispensable by procuring supplies of scarce provisions and other things that were difficult to come by. It was a role he was to play more and more in the following years and one that he was to retain until the end of the Third Reich.

5

'On Friday We're Going Shooting':
The Brothers in the Freikorps

Gebhard did not have much time to recuperate from the war; the semester had already begun. And they were unsettled times. Millions had come back from the war and didn't know what to do. The country was racked with disturbances. On 29 October 1918 sailors in Kiel and Wilhelmshaven mutinied, and within a few days the rebellion had spread throughout Germany. In all the larger towns revolutionary workers' and soldiers' councils ('soviets') were formed, demanding the abdication of the Kaiser and the proclamation of a republic. On 15 January 1919, when Gebhard was starting his course in mechanical engineering at the Technical University in Munich, Karl Liebknecht and Rosa Luxemburg were arrested and murdered in Berlin. Four days later elections to the National Assembly were held, accompanied by violent street battles in the capital.

The uncertainty of the political situation made it difficult for Gebhard to concentrate on his studies and his future career. Added to that, his living conditions were not particularly pleasant: 'An uncomfortable bed-sitter in Schellingstrasse, not enough coal to heat it, not enough bread for your coupons . . . not pleasant times at all.' The war had accustomed Gebhard to going short of things; what disturbed him more was the 'unsettled atmosphere in the city', the absence of order, the chaos of the postwar period. In Bavaria, too, 'the "soldiers' councils" were shooting their big mouths off'.

Munich was a centre of the 'soviet movement'. Since 8 November there had been a coalition government in the Bavarian capital between the Majority Social Democrats and the Independent Social Democrats under the Independent Socialist Kurt Eisner. Eisner, a journalist born in Berlin, had left the Social Democratic Party in 1916 in protest against its support for the war. In early 1918 he had organized strikes in various Munich armament factories, had been arrested, then released after a few months. On 7 November, after a large demonstration on the Theresienwiese (where the October beer festival is still held), he succeeded in occupying the ministries and the royal palace. The King fled, and the republic was proclaimed.

Eisner became Prime Minister of the Bavarian Republic, but had to struggle against considerable resistance. For socialists such as Ernst Toller and Max Levien and anarchists such as Gustav Landauer and Erich Mühsam, the revolution had not gone far enough. They demanded a strengthening of the position of the workers' and soldiers' councils. With only 2.5 per cent of the votes, Eisner's Independent Socialists suffered a devastating defeat; the Majority Social Democrats received 33 per cent. The election was won by the newly founded Bavarian People's Party, the political arm of Catholicism, which presented itself as guaranteeing stability and order in the unsettled

times. At the elections to the Bavarian Parliament on
12 January Bavarian women, including my great-grandmother, were allowed to vote for the first time. Presumably
the Himmler family voted en bloc for the Bavarian People's
Party.

On 21 February 1919 Eisner was assassinated on his
way to the Bavarian Parliament by a young right-wing
nationalist officer, Count Arco-Valley. On 17 March the
Social Democrat Johannes Hoffmann became the new
Prime Minister. During the weeks that followed anarchy
broke out, above all in Munich. On 7 April in the
Wittelsbach Palace, the Central Council, formed of Independent Socialists and anarchists, proclaimed the Bavarian *Räterepublik*; shortly afterwards it was overthrown
by the second, 'true' *Räterepublik* of the Communists
under Eugen Leviné. That republic lasted barely two
weeks and ended in violence and bloodshed. The hastily
assembled 'Red Army' had no chance at all against the
units of the regular army and the Bavarian Freikorps
marching on Munich.

In the meantime, after the fatal attack on Kurt Eisner,
whose real name was Salomon Kosmanowskis, the
soviet republic was launched [Gebhard noted in his
'Reminiscences']. Several times already, often within a
few hours, not only the political but also the criminal
underworld in Munich had crawled out of the wood-
work and started taking over the city – dark figures,
so-called sailors – until eventually, on 1. 4. 1919, the
city was in their hands. My studies were interrupted
again, of course . . . Munich, from which the weak
Hoffmann government had fled to Bamberg, had to be
liberated from outside.

In fact, it would have been possible to take Munich without armed intervention. The 'Action Committee', especially Ernst Toller, had several times offered to negotiate with Hoffmann, and on 1 May the 'Red Army' had been given the order of the day to lay down their arms. In the course of the 'comprehensive operations' which, as Gebhard put it, put an end to the 'red nightmare', an army of 33,000 men with artillery, flame-throwers, armoured cars and even aeroplanes took to the field against workers armed with completely inadequate equipment. Even decades later, Gebhard's description still puts the attitude of the Freikorps in a nutshell: there was no negotiating with left-wing revolutionaries who, in their eyes, were 'criminals'. The campaign, which had the mood of a pogrom, claimed some 650 dead, more than half of them civilians; during the state of war in the months that followed hundreds were the victims of on-the-spot executions.

Heinrich took part in the march on Munich with the Schaaf Detachment of the Landshut Freikorps, even though at the time he was supposed to be doing a crash course that would enable him to finish his school-leaving certificate. Finally he had the opportunity to prove himself as a soldier. His unit fought its way from the east of the city, along Rosenheimer Strasse and across the bridges over the River Isar, through to the centre. On Karlsplatz he was involved in heavy fighting against the poorly armed revolutionary workers. On 3 May Munich was 'liberated'.

This meant the end of the 'rule of the writers from Café Megalomania, Toller, Erich Mühsam and that mob', Gebhard noted with relief – Mühsam had been arrested

and imprisoned, Gustav Landauer had been murdered in
Stadelheim Prison – but added his regret that 'the criminals had still managed to murder the hostages in the
basement of Luitpold Gymnasium'. As a student Gebhard
was once more living in the district where he had spent
his childhood, and 'Café Megalomania' was the same
Café Stefanie behind the university, through the windows
of which he had watched the chess players as a child.

The chaotic conditions, especially the shooting by the
'Red Army' of the twenty-two hostages – including seven
members of the anti-Semitic and nationalist Thule Society
– in Luitpold Gymnasium had terrified the people of
Munich. It overshadowed the atrocities committed by the
'liberating' forces, which tended to be regarded as measures necessary 'to restore order'; henceforward the memory of the terror of the Soviet-style republic, exaggerated
for propaganda purposes, would serve to idealize the
'liberators'.

This was despite the fact that, as Sebastian Haffner
wrote in *Defying Hitler: A Memoir*:

> The Freikorps resembled the later Nazi storm troops
> which most of them later joined. They certainly had
> the same outlook, behaviour and fighting methods.
> They had already invented the device of 'shooting
> while attempting to escape', and had made significant
> advances in the science of torture. They also antici-
> pated the events of the 30th July 1934 with their bold
> habit of lining less important opponents up against a
> wall, without many questions or distinctions.

The weeks of the 'soviet republic' went down in the
collective memory as a 'reign of terror', summed up as a

plot visited on Bavaria by Jews, outsiders and a few writers from the Schwabing coffee houses. Thus Gebhard's claim that Kurt Eisner's real name was Salomon Kosmanowskis reflected the right-wing propaganda of the time that tried to smear left-wing politicians by turning them into that bogey of the middle classes, the 'Jewish Bolshevik'. In Georg Schott's *Volksbuch vom Hitler* (The Hitler Chapbook, published in 1924), which was famous in right-wing circles and would be important for Heinrich a few years later, Eisner also appears as a Galician Jew called Salomon Kosmanowski. The true victors to emerge from the catastrophic weeks of the Bavarian 'soviet republic' were the right-wing radicals. During the years that followed they succeeded in stirring up hatred of 'bolshevism' and fear of 'an international conspiracy of the Jews'.

In the summer of 1919 Professor Himmler was offered the position of head of the Gymnasium in Ingolstadt, to the north of Munich. It meant another move, with all the attendant hassle, and another change of school for their youngest son. Added to this, Ingolstadt was a not particularly attractive garrison town. But the social advancement the position of headmaster would bring must have made it attractive to Gebhard senior.

Initially he went there alone, his wife following with Ernst at the end of September, by which time the official apartment in the school had been made ready. Ingolstadt is on the Danube, only about twelve miles from Neuburg an der Donau, where Gebhard senior had attended boarding school. And Abensberg, the small town where Anna

Himmler's father came from and where she still had relatives, was not far away either.

By this time Heinrich had passed his *Abitur*. Now, to everyone's surprise, he suddenly announced he wanted to study agriculture, which was doubtless well outside the range of what his parents thought of as a suitable career for their son. But they respected his decision and, as always, gave him what assistance they could; they found him a place for work experience, so that he was able to start immediately that August on an estate to the north of Ingolstadt.

Heinrich clearly had just as idealized a picture of country life as he had of life as an officer. His parents' scepticism about his choice seemed to be confirmed when, with his susceptibility to illness, he proved unable to cope with the rigours of physical labour despite his dogged determination, and came down with paratyphoid after only four weeks. He spent September in hospital at Ingolstadt, where his father visited him every day while his mother worried herself sick in Munich. He was doing fine, Heinrich reassured her in a letter of 11 September – she didn't need to worry in the least about him. He added a disdainful message to Ernst, who had obviously not written to him for a long time: 'If that bone idle so-and-so Ernsti is presumptuous enough to imagine I'm going to reply to his first letter for 6 weeks, he is terribly mistaken.' And, taking it upon himself to include his father in the decree, he went on, 'Neither Daddy nor I will write to the lazybones.'

After his severe illness he had to postpone his work experience, and in the autumn of 1919, only one semester after Gebhard, he enrolled at the Technical University in

Munich to study agriculture. At first he took a room in the student hostel in Schellingstrasse, as had his brother, but a little later the two of them moved one block away, to the street of their childhood: 'Once both of us, Heinrich and I, were studying in Munich, we had very cosy lodgings with two very charming aristocratic canonesses, the Countesses Castell, on the fourth floor of a house on the corner of Theresienstrasse and Amalienstrasse. For lunch and dinner we were well looked after in the Pension Loritz in nearby Jägerstrasse, where we were soon part of a very pleasant, friendly circle,' Gebhard recalled.

Financially they were kept on a relatively tight rein: the Himmler family were by no means as well off as before the war. All the same, their parents made every effort to allow them to pursue their university studies under conditions that can certainly be described as comfortable.

The Pension Loritz was only a few streets away from the university and five minutes from their room. There they had a home from home in a socially acceptable environment – their parents knew Frau Loritz from the time when they had lived in Amalienstrasse themselves. There they met people of their own age, including the Loritzes' daughters, Kätha and Maja, and a distant cousin, Ludwig Zahler, known as Lu. The Himmlers had been close friends of the Zahlers since their time in Landshut; they are repeatedly mentioned in Heinrich's diary and letters. At the Loritzes' the young people would often sit together chatting after the meal, and the two brothers had the opportunity for their first, cautious experiences with women of the same age. This generally took place under the supervision of an older person.

Things were a little more relaxed during *Fasching* (carnival), which was celebrated exuberantly in Munich.

On 2 and 3 November – the semester had only just begun – the brothers wrote their first joint letter home. First of all Gebhard: '. . . we would both like our *ice-skates* together with the *keys* now; if it should get really cold and we have time we'd like to have our skates *here*. So if you would, Mummy dear, put them in your next parcel.' Couldn't they have taken their skates when they left home only a few days previously, after the vacation? But the young men seem to have been used to having their mother at their beck and call. Her main occupation for years must have been sending parcels non-stop.

In the same letter Heinrich moaned at great length about the 'outrageous amount of work' he had to do for his courses. He felt constantly under pressure from his parents to prove he was working hard. Perhaps, however, the motivation here was simply his need to make himself seem important and his compulsion to describe anything, however banal, in minute detail. At the same time he was the one who undertook errands for the family: he got pills from the pharmacy for Ernsti, regularly visited old family friends and frequently wrote Gebhard's letters as well, so that his elder brother just had to sign.

At university their interests developed in ever more different directions. As soon as he started, Gebhard joined the Academic Choral Society, the majority of whose members were law students. This was a student fraternity where, besides going to concerts and the theatre together, the members made lifelong contacts. It was here that Gebhard became acquainted with Richard Wendler, a law student of the same age who was to become his brother-in-law. We will come back to him later.

Heinrich spent most of his free time with the Apollo student fraternity, of which – like his father, who still belonged to it as an 'old boy' – he became a member. A number of family friends were also members, including Professor Rauschmeyer, a former colleague of Gebhard Himmler senior at the Gymnasium in Landshut whose daughter Mariele the two brothers met again in the Pension Loritz circle. The formal duels, however, soon brought Heinrich into possible conflict with his Catholic faith. He was unsure whether this 'purification rite', by which the fraternity members had to prove their manliness and fitness for an elite group, was not a grave sin in the eyes of the Church. He had many discussions about it with Gebhard and Lu, and with his father, who clearly managed to reassure him.

In Heinrich's diary, entries reflecting his longing for the warmth of the family and the romantic feelings of his first love for the Loritzes' daughter Maja alternate with his programmatic plans to toughen himself up, to practise discipline.

After Maja had left Munich to spend a year with another family learning how to run a household, Lu and Kätha (who soon married) became his closest friends. Kätha often signed the numerous letters to Heinrich 'your little sister'. She was also the one Heinrich was most likely to talk to about his problems. On 6 December 1920 she wrote, 'If you follow your emotions, then you mostly have the feeling you are giving way, that is, showing weakness. Are you not forgetting the strength that flows from your moments of quiet? . . . Do not keep too tight a rein on yourself, Heini, so as not to lose the best things life can give.'

Even though Heinrich made great efforts to be sociable – he learnt to dance, became a member of the Alpine and Rifle Clubs, cultivated his relations with other members of the fraternity as well as many of his parents' old acquaintances – during his time as a student he frequently suffered from a sense of not belonging. 'They think of me as a cheerful, amusing lad who takes care of everything – "Heini will see to it",' he wrote in January 1922. He was aware that his often very harsh criticism of the behaviour of others made them keep their distance. 'I just can't keep my trap shut,' he wrote in his diary. He was constantly exhorting himself to adhere strictly to religious command- ments in order to make himself into a 'good person', and believed he had the right to make similar demands on others, or guide them along those lines.

His Sundays were often spent on solitary excursions to family graves or unannounced visits to his old nanny Thilde and her 'decent, conservative husband' – 'I simply feel at home with these dear people.' And yet in the long run this was hardly sufficient for the twenty-two-year-old. 'I'm in such a strange mood,' he noted shortly afterwards in his diary. 'Melancholy, yearning for love.' He categor- ically rejected sexual experiences before marriage, basing his ideas on one of his favourite books, Hans Wegener's *Wir jungen Männer. Das sexuelle Problem des gebildeten jungen Mannes vor der Ehe* (We Young Men: The Sexual Problem of the Educated Young Man before Marriage). At the same time he showed a keen interest in anything to do with sexuality. His diaries are full of notes on conversations with Lu and another friend about 'the problem of nudity', 'sexual intercourse', 'avoiding fertilization' and so on. He sometimes found his renunciation of physical relationships with the opposite sex hard to bear, but he was afraid of the harm they would do to his character and comforted himself with theories he thought up himself:

> It just happens to be the case that there are two kinds of person [he noted in his diary on 22 May 1922]. On the one hand the phlegmatic, severe ones, among which I include myself, and which are necessary in the racial community. And then there are the light-hearted ones, to which whole nations belong, fiery and with a free-and-easy attitude to life but without going to the bad; married or single, they flirt and kiss without seeing anything in it, since it is only human and since it is enjoyable.

He must often have got on the much more easygoing Gebhard's nerves with these inhibited views. Gebhard was much more relaxed in his relationships with women.

But despite this difference, the two brothers remained close, not least in their right-wing nationalist opinions and their patriotic, military sense of duty. While Heinrich, as a member of the Landshut Freikorps, took part in the battle against the Munich *Räterepublik* in May 1919, Lieutenant Gebhard Himmler had already become a member of the Munich 'Citizens' Militia' founded on 10 May that year. There had been an intensive recruitment drive for the Citizens' Militia, which was responsible for public order and security. 'No fit man is too old!' it said on one of its posters. By the end of 1919, two hundred thousand members had already been recruited; they were given a Militiaman's identity card as well as guns and ammunition.

But Gebhard and Heinrich, as did many former soldiers with front-line experience, soon found the Citizens' Militia too staid, and so at the beginning of November 1919, the week after Heinrich started at university, together with Ludwig Zahler they joined the 14th Volunteer Company, Rifle Brigade 21, which had been absorbed into the regular Army that summer. This Rifle Brigade 21 was led by Colonel Franz Ritter von Epp, who had brutally put down the Munich *Räterepublik* with his Freikorps Epp and since then been fêted as the 'liberator of Munich'. The Freikorps Epp had been combined with others to form Rifle Brigade 21. Ernst Röhm, the later leader of the SA, was Epp's adjutant; Rudolf Hess, Gregor and Otto Strasser and others, who were to be leading figures in the Nazi regime only a few years after, were also members of the Freikorps. Epp's authority extended well beyond the Rifle Brigade: not only was the regular Army in Munich/Upper Bavaria under his command, but also the city police, the Munich Citizens' Militia and the technical emergency service, of which Gebhard was also a member.

Gebhard and Heinrich took part in weekend exercises and target practice, were assigned to street patrols and were always on call for emergencies. Heinrich enthused about his new commitment. On 3 November 1919 he wrote home, 'On Friday we're going *shooting*. I'm looking forward to it terribly, especially to being able to wear uniform again.' In this he corresponded perfectly to Franz von Epp's ideal kind of man, one 'who enjoys the trade of soldiering . . . who enjoys measuring himself against an opponent . . . A convinced and determined *landsknecht* with the sense of honour of his trade.' Neither Gebhard nor Heinrich had any problem identifying with the romantic image of the determined *Landsknecht*, the mercenary foot-soldier of the sixteenth century, and with the concomitant contempt for the stolid bourgeois. They saw themselves as political soldiers who had to fight – and did so willingly – in a permanent civil war.

Even decades later, in his 'Reminiscences', Gebhard still defended this step: 'Anyone who did not go through those times will probably not be able to comprehend how we, hardly back from the battlefield or the garrison, were soldiers again. We were not doing it for pleasure, however, but out of harsh necessity.' The political situation after the November Revolution, he said, was still very unstable; left-wing extremists in the Spartacus uprising in Berlin, in Thuringia and in the Ruhr had constantly tried 'to undermine the free state, which was still rather shaky. We had to be on our guard against that.'

The more the Freikorps drifted into opposition to the new republic and became isolated, the stronger the 'Freikorps spirit', their sense of belonging, became. Many members shared the disillusionment brought on by front-line experience and the consequent feeling of pointlessness, a loss of belief in values; at the same time, there was a sense of comradeship transcending class differences, even between officers and the common soldiers. Leadership did not come from rank, but solely from 'actions performed in battle'. Most members of the Freikorps saw the lost war as the collapse of the 'phoney bourgeois system'. The figure of the comfortable, noncombatant 'bourgeois' was seen as their real enemy, often even more than that of the Communist or proletarian. This contempt for the middle-class civilian was transferred to the liberal bourgeois state – was directed, indeed, against the whole system. While the older officers tended to be monarchist in outlook, the younger ones longed for a new form for the Reich, which found expression in the combination of nationalism and socialism. National Socialism combined the dream of a great nation with the ideal of comradeship and the principle of authority vested in a *Führer*, a leader; it saw itself as the antithesis of both Marxism and capitalism.

The members of the Freikorps saw themselves as the real Germany, they 'felt' themselves to *be* Germany, in the words of Ernst von Salomon, a Freikorps fighter who would be sentenced to five years in prison for his part in the murder in 1922 of the Jewish Foreign Minister, Walther Rathenau. In his later novel, *The Outlaws*, Salomon described his development from a Prussian nationalist cadet to an anti-democratic fighter: 'We believed that it was we who were meant to have the power and no one else, for Germany's sake. For we felt that we embodied Germany. We believed that we were entitled to have that power. The people at the head of affairs in Berlin had no such right.'

It was a male fellowship; more than that, they saw themselves as the fellowship of the best, toughest, most soldierly men under the command of the best man, their leader, their Führer, and they were now laying claim to power. It was precisely the mixture of contempt for the Weimar state, confused dreams and wild determination to fight for any goal their leaders decreed, together with their us-and-them attitude, that made the Freikorps an extremely explosive ingredient in a democracy whose foundations were shaky anyway.

At Christmas 1919 the two elder brothers came home, which was now in Ingolstadt. On 23 December the family celebrated Ernst's birthday and – as was and still is traditional in Germany – Christmas on the following day. The presents that year were modest: the boys were allowed to choose books for themselves from their father's library and Ernst, who was keen on science, was given a chemistry book by his brothers. Every year Christmas was celebrated according to a fixed ritual. While Gebhard and Heinrich decorated the tree, Ernst had to savour the anticipation until the door to the Christmas room was finally opened. 'It was lovely, really lovely,' Heinrich noted on the 24th in an outburst of emotion unusual for his diary. That morning the elder boys had been out to fetch moss for the crib and later on helped their mother with the cooking. After they had had their presents, Gebhard played the piano, then they sang songs, accompanied by Gebhard and Heinrich on the guitar. 'Then we drank punch and went to midnight mass,' which Heinrich found 'powerfully moving'.

During the holiday the two elder brothers went their own ways. Gebhard retained enthusiastic memories of vacations in Ingolstadt, for which a so-called vacation association, the Ingolstadtia, had been founded, 'which brought together students of every political hue, from members of the duelling fraternities to the Catholics, just as in a fraternity, for very pleasant student get-togethers and, very soon, general social intercourse'. Graduates of all professions – doctors, lawyers, civil servants – were members of Ingolstadtia, just as they were old boys of various fraternities, 'and if we organized a summer or a winter party during the vacation, then everyone came, it was more or less the done thing to attend'.

Starting in September 1920 Heinrich spent time on a farm in Fridolfing, close to the Austrian border, to make up for the period of practical experience he had had to cancel the previous autumn. It was arranged through Frau Loritz, who was related to the owners, the Rehrls, and Heinrich was treated like one of the family. He was largely spared hard physical labour and could indulge in his romantic enthusiasm for the traditional 'tranquil' country life during numerous walks and animated discussions with Herr Rehrl. He had acquired a motorbike and at weekends went to visit old friends of the family in Munich, Ingolstadt and elsewhere, and often made excursions into the Austrian Alps. His Munich friends kept him up-to-date by letter, but he also had frequent visits from acquaintances and relatives. Parcels were constantly being sent back and forth between him and his mother – in exchange for books he'd read, worn-out underwear and similar 'rubbish', he was sent clean clothes, tobacco and food parcels, even though the food at the Rehrls' left nothing to be desired.

During this time Heinrich also regularly exchanged letters with Ernst, who by now was fifteen. His younger brother often sent caricatures he'd drawn himself, with which both Heinrich and the Rehrls were delighted. 'You can't imagine how much I enjoyed your splendid, outrageous drawings,' Heinrich wrote on 14 November. 'Even

though you're at the awkward age, you're still all right.'
Clearly 'Ernsti' was not only a well-behaved model pupil,
but also something of a comedian. In the photos in the
family album one can see how he liked pulling faces and
playing the clown. Even though Heinrich enjoyed his
brother's pranks, however, he could not resist bombard-
ing him with exhortations and telling him how to behave.

> I was delighted at your good marks. But don't let them
> go to your head, you only owe them to the fact that
> the others are a little bit more stupid than you are
> (which actually must be quite difficult). By the way,
> I expect you to do something in history as well, not
> because it's required at school but out of genuine
> interest, because you need it for life. Don't get too
> one-sided now. And behave yourself and don't annoy
> Daddy and Mummy, or else . . .!

He still felt superior to Ernst, but seemed already to fear
his head start on him might melt away. This was presumably why he made Ernst out to be 'small, insignificant
and ugly' and demanded regular letters as proof of his
love; if they failed to arrive, he punished Ernst with
demonstrative disregard.

Despite the thriftiness ordained by his parents and his
meticulous bookkeeping, Heinrich constantly complained
of a lack of money at Fridolfing. This is no surprise, given
the fact that notwithstanding the difficult times, he continued to live in the style he was used to at home. Frau
Rehrl took care of his bodily needs and his washing, and
a woman paid for by his parents cleaned his room, so
that he needed money only for special expenses. And
these were not inconsiderable, including his motorbike,

his many trips and other pleasures. He spent almost twenty marks on a visit with friends to a festival in nearby Tittmoning – travel, sausages and beer, a programme – a considerable sum in those days for a young man whose parents had lost a large part of their former wealth through the war.

In the autumn of 1921 Heinrich returned to university in Munich. He was back in the same district as before, in a pension in Briennerstrasse run by another acquaintance of his parents, Frau Wolf. Now he sometimes had to cook for himself. In May Gebhard had passed the preliminary examinations for his diploma – as a soldier who had seen active service he was exempted from certain exams. His somewhat moderate grades suggest he had spent more time playing at soldiers than studying. Progressive inflation was making conditions more and more difficult, even for the Himmlers. By 1921 groceries cost almost eight times more than at the end of the war, which only increased their parents' exhortations to be thrifty.

Heinrich clearly found this more of a burden than his brother. On 24 November that year he noted in his diary that he had talked a lot with Lu about their deprivation and 'dire poverty'. 'But we are determined to preserve our honour; it is our greatest good.' And two weeks later, on 9 December: 'What a poor devil a student is! Everywhere there are fine things and we cannot afford to buy even the cheapest – and yet life is all right at the moment. But who knows what lies in store? – indigence, imprisonment, war.'

During these years he seems to have been genuinely convinced things would 'ignite' at any moment, either in a civil war or in another conflict between the nations. But this ominous 'struggle' he believed he was faced with also included the personal test awaiting him: to have to stand on his own two feet in the near future, to become grown up. It was a prospect he found disturbing: 'I am a long way from the refined assurance of behaviour I would like to have,' he had noted in November. He spent a good deal more time perfecting his 'social polish' in the fraternity or chatting to 'useful acquaintances' than in serious study, to which he devoted himself only in short bursts before examinations. He feared the end of this calm before the storm as much as he longed for the 'struggle to prove myself'. 'How time flies. My lovely, blissful student days will soon be over,' he complained in his diary on 21 February 1922. It is clear from many of his entries how unsure of his future he was, how often he changed his vague plans. On 22 November he had noted, after a lecture in the Hofbräuhaus on military issues of the First World War, 'I am now more certain than ever that if there should be another campaign in the east, I will be part of it. The east is the most important area for us. We must fight and settle in the east.' Only one day later he was already wavering, asking himself where life might take him: 'Spain, Turkey, the Baltic states, Russia, Peru? God willing, in two years' time I will no longer be in Germany, unless there is struggle, war again & I a soldier.' He was torn this way and that in his dreams between emigration and being a soldier.

While Heinrich was battling with constant changes of mood, with depression, with his doubts and his rigid moral concepts, Gebhard clearly enjoyed student life in a much more relaxed way. He 'calmly accepted the frugality of life in those days', and enjoyed 'simple pleasures' such as when he and his friends would 'often manage to conjure up delightful evenings on the stage and the rostrum from literally nothing'.

In the autumn of 1921 Gebhard had fallen in love with Paula Stölzle, a distant cousin from Weilheim, south of Munich, probably when she visited Ingolstadt. The following winter he was doing a period of practical training in a factory there. In November Paula also went to see Heinrich in Munich. They had tea in his room, smoked, and chatted about her relationship with Gebhard; 'and then we kissed and agreed to call each other by the familiar *du*. She is the dearest of girls. Very lively, a little frivolous. She's definitely just the girl for Gebhard.' They got engaged during the Easter vacation, 1922. The Himmler parents seemed delighted at the connection with the daughter of the well-respected banker Max Stölzle, and the engagement was announced surprisingly early – Gebhard was still a student.

6

'They All Went Wild with Excitement':
The Putsch

The year 1922 brought other great changes for the Himmlers. At Easter Gebhard senior was promoted to the headship of the highly regarded Wittelsbacher Gymnasium in Munich. It must have been a triumph for this man who had risen from a poor background – the culmination of his life's work, even if, in those difficult times, the promotion did not mean any improvement in their material circumstances. Inflation ate up everything. In that year food was already a hundred and thirty times more expensive than at the end of the war. Added to that, the new headmaster had to take a flat for himself in Munich, which involved an additional expense as his wife and youngest son had to stay in Ingolstadt until the end of the school year.

Heinrich and his father saw a lot of each other during this period; on Sundays they went for walks and ate together in a restaurant. From his letters to his mother it is clear that it must have meant a lot to him to have his father to himself for once. 'Daddy & I get on well and have a good time together,' he wrote on 9 May; 'Daddy has settled down very well, goes for regular walks and is not overworking.' Heinrich, who was quick-tempered, and his father did not always get on that well together. When, in Ingolstadt in 1921, he had asked his father for a fairly large sum of money for books, there were 'great, heated debates about it, unfortunately I got rather worked up'. The following day he discussed the matter of the book money again with his mother – 'unfortunately got worked up again'. Following such disagreements, though, Heinrich always quickly made an effort to make up. As he had done earlier on for Gebhard, he now took on some correspondence on behalf of his father. On 13 June he wrote to his mother, 'Many thanks from Daddy & me for the excellent cake. I took two-thirds of it straight out to Daddy yesterday afternoon.'

The next day the two of them went to the Zirkus Krone, the only circus in Germany with a permanent building, which was right next to the Wittelsbacher Gymnasium, in order to attend a meeting in protest against the 'Black Insult'. What was seen as the 'black insult' was the use of black French colonial troops in the occupation of the Rhineland after the war. In the eyes of many, and not only those of the conservative camp, the mere presence of these soldiers was an offence against 'all the laws of European civilization'. Not only had Germany lost all its colonies as a result of the war, the former subject races were now part of the victorious occupying forces. Heinrich noted in his diary: 'Quite a lot of people. They were all crying, "Vengeance!" Very impressive. But I've already been to better things of this kind, with more atmosphere. Afterwards 10 o'clock in the Augustinerkeller. Discussion about women, love, life – life today, that is – about the secret matters, about patriotic activity.' Heinrich knew about the 'secret matters', presumably a reference to the activities of secret military and extreme right-wing organizations in Munich, through his membership of the Freiweg Rifle Association. Then, the following day, Heinrich, his father and others, presumably all fellow members of the Apollo fraternity, met in a beer cellar and had a discussion about 'the past, the war, the revolution, the Jews, anti-officer agitation, the *Räterepublik*, liberation'.

In Munich in the 1920s the right wing organized countless mass demonstrations, often staged as pompous military parades. In them lived on the military tradition of the Empire, with its parades, uniforms and military bands. Rallies against the Treaty of Versailles and against 'the war-guilt lie' were regular events. Heinrich took part in a protest rally on Königsplatz on 28 June 1922. Deeply moved, he sang the '*Wacht am Rhein*' ('Guard on the Rhine') together with sixty thousand others. 'It was magnificent,' he enthused in his diary. He had a definite weakness for anything military, which was capable of arousing uplifting, sometimes truly ecstatic, feelings in him. 'Soldiers marched past. Oh my God!' he had written on 26 February.

What was Heinrich's father's attitude to his increasingly radical political stance? Did they argue about it? Heinrich's diary entries show that at their frequent meetings his father was 'deeply depressed about Germany's situation'. But even if the two of them may not have seen eye to eye on all political questions, they were united in their opposition to the Weimar Republic and in their dream of 'national liberation'. Otherwise Gebhard senior would hardly have accompanied his son to the meeting at the Zirkus Krone. As early as 1920 Heinrich must have assumed his father's tacit agreement with a protest rally at the university against the death sentence passed on Count Arco-Valley, Kurt Eisner's murderer, in which he took part. It 'was truly refreshing. I wish Daddy could have seen' how 'the German nation's hope of resurrection' had found expression there, he wrote in his birthday letter to his mother on 18 January. 'The gentlemen in the cabinet will know why they pardoned Arco. Otherwise they'd have been in for it. We were all ready – in fact, we were sorry everything passed off so smoothly.'

In the summer vacation Heinrich and his father both returned to Ingolstadt. Heinrich, however, had little time to enjoy the pleasures of the student fraternity because his final examinations were looming. On 22 July 1922 their parents celebrated their silver wedding with a small gathering, the only guests apart from the family being their old nanny, Thilde, Gebhard's fiancée Paula and her parents. The menu for this celebratory meal was still in accordance with comfortable middle-class pretensions, even if, given the times, it was distinctly more modest than before the war. And even though the menu card itself was handwritten rather than printed, its very presence was a clear demonstration that the family continued to set great store by correct etiquette.

Ernst had clearly not been troubled by his further change of school; he was hardworking and his marks continued to be outstanding. He was also learning a remarkable number of languages; as well as the compulsory Latin and Greek, he was doing optional courses in English, French and Italian with great enthusiasm. I do wonder, though, how he coped with always having to find new friends, especially as it was probably twice as difficult when, as the headmaster's son, he would have to fight to gain the respect of his fellow pupils. It was presumably not mere chance, therefore, that Ernst sought closer contact with his brothers at this time. The result was that even while still at school he joined their circle of student friends and, despite being considerably younger, was quickly accepted by them.

By this time he was sixteen, and during these summer holidays he did a course of training as a 'short-term volunteer'. He was unusually young to be a member of one of these reserve units of the Freikorps. He would certainly not have been able to do the military training course without his parents' consent. It is, therefore, safe to assume that they at least tolerated, if not approved of, their three sons' engagement in the right-wing nationalist Freikorps.

Clearly, Ernst too could hardly wait for a chance to defend the Fatherland with his gun. Or did he join the Freikorps to prove to his brothers that he was no longer the spoilt baby of the family, which was still their image of him? Gebhard in particular clung to that image; in his 'Reminiscences' he wrote, 'It was quite natural, given the difference in age and the sphere that Ernst inhabited as a schoolboy, that his relations with Heinrich and myself were not as close as those between us two. In addition, as a late arrival he was very much spoilt by Mother, which often irritated the two of us, who had already been through all sorts of things.' So even his 'Reminiscences', written when he was an old man, reflect this slightly patronizing attitude towards his youngest brother, whom he seemed to envy for the special affection their parents had for him, and perhaps also because the First World

War had brought his own childhood to such an abrupt end.

At the end of July Heinrich passed his examinations, completing his diploma in agriculture in only three years. He had managed to shorten the normal course by a year, since at the Rehrls he had found time, while doing his practical training, for some intensive study. He then set out on the almost hopeless search for a job. His father still had influential contacts; in this case Hudezeck, Gebhard and Heinrich's former teacher, who found him work in a fertilizer factory in Schleissheim, to the north of Munich. The relationship, based on mutual assistance, was to continue for many years. Fifteen years later Heinrich, at his father's request, used his influence as Reichs-führer SS and head of the German police to help Hudezeck get promotion to a school headship. A further fifteen years later Hudezeck did Gebhard a favour by providing him with an exonerating testimonial for his Nazi years.

According to Gebhard, Heinrich's pay in Schleissheim was 'lousy', but at least it was a permanent post, something that was almost impossible for someone entering the job market at that time to find. Schleissheim was too far from Munich for Heinrich to commute, so he had to move.

In the meantime Gebhard senior had been given an apartment on the top floor of the Wittelsbacher Gymnasium, and in the autumn his wife moved with Ernst to Munich. It was a huge apartment, with a long, gloomy hall. There were enough rooms for all the family, which at least saved them the expense of Gebhard's bedsitter.

The Marsplatz, where the Gymnasium was situated,

was close to the centre, but it was not a particularly attractive residential area. The school, which still exists today, is on a wide arterial road leading out of the town and close to the main railway station. At the time there was a barracks with a large parade ground opposite the school. There would have been little motor traffic then, but the noise of the pupils, the bellowing of orders from the parade ground and the shunting of the locomotives would have been audible in the apartment, not to mention the shouting from the mass rallies at the Zirkus Krone.

Heinrich frequently came into Munich from Schleissheim, not only to see his family and friends, but also to attend political meetings of various right-wing groups. He was there on Königsplatz on 16 August when Hitler spoke at the great protest demonstration of the *Vereinigten Vaterländischen Verbände Bayerns* (United Patriotic Associations of Bavaria). The rally, comprising around thirty thousand armed members of various extreme organizations, took place under the slogan of 'For Germany – against Berlin' and was directed against the 'Jewish Bolshevism' which, they claimed, was using the republic as cover to strengthen its own position.

The rival right-wing groups in Bavaria were united in their opposition to the Berlin government. The NSDAP – the *Nationalsozialistische Deutsche Arbeiterpartei*, National Socialist German Workers' Party, founded on 5 January 1919 as the German Workers' Party, which it remained until February 1920 – held its first mass rally on 24 February 1920 in the Hofbräuhaus, an old-established beer hall right in the centre of Munich. Before two thousand fans, the Party's new head of recruitment Adolf Hitler, who called himself the 'drummer' of the right-wing movement, announced the twenty-five points of the Party programme. These included a 'Greater Germany' for all ethnic Germans, the annulment of the Versailles treaties, plans for 'land and soil' (colonies) and a fight against 'Jewish' capitalism. Essential to the realization of these demands, he insisted, was the creation of a strong central power, the replacement of democracy by an authoritarian, dictatorial system. Hitler's ceaseless outpouring of hatred against the 'November criminals', the politicians who he claimed had betrayed Germany by requesting an armistice, found increasing acceptance. Soon his appearance as a speaker could fill the huge Zirkus Krone building where, between May and August 1923, he addressed packed meetings five times.

By now conditions in Germany were worsening, and at increasingly breakneck speed. The middle classes, with their long tradition of saving, were particularly hard hit by the effects of inflation. They were practically dispossessed, which caused great bitterness. Nothing prepared the German middle classes for Hitler so much as the inflation of 1919–23, wrote Stefan Zweig. Even for a comfortably-off family such as the Himmlers, the dramatic hyperinflation of 1922–3 was a new shock. Since so much of their former wealth which, in the first years of their marriage, had meant security as well as affluence, had been lost in the war loans, it is highly likely that as soon as the war was over they would have started to save more strenuously than ever. And now these new savings were swallowed up by permanent inflation. Thanks to Himmler senior's income as a headmaster, they had more money at their disposal than many others; but there was literally nothing to be bought with money. In August

1923 the dollar had an exchange value of a million marks; by September people were talking in thousands of millions, by the end of October in billions.

In July that year Gebhard completed his diploma in engineering. During his final years he had concentrated on his studies and taken a very good degree. Despite this, the chances of finding work were almost nil. In order not to spend his time sitting around idly at home, he spent the last months of 1923 in a Munich mortgage and exchange bank, which was taking on temporary staff 'to deal with the flood of worthless paper'. Heinrich resigned from his job in Schleissheim on 1 September; by this time his wages, meagre anyway, had lost all purchasing power. Above all, however, he saw an opportunity of proving himself in another armed struggle. His diaries of the time are full of entries about his most ardent wish to put on his 'favourite garb', a soldier's uniform, again. On 15 September he joined Werner Company, a Bavarian volunteer reserve company of the Army.

His parents would not have been exactly delighted by his resignation. But perhaps the times were so chaotic they no longer attached great importance to such a step. Gebhard and Anna Himmler's world had been rocked to its foundations by the losses in both material and cultural values brought about by the defeat in war and the downfall of the monarchy. The difficulties of the initial years of the republic, above all the crisis that reached a dramatic climax in the autumn of 1923, may only have served to increase their scepticism about the young democracy. Their heartfelt wish would presumably have been for the restoration of stability and order. And, like many other bourgeois, they probably saw the Army and its officers,

who, moreover, often came from old-established aristocratic families, as the only group that could ensure that.

Their concern about their own future was exacerbated
by the poor prospects for their sons, since they were both
already getting on in years. Their two eldest had graduated, but there was no work for them; what work there
was did not bring in enough to live on. Their youngest
son, on the other hand, was preparing for his school-
leaving examination and despite his very high grades, it
was even doubtful whether he would be able to go to
university at all. By the end of the year the mood in the
Himmler household was sombre. Gebhard wrote:

> The losses suffered by the German people went into
> the thousands of millions. As the situation deteriorated
> at ever increasing speed, people said things couldn't
> go on like that, but no one knew what needed to be
> done to halt the catastrophe. Heinrich transferred to a
> *Reichsflagge* [Reich Banner] unit before I did because
> the 14th Reserve Company seemed too innocuous.
> All sorts of strategies pulled this way and that; thus
> in October 1923 the Reichsflagge split into the Old
> Reichsflagge, which remained in Nuremberg, while we
> in Munich joined the *Reichskriegsflagge* [Reich War
> Banner] under Captain Röhm.

In the spring of 1921 Gustav Ritter von Kahr, the
Prime Minister of Bavaria, under pressure from the central government in Berlin had had to disband the Bavarian
Citizens' Militia. The Treaty of Versailles demanded the
reduction of the German Army to a hundred thousand
men by January 1921. The result was the emergence of a
multitude of radical 'patriotic associations', including the

Bund Oberland (Oberland League) which had emerged from Epp's Freikorps, and the Reichsflagge. The Munich group of the Reichsflagge was a military unit practising strict discipline which initially opposed all left-wing groups, then later the whole system of the Weimar Republic, and supported the reintroduction of the monarchy in Bavaria. At its head was Ernst Röhm.

It was at his initiative that the Oberland League, the Reichsflagge and the Nazi SA founded the *Deutscher Kampfbund* (German Combat League) on 1 and 2 September 1923 in Nuremberg, with the aim of 'breaking that shameful disgrace, the Treaty of Versailles, at all costs'. The Combat League was determined to fight against 'Marxism, the Jews and the parliamentary democratic system'. Adolf Hitler took over the political leadership on 25 September 1923, which led in October to the Reichsflagge split. Large sections left the Combat League, but the Reichskriegsflagge under Röhm remained, and accepted Hitler as their political leader, their 'Führer'.

Since 1921 Ernst Röhm, a typical representative of the generation that had served at the front, had been one of the key figures in the transformation of the section of Hitler's NSDAP responsible for security at public meetings into a paramilitary organization, the *Sturmabteilung* (SA), and he had excellent contacts with all of the paramilitary associations. As 'arms adviser' he was initially responsible for the secret – and in demilitarized Germany, illegal – arsenal of Epp's Rifle Brigade, and from 1921 onwards for that of the whole of the Bavarian military district, which brought him the nickname of 'machine-gun king of Bavaria'.

In 1919 Gebhard and Heinrich had transferred from

the Munich Citizens' Guard to Rifle Brigade 21; now both of them – Heinrich in 1922, Gebhard at the beginning of 1923 – joined the Reichsflagge. Over the previous few years their rejection of the parliamentary republic had become a distinctly radical stance, and their willingness to 'solve' the untenable political and economic situation by force of arms had grown steadily stronger. There is no evidence to indicate their parents' attitude to their sons' political evolution, but it is difficult to imagine them all continuing to live together under one roof if there had been serious differences of opinion. Neither in Gebhard's 'Reminiscences' nor in Heinrich's diary are there any indications of parental objections, not even when the two brothers eventually took part in the Hitler Putsch.

As early as September 1923 there had been rumours in Munich of a forthcoming *coup d'état*. There was a pervasive feeling that something had to happen, and the members of the Combat League in particular were straining at the leash. Adolf Hitler, too, was urging swift action. He was running out of funds to support the SA, the nationalist associations were threatening to go their separate ways, and his prestige among the right-wing combat troops was in danger of fading if he did nothing.

During these months Bavaria was ruled by a triumvirate: Kahr, since 26 September 1923 Commissioner of State with almost dictatorial powers; Hans Ritter von Seisser, head of the Bavarian police; and the Army GOC for Bavaria, von Lossow. They, too, dreamt of a 'march on Berlin' – on the model of Mussolini's 'march on Rome' – to install a nationalist government there. Hitler attempted to get the three of them on his side – he needed military support and at least the tacit connivance of the police. Eventually, however, he decided to proceed without them, even though going it alone meant his putsch had virtually no chance of success. The decision to strike earlier than planned was taken on 7 November. Hitler wanted to give a rousing signal. On the 8th all the leading Munich politicians were gathered in the Bürgerbräukeller to hear an address by Kahr.

With an audience of three thousand, the Bürgerbräukeller, a beer hall in the eastern part of the city, was full to bursting. Kahr had already finished the first part of his speech when Hitler and his SA stormed the building, and in the ensuing tumult, waving his gun, proclaimed the 'national revolution'. General von Lossow and Hans von Seisser took countermeasures, which more or less stifled the putsch at birth. Now Hitler and the SA were going to pay the price for the rushed, improvised preparation.

That evening, Captain Röhm and his supporters in the Reichskriegsflagge had assembled in the Löwenbräukeller on the other side of Munich, awaiting Hitler's orders from the Bürgerbräukeller. A courier arrived with instructions to occupy Army headquarters, which were in the centre of Munich between Odeonsplatz and the university. Röhm succeeded in this, but he omitted to take the telephone exchange, via which during the night Lossow requested support from troops loyal to the government in the surrounding area. The attempt by the putschists to occupy other government buildings and barracks foundered on their own lack of organization.

When, late in the morning of 9 November, Hitler set off with two thousand mostly armed men for a demonstration in the city centre, the putsch was as good as over. This 'national revolution' attracted only the occasional spectator to cheer them on, while others mocked them. When the procession arrived at the Feldherrnhalle on Odeonsplatz a furious gun battle broke out, in the course of which fourteen putschists and four policemen were killed. Hitler was narrowly missed by a bullet. Hermann Göring, wounded in the leg, managed to flee across the Austrian border with other leading putschists. Julius Streicher, Wilhelm Frick, Ernst Röhm and others were arrested. Hitler was caught the following day in the house of the publisher Ernst Hanfstängl and taken to Landsberg Prison, where Count Arco-Valley had to vacate his spacious cell for the new high-ranking prisoner.

Gebhard and Heinrich, too, were at the meeting in the Löwenbräukeller, 'a social evening for the comrades of the Reichskriegsflagge', as Gebhard put it in his 'Reminiscences'. His formulation suggests they just happened to be in the Löwenbräukeller, but the likelihood is that they were with Röhm, waiting for Hitler's further orders. Suddenly, Gebhard records, a messenger from the Bürgerbräukeller appeared and announced that Hitler

> together with Kahr, Lossow and Seisser, had proclaimed a nationalist government! Today it is impossible to imagine the enthusiasm with which the news was greeted by everyone in the place. Old men and women had tears running down their faces, young people jumped up on the tables, everyone went wild with excitement. The Reichskriegsflagge was given the task of occupying the Army District Headquarters on the corner of Ludwigstrasse and Schönfeldstrasse. In next to no time the company had fallen in and marched off to the city centre under the leadership of Captain Röhm.

When they arrived there after a half-hour march, accompanied 'by the excited crowd from the beer cellar', it looked as if 'everything was in order. We didn't worry about what was going to happen next, the important thing was that something *had* happened.' At the time they had gone there 'purely as patriotic soldiers, students and workers', not 'with a clear allegiance to Hitler'.

In his 'Reminiscences', written in the 1970s, Gebhard gives a detailed description of the heroic epic of the Hitler Putsch, in which he took part in the front line, side by side with Heinrich. It is a report full of nostalgic memories of their great days and his own role in them. He describes the course of events during the night, their gradual encirclement by government troops; in loving detail he remembers the exact position of every machine-gun. I look at the famous photo of Heinrich at the barbed-wire barricade, bearing the standard of the Reichskriegsflagge. Suddenly I'm certain I can see Gebhard, further to the right of the picture, in his cap. Later on I have my doubts again, the photo is not clear enough. It's possible, though.

Gebhard goes into the greatest detail about moments he clearly found moving: especially one of his comrades 'planting his Annaberg pennant' on the barricade. This pennant had been awarded to the members of Epp's Freikorps and the Oberland League who had tried to prevent the cession of the eastern parts of Upper Silesia to Poland and had taken part in the successful and brutal suppression of Polish uprisings in Upper Silesia. The battle of Annaberg, in the Erzgebirge, the mountains on the Czech–German border, was accorded almost mythical status in right-wing circles.

Gebhard even manages to describe as a secret triumph

the moment when the putschists had to capitulate: 'we had to hand over all our weapons and ammunition, then we were free to withdraw. I have to say, hats off to the infantry company to whom we had to surrender our weapons. They didn't move a muscle, even though, after we'd handed over our rifles we threw our cartridges down at their feet with one hell of a clatter.' Years later he still seemed proud of that demonstrative gesture. Clearly Gebhard too, like Heinrich, had a weakness for uplifting feelings when it came to the German people and nation, the military, and male comradeship.

> And then came the withdrawal. In the middle was our fallen comrade Faust, carried on a stretcher. We wanted to take him out to his parents. In silence we marched through the streets. I remember the smirks on the faces of many a worthy citizen, while the previous evening they had cheered us on. At the Theresienwiese we saw a crowd of workers, who had just finished work at the factories in Sendling, coming towards us. We expected there would be another brawl. How wrong we were! Not one harsh word. The workers stood in silence and took off their hats and caps as we marched past with the dead man; a few women went up to the stretcher and gently stroked the canvas sheet covering the dead body.

A few days after the failed putsch, on 15 November, the Rentenmark was introduced as the new monetary unit (to be replaced the next year by the Reichsmark). This finally stabilized economic life, even if at the cost of increased unemployment. Heinrich and Gebhard were affected by this too, since Gebhard's work at the bank finished with the end of the flood of worthless paper, and the Werner Company, of which Heinrich had had such high hopes for a career as a soldier, was disbanded after the *coup d'état*.

Many of the inhabitants of Munich had sympathized with the putsch. After its failure, however, the swastikas and storm troopers vanished from the city. Hitler, Röhm and others were now in prison, the NSDAP was banned and the nationalist movement fragmented. The sympathy for right-wing radicals remained, however. At the regional elections in the city on 6 April 1924 the *Völkischer Block*, the largest grouping within the extreme right-wing nationalist movement, received 33 per cent of the votes, more than the Social Democrats and the Communists put together. With the currency reform the political situation also gradually stabilized, and at the general election in December 1924 the nationalists were no longer a force to be reckoned with. Though only for the time being.

7

Service and Sacrifice:
The Years following the Putsch

Gebhard was lucky. In January 1924 he found new employment in the drawing office of Neumayer's Engineering Works in Freimann, a district in the north-east of Munich. There 'preparations were being made for the production under licence of the little English air-cooled Rover car, a small car that was to be a sensation on the German market'. He earned a whole hundred and twenty marks a month. Heinrich, on the other hand, could not find work, even though he mobilized all the family's contacts with friends and acquaintances. His parents, too, made efforts to find a suitable position for him with the Farmers' Association or as an estate manager. It must have been a new experience for Heinrich to discover that for once the family's extensive connections could not help him.

Once more he was living with the family in the school apartment on Marsplatz; during the day he was mostly going round looking for work or visiting friends. Together with Gebhard and Ernst he often popped in to see Kätha and Lu Zahler. By now they were married and had a little daughter called Lotti. Heinrich also used to go

{ 100 }

by himself to chat to Kätha, sometimes about his first love, her sister Maja, who had been married since the beginning of 1921. Käthe told him Maja's husband suffered from a 'nervous disease' and that she had therefore decided not to have any children by him – a sensible decision, Heinrich thought, though it was 'a crying shame for that admirable woman'.

He also saw his friend Falk Zipperer regularly. They would talk about National Socialism or read out pamphlets to each other. While Falk had serious ambitions as a writer, about which Heinrich made admiring comments, Falk responded by praising the nationalistic articles Heinrich was writing for provincial newspapers.

Heinrich was committing himself more and more to the nationalist movement; he joined the National Socialist Freedom Movement of Gregor Strasser and General Ludendorff, appearing as a speaker for it in various towns around Bavaria during the February elections. On the 15th he went to the Stadelheim district of Munich to visit Ernst Röhm in prison. 'We had an excellent and fairly uninhibited chat. I had taken him a pan-German newspaper, which pleased him immensely.' For his part, Heinrich was relieved that 'the good Captain Röhm' had not lost any of his good humour. In all Heinrich's visits that February to friends of the family, to the Zahlers, to his father's former student Ernst Fischer and his wife whom the Himmler brothers called 'Uncle' and 'Aunt', and to other members of the Apollo fraternity, the conversation kept coming back to questions of politics, especially the forthcoming trial of Adolf Hitler. The brothers also had many a 'heated discussion' with their father, as Heinrich noted in his diary. These were probably on the topic that was closest to their hearts: the longed-for rebirth and renewed greatness of the German nation.

The trial of Hitler and of the others responsible for the putsch began on 26 February 1924. From the very beginning the court treated the accused with great leniency, allowing Hitler to dominate proceedings with his long-winded speeches and, when the sentences were pronounced, assuring the putschists that they had acted 'in a patriotic spirit and with the most noble, selfless of intentions'. In his final hour-long address Hitler presented himself as the future 'destroyer of Marxism'. On 1 April, together with three of his fellow accused, he was given the mild sentence, including the time spent on remand, of five years' *Festungshaft* (confinement in a fortress), a scandalous verdict that was compounded by the extremely comfortable conditions in which he served his sentence. He was released only nine months later. Hitler's self-assured conduct in the courtroom and his bellicose speeches against Marxism, which was particularly hated by the Munich middle classes since the revolution, as well as what amounted to carte blanche given him by the court, brought him widespread admiration far beyond the circle of his immediate followers.

Hitler had become a secret folk hero. He was given preferential treatment during his time in Landsberg Prison, where he received streams of visitors and baskets of letters from admirers. In that year Georg Schott's *Volksbuch vom Hitler* (The Hitler Chapbook), in which the author transformed him into a kind of demigod, was published in Munich. Hitler, Schott wrote, was 'the living embodiment of the nation's longing'.

*

In view of the hopelessness of his search for work, Heinrich once more entertained dreams of emigrating. He was a member of the *Bund der Artamanen*, a group that had developed its own 'blood-and-soil' theories and planned to colonize the 'east' with farmers living in fortified villages. For a while he even learnt Russian and Spanish, but whenever the prospect of work abroad took on a more concrete form, he shrank from it – either because he lacked the courage to take such a step, or because he increasingly saw himself in the role of the selfless fighter for his people and consequently had to stay in the country.

To support and strengthen his ideology he looked for suitable reading, following Hitler's advice in *Mein Kampf* (My Struggle), written while he was in prison, that his followers should read books that confirmed their faith. Heinrich now had plenty of time for reading. He showed a distinct preference for works on nationalist ideology, with their glorification of 'German qualities' – fighting spirit, loyalty and a refusal to compromise – and of their 'racial superiority', such as Werner Jansen's *Das Buch der Treue* (The Book of Loyalty) and *Ritter, Tod und Teufel* (Knight, Death and Devil) by Hans Günther. In 1923 Adolf Viktor von Koerber's *Adolf Hitler. Sein Leben und seine Reden* (Adolf Hitler: His Life and His Speeches) was published in Munich. Here was another book that fired Heinrich's enthusiasm and from which he read out during cosy evenings together with his uncle and aunt Hugo and Friedel Höfl when he visited them in Apfeldorf in February 1924. In his comments on the book in his reading list, Heinrich wrote that Hitler was 'a truly great man & above all a genuine & pure man. His speeches are magnificent examples of the German & Aryan spirit.'

In his regular comments on his reading, attacks on the Church now increasingly appeared. He criticized books on Catholicism as 'too doctrinaire' or 'hypercatholic'. His need for a belief in the supernatural shifted ever closer to spiritualism and occultism, an interest that he was to pursue during the following years in a variety of ways. Heinrich still went with the family to mass on Sundays and enjoyed a good sermon, but he also talked a lot about his doubts – with Hugo Höfl, for example, and with Wilhelm Patin, another distant relative. Patin had taught religion at a Gymnasium and for a while was a canon of the cathedral chapter; he had often visited the Himmler family while studying theology in Munich and had been Heinrich's sponsor at confirmation. In 1924, by which time he had qualified as a lawyer, the two frequently met and discussed such things as 'the great significance of the NSDAP for the deliverance of our oppressed Fatherland'; together they attended political meetings in the Hofbräuhaus. Patin was to remain in close contact with Heinrich later on. In 1933 he would join the SS, working initially for its security service in Munich, where he was in charge of the section dealing with ecclesiastical questions; later he transferred to the Central Security Department where, among other things, he gathered information on the activities of the Polish Catholic Church, which proved valuable to the intelligence service.

During this period Heinrich again showed his willingness to sort out affairs for other members of the family. Presumably this was not just because he had plenty of time, but also because he saw it as a way of improving the rather pathetic figure he cut just then. An opportunity arose when, shortly after Gebhard had started his new

job, he and his fiancée Paula Stölzle broke up. There had
already been one serious crisis in their relationship in the
spring of 1923. At a carnival ball Paula had been 'unfaith-
ful' to Gebhard – which probably just meant that she had
flirted with another man. Gebhard had asked Lu to get
Heinrich to go to Weilheim, where Paula lived, in his
support, and Heinrich had immediately 'dealt with' the
problem. In a letter from that time he warned Paula:

> You have most ignominiously failed a test [of faithful-
> ness, K.H.] . . . If your union is to be a happy one for
> you and for the nation, which must be founded on
> healthy, moral families, you will have to be kept on a
> tight rein, on a barbarically tight rein. Since you are
> not hard and strict enough on yourself . . . and your
> future husband is too good for you and has too little
> knowledge of human nature . . . I feel it is my duty to
> do this.

Despite his lack of experience with the opposite sex,
Heinrich clearly had absolute confidence in his judgement
of women. Even while he was a student, he had repeatedly
quarrelled with his friend Kätha because he was too harsh
in his judgement of others:

> I provoke other people with everything I say [he noted
> in his diary]. I'm going to break with Frau Loritz and
> Kätha, and this will last some considerable time. Our
> relations are strictly formal. I have my doubts whether
> [Lu] will be all that happy. But I hope that Kätha can
> be trained. K. & her mother suffer from incredible
> fem. conceit . . . I have too much self-respect to play
> the clown to fem. whims – this is why I'm breaking
> with them. I do not find it easy . . . but I must finally

act in accordance with what I think. I intend to strive every day to train myself: there is still such a terrible amount wanting.

He soon made it up with Kätha and her mother, but their relationship remained difficult. When Lu once told him that Kätha thought he totally despised women and never gave them their due, he confided to his diary – and presumably also to Lu – that such was not his opinion – his only objection was 'to female pride wanting to rule in areas which are beyond its abilities'. He went on to define his concept of the ideal relationship between men and women:

> A woman is loved by a proper man in 3 ways. As a dear child that one has to scold & perhaps punish in its irrationality, that one protects & cares for because it is delicate & weak & because one loves it so much. Then as a wife & as a faithful, understanding comrade who fights her way through life at one's side, ever loyal and without hampering the man's spirit & putting him in shackles. And as a wife whose feet one kisses and who, through her feminine softness and childlike, pure sanctity, gives one the strength not to weaken in the hardest struggles, & grants one at ideal moments of the soul the most divine bliss.

The parallels in his clashes with Kätha and Paula reveal Heinrich's perversely unrealistic view of the 'ideal woman' in which adoration and disdain sit side by side. He rejected female strength and self-will, such as Paula showed – they were menacing signs of female independence, which had almost the taint of 'whorishness'.

Paula's reply to Heinrich's harsh and arrogant letter

had been full of remorse, and she had promised contritely to mend her ways. But the relationship between her and Gebhard kept on hitting difficult patches, and during one of Paula's visits to Munich in February 1924 the coolness between them was clear for all to see. Paula had supposedly been 'talked about' again, and this time a family council was held over lunch at which Heinrich argued vehemently that the engagement should be broken off so as to restore the family honour. Once more he was the one who undertook to adopt the 'right' tone with Paula, since he felt Gebhard was too polite. In this he behaved in the way he frequently did later on as Reichsführer SS. He would overlook human weakness once, generously giving the 'sinner' the chance to redeem himself; if, however, the miscreant did not take that chance, then he was out of favour with Himmler once and for all, and consigned to outer darkness.

So intent he was on his task that he completely failed to see that Gebhard and Paula had long since realized they were not suited to each other. If Heinrich had not been there, adding fuel to the fire, they would probably have parted with mutual respect and little fuss. While Gebhard increasingly left things to his brother, Paula resisted Heinrich's attempts 'to try and train her for Gebhard' and accused Gebhard of being 'hopeless' because he put up with Heinrich dictating to him.

But admonishing Paula was not enough for Heinrich. In May that year he informed her, through their aunt Friedel Höfl, that she should take care not to stir things up against the Himmlers. He was, he warned her, 'a most good-natured person', but there was 'another, quite different side to him' which he could show if people forced him to. His letters to Paula reveal how arrogant and intolerant Heinrich had become in the last few years. Only those who bowed to his ideals were accepted as 'our kind of people', and he drew a sharp distinction between 'us' and 'the rest'. 'Us' were his family and friends, those who were of a like mind politically and his 'racial equals'; with these people he did everything he could to maintain good relations. 'The rest' were those who disagreed with him politically or who were his 'racial inferiors', but also those who had fallen into disfavour, who had been excluded from the circle of those who belonged because of behaviour he disapproved of. With a thirst for vengeance that had something archaic about it, he sought to destroy such people socially; if necessary, as he informed Paula Stölzle, he would not rest until 'the opponent in question has been shut out from all society, in both civic and moral terms'. At the time, given his age and his social position, such a threat sounded as ridiculous as it sounded arrogant, and Heinrich must have suspected it. 'Stay firm & and do not allow yourself to be laid low by doubts,' he urged himself in his diary. Later, when such was the attitude of the Reichsführer SS, the consequences could be fatal.

The break with Paula and the Stölzles clearly created no ill-feeling within the family. Everything continued as normal: the family ate together and exchanged news, on Sundays the men went for walks together during which they often had animated discussions about politics, and while Heinrich kept on chewing over the events of 9 November with his elder brother he also enjoyed fooling around with Ernst. After one Sunday breakfast he noted: 'High jinks with Ernst, who's a little devil.' And on the same day after lunch he noted once more: 'high jinks'. It doesn't sound as if the clash with Paula Stölzle had seriously affected the mood of the Himmler household.

Much more depressing was the fact that Heinrich still had not found work. The problem was increasingly urgent because Ernst's studies had to be financed. He had passed his *Abitur* at Easter 1924 with outstanding grades in all subjects. The pressure Heinrich felt after months of unemployment can be seen in his complaint to his Uncle Hugo in May 1924: 'Unfortunately I'm still here,' he wrote. 'The way things drag on is terrible. These weeks of waiting are really wearing me down.' His opportunity finally came at the end of June: Gregor Strasser, *Gauleiter* (regional head) of the National Socialist Freedom Movement in Lower Bavaria, needed a secretary and assistant for his office in Landshut. Heinrich applied and was appointed. He left Munich at the beginning of July.

Even though his parents must surely have been delighted that he was once more in employment, this new position would certainly not have corresponded to their ideas of a proper occupation. Consequently Heinrich had to emphasize the importance of his work all the more. As Strasser's assistant he had 'to build up and run the organization of the whole of Lower Bavaria', he wrote, two months after starting work, to Robert Kistler, a former member of the same regiment. Even then he was complaining, as he kept doing later on, that he had 'an awful lot to do'. On the other hand, the position seemed to fit his inclinations: 'the organizational work, for which I bear full responsibility, suits me very well'. One part of this was office work, but he also spent a lot of time riding around on his motorbike, distributing newspapers and propaganda material and making speeches in small towns. In his pocket diary he noted journeys all over Bavaria, but he also travelled to Saxony, Baden and as far afield as the Baltic, everywhere there were Party cells and interested supporters.

Heinrich was exactly the right man for this work, which demanded idealism, dedication to the cause and conscientiousness in carrying out the appointed tasks – but was very poorly paid. He himself described the 'work of us nationalists' as 'a labour of self-denial', of which 'the fruit will ripen only after many years'. Nonetheless, he went on, he carried out this 'hard work unwaveringly and now more than ever out of this boundless love for the land of Germany, which today is sick unto death'. And he concluded his letter to Kistler: 'It is selfless labour in the service of a great idea and a great cause for which we will quite naturally never receive recognition. Nor do we expect any.'

The thought that he was sacrificing himself for his people, his country and an idea, that he was serving them without expecting any recognition for these services, was a leitmotif running through Heinrich's life. He clearly needed this conviction for his self-image. And recognition of his work from others was not slow in coming. After the failed putsch, a university friend, Mariele Rausch-meyer, commemorated his action in a letter: 'I would like to thank you and your people for that one glorious moment on the morning of 9 November.' They had all gone out into the street 'wild with happiness and rejoicing. There was nothing one would not have sacrificed with thousandfold pleasure for the freedom of the nation.'

At the university, she went on, people no longer greeted each other with 'Good morning', but with '*Heil!*' When they reached the War Ministry in Ludwigstrasse, 'the tears came to her eyes' at the sight of the black, white and red flag (the flag of the German Empire, retained as the war ensign by the Weimar Republic), then the troops of the 'Reichskriegsflagge, with Heinrich Himmler in the vanguard, the flag on his arm – one could see from the flag how safe and secure things felt'. For her the connection with Hitler was of secondary importance; Ludendorff was the man she worshipped.

She sent the letter to Heinrich in June 1924 as 'a small token of warmest gratitude and faithful remembrance, for the hours during which we learnt to hope once more'. Now, Mariele continued, they were all beyond that and had 'become harder'. What, however, had remained the same was 'our iron will for the future, our loyalty to the dead since 1914 and our angry love for a land that rebuffs that love as does no other land'. With a 'confident *Heil!*' she expressed her pleasure that Heinrich was hard at work again with the nationalists. Mariele Rauschmeyer was a woman Heinrich would have no qualms about counting as 'one of us'.

On 2 August, shortly after he took up his position in Landshut, she wrote to him again, just after she had taken her degree as doctor of medicine. She was surprised that he had made politics his profession, especially as in the spring she had used her contacts to try and find him a post as estate manager. She expressed, though, her complete agreement with his conviction that being a German nationalist and 'Teutonic in the full sense of the word' did not simply consist of anti-Semitism and opposition to the Bavarian People's Party: it had to be fought for, and at the same time young people had to be brought up to believe in it. She herself, she said, wanted to make her contribution, 'to be the way the fighters visualize German women, the work at the front for the man, and at home for the woman'.

An old 'fellow combatant and fellow sufferer', Emil Wäckerle, also expressed his delight in a letter of 1 August: 'I am exceptionally pleased that the nationalist movement in Lower Bavaria is in your hands. I wish you luck and fruitful labours.' The warmest sympathy and encouragement also came from a distant relative from Weilheim, Marianne Nässl, a teacher who was living in the house of her brother-in-law Hugo Höfl in Apfeldorf until she emigrated to Brazil in 1926, where she also worked as a teacher. 'Mariandl', as she was called, had obviously kept in touch with the Himmler family and had met Heinrich a few times. On 8 September 1926, shortly after her arrival in Rio, she wrote to 'Dear Heini'. Heinrich, given his dreams of going abroad, was probably enthusiastic about her bold step; at the time when Marianne was emigrating he was reading a book called *As a German Settler in the Brazilian Jungle*. For her part she showed a keen interest in Heinrich's activities, and got him to send her German newspapers, presumably including the Nazi Party paper, the *Völkischer Beobachter* (Nationalist Observer), which she distributed among her German acquaintances in Rio.

'Living here abroad, I am really keen to see how things will develop in Germany in the near future, things you are so actively involved in! But think about what you are doing and be very careful!' she wrote, only to conclude

that it was 'pointless and ridiculous' of her to give him
advice – he would get more than enough of that from his
parents and, after all, he knew what he wanted. 'Your
purpose is a good one, based on ideals . . . and no one
can ever deflect you from the goals you have set yourself.'
Her own wish, she said, was 'for the German nation to
recover its health again and be purged of all the vermin
and bad elements there are in it, so that it can fully
recover its position in the world and once more take its
rightful place among nations. But with all this Jew-trash
there is today, it is impossible to get anywhere.' At the
end she sent him 'thousands of true-German greetings'.
Images such as the equation of the 'Jew-trash' with the
'vermin' of which the nation must purge itself found a
ready ear in Heinrich. Four years after this letter, on 1
September 1930, Marianne Nässl joined the NSDAP Foreign Organization, Brazilian section. Some years later she
was to return to Germany, where she became a close
friend of my grandparents.

Heinrich's political commitment to a party which at
the time was tiny and in danger of being banned won him
the sympathy of friends and 'comrades', who admired
him as a man who was prepared to fight for his ideals.
During the mid-twenties electoral support for right-wing
radical parties was low. However, such groups clearly –
and correctly – believed that their potential backing
among voters who secretly sympathized with their ideas
was much greater, and that they would regain their open
support when the time came.

There is much to suggest that Himmler's parents
agreed with this broad nationalist consensus. But at the
same time they were concerned about Heinrich's future.

His choice of profession went against the conventions of his respectable bourgeois background; however, it did not, as some of his biographers suggest, lead to a break with his family. His parents probably urged him to look for a 'proper' position, for there is a letter he wrote from Landshut at the end of October 1924 as a member of the Reich Association of Graduates in Agriculture, clearly looking for employment. On 5 November he received a reply: he should not set his sights too high, he was told; with his qualifications 'a *senior* position is more or less out of the question because of your lack of experience'.

For his work for the Party Heinrich was not very well paid, but no worse than his brother. His parents may well have been sceptical, but they probably did not start thinking of him as a failure or a 'dreamer' until later on, when he was still on a minimal living wage while Gebhard was gradually rising in the world. Heinrich continued to come to Munich now and then to see friends, and on those occasions he stayed in his parents' apartment. He always came for his mother's and father's birthdays and they continued to correspond. Until the end of the twenties Heinrich kept a note of all the letters he sent and received, meticulously numbered and with the date and place they were sent from. From this list it is clear that even after his departure from Munich in the summer of 1924 he received a letter from home roughly every two weeks and replied about once a month. Mostly he sent postcards from his travels.

These ties between Heinrich and his family, which remained stable and unbroken, are misrepresented both in historical and biographical research as well as in the family folklore – perhaps because they all wanted to keep their distance from such a criminal character as Heinrich Himmler, to see him as a 'one-off', as someone abnormal that they and their 'normal' environment had nothing to do with.

By the end of 1924 Gebhard was unemployed again because his firm, Neumayer's Engineering Works, was down-sizing. But early the next year he found a position as assistant teacher at the City Technical College for Precision Engineering, which was situated next to the Wittelsbacher Gymnasium. This suggests that his father, as head of the Gymnasium, had used his influence with his opposite number in the technical college. Gebhard taught technical drawing, physics and the science and use of instruments; his position was made permanent as early as April 1925. This change to teaching seems to have been a happy one: 'I settled in very quickly, teaching suited me perfectly. I was very soon on excellent terms with my pupils as well as with those on the evening courses for apprentices.' He continued to live with his parents, doubtless for practical reasons: the headmaster's apartment in the Gymnasium was huge and there was a maid and a cook to keep things tidy, do the laundry and provide meals.

Gebhard had become friendly with the sister of an old friend from university, Richard Wendler. One year younger than Gebhard, Mathilde Wendler, known as Hilde, had qualified as a bookkeeper and worked in a Munich bank. According to Gebhard's daughter, her parents met at a fraternity ball and fell in love; they got married on 18 September 1926. Heinrich, who had just moved back to Munich, was at the wedding. On 12 September Gregor Strasser had been made head of propaganda for the NSDAP; Heinrich followed him to the Party headquarters in Munich, where he was given an office post. Here, at last, he had the prospect of at least modest advancement.

Strasser, a pharmacist from Landshut who, like Heinrich, had been in Epp's Freikorps, had been in the Party since 1921 and had also taken part in Hitler's 'Beer Hall Putsch'. The two Strasser brothers – though Otto would leave the NSDAP in 1930 – had the 'left wing' behind them and enjoyed considerable influence in the Party up to 1933. At the conference of Party leaders in Bamberg on 14 February 1926 the so-called left tried to push through a reform of the old Party programme, a move which Hitler categorically rejected. Strasser gave way, especially as the meeting showed that for most of the Gauleiters the Party programme was less important than the figure of Hitler as Führer. During the last six months of 1932 Strasser, as head of the political organization of the NSDAP, was looked on as second only to Hitler. In December of that year, however, there was a disagreement between them, one of the reasons being Strasser's persistent demand for the nationalization of the banks and heavy industry, on which Hitler was reliant for funds. In 1934 Strasser was murdered during the so-called Röhm Putsch – by Heinrich Himmler's SS.

8

'We Must Be Happy':
Heinrich and Marga

With his transfer to the Party Central Office in Munich, Heinrich saw his chance of developing his career independently of Strasser. Despite the increased office work at Party headquarters, he continued to travel around a lot on propaganda tours. In December 1926 he went to Bad Reichenhall, where he met his future wife.

As Gebhard told *Der Spiegel* editor Heinz Höhne years later, Heinrich went into a hotel lobby to avoid a downpour and doffed his Tyrolean hat so vigorously to a lady that he soaked her with the spray. With her blue eyes and thick blond hair, Marga Siegroth, née Boden, who was taking the waters there, corresponded in outward appearance to Heinrich's ideal woman. She had grown up with her four brothers and sister on an estate in Pomerania, had worked as a nurse in a military hospital during the war, and now ran a small private clinic in Berlin-Schöneberg funded by her father. One problem was that she was, after a short marriage, a divorcee. For the moment their romance remained a secret, since they knew that it would meet with the disapproval of his parents at least. Marga was not only divorced, she was seven years older and a Prussian Protestant into the bargain. Gebhard and Hilde were the first to be told about their relationship. Heinrich admitted to his brother that he would rather 'clear a hall of a thousand Communists on his own' than confess his relationship to his parents.

Unfortunately, Heinrich's letters to Marga have been lost, but Marga's letters written during their engagement make it clear what it was that united the couple, who were dissimilar in so many respects: they were both interested in herbal medicine and homoeopathy and dreamt of having some land of their own, keeping hens and growing vegetables and herbs. Heinrich supplied Marga with literature on the Freemasons and the 'international Jewish conspiracy'. On 22 June 1928, when she was clearly annoyed with the co-owner of her clinic, the gynaecologist and surgeon Dr Bernhard Hauschildt, she wrote to Heinrich: 'That Hauschildt! Those Jews are all the same!' They were united in their anti-Semitism, even if Marga felt it was pointless to waste time 'moaning about the Jews', since 'the facts themselves speak volumes' (a letter of 2 November 1927). In addition, they both liked puzzle magazines; indeed, even during their short visits to each other they seem to have been an indispensable antidote to boredom. Once, weeks before they were due to meet, Marga asked Heinrich to start collecting puzzle magazines – 'otherwise, we won't have enough and we won't know what to do in T[ölz]'.

At first Marga's letters were self-assured and full of humour. 'Today I feel like a fight, like mocking things,' she wrote to him on New Year's Eve 1927. 'You aren't against that, but you are more for peace.' And when she told Heinrich how enthusiastic her father had been about their plans to marry, she added an ironic rider: 'For him women have one sole justification for their existence, and that is to get married.' She called Heinrich pigheaded, her '*Landsknecht* with the hard heart', 'tough on the outside [but] sweet and kind' to her; she mocked his aversion to the metropolis – 'There you are, stuck in Bavaria, afraid of the metropolis of Berlin, while I'm not at all afraid of small towns.'

She was impressed by his honest love for her and his romantic letters, which he spent half the night composing, and envied him his greater facility with words. And her own letters do, indeed, often sound thin, the same repeated assurances of love like empty clichés. Even though she more than once criticized his pessimism and sombre brooding – 'to put it bluntly, I beg you to stop it' – they were basically in agreement that people were 'false and vile'. This meant that they clung even more closely to each other and to their 'pure love'. 'We must be happy,' Marga wrote imploringly in March 1928, only to admit a few days later, in a gloomy mood, 'Do you know, darling, sometimes everything fills me with dread. So much that is new! People and things, the whole environment. Then I'm sometimes even a little glad it's still some way off.'

The more their plans for the future took on concrete form, the less importance Marga attached to her independent life as head of the clinic, where she had worked for years. More and more frequently now she wrote that she would have no regrets at leaving, since she had had 'nothing but trouble' there because 'the people are so horrible'. However, her longing for their happiness together was constantly disturbed by fears, not least of being alone in a strange environment.

Heinrich resisted her demand that she have him all to herself. Even before the wedding they often argued – about whether the wedding should be in Berlin or in Munich, about arrangements such as the honeymoon, selling the clinic, buying a house near Munich, about tradesmen, and also about whether Heinrich would be allowed to cook when they were married, which she banned. 'You'll be wanting to keep an eye on what's cooking. No, I'm not having that. If you insist on cooking you'll have to do all the other housewife's chores as well.' They would have to swap roles, she said: 'No half measures.'

These letters also make clear Marga's reserve with regard to his family, her absolute phobia about contact with people she did not know – and of whom she was not wrong in assuming they rejected her. On 20 April 1928 his mother wrote to Heinrich, after he had finally told his parents of his decision to marry Marga:

My dear, dear Heinrich,
Only now can I bring myself to write you these few lines – I had to calm down a little first. First and foremost let me wish you, from the bottom of a mother's heart that truly loves you, every, every happiness, my dear son. May you find, in the bride you have chosen, a loving companion, a faithful comrade who will understand you and share in your joy and sorrow with all her heart. That this mother's heart is filled with deep sorrow as well as joy is something you will know and feel yourself, otherwise you would not have found it so difficult to tell us.

Her heartfelt wish was to talk to him, and she suggested a day when his father would also be there. The latter added no word to the letter, apart from getting his wife to send 'all his love' – but perhaps she had added that of her own accord.

His mother's reaction in her letter was as horrified as was to be expected, faced as she was with a proposed union which, given the conventions and moral outlook of the time, must have been shocking to the Himmlers and their circle of friends and acquaintances. A divorced woman, older than him, and a Protestant into the bargain! His mother, a devout Catholic, probably found the last point harder to bear than his father.

With heavy hearts, Heinrich's parents gave their approval to his decision and made an effort to give Marga a friendly welcome. When, in May, she planned to spend a few days in Munich they insisted she stay with them – which Marga accepted only with great reluctance. After the family had got to know her, they all wrote her friendly letters. Again she found it difficult to respond: '. . . I was quite speechless – give them my thanks, but it's impossible for me to write myself. My dear, what troubles you're going to have in your relationship with me, I'm really afraid of new people,' she told Heinrich.

Clearly his parents had come to terms with their new daughter-in-law, and his father started to look around for a suitable house for the couple. He sent Heinrich adverts from the newspapers with his comments: 'House in the country with poultry' or 'Cheap. Dirt cheap!' and notes about prices, situation and anything else he had been able to find out.

Marga's share in the clinic had already been bought

out by the co-owner Dr Hauschildt, and after some searching Heinrich acquired a modest wooden house in Waldtrudering, at the time still an out-of-the-way suburb in the east of Munich. He not only saw to the purchase of the house, but also organized workmen for the necessary alterations, since Marga had to continue working in Berlin until just before the wedding. While Heinrich, after all the lean years, obviously enjoyed handling relatively large sums of money, Marga, in far-off Berlin, was worried there would be nothing left. 'I'm at my wits' end how we're going to pay for all this. I did ask you not to buy anything else,' she wrote on 27 June, in her last letter before the wedding.

Heinrich and Marga were married on 3 July 1928, first of all in a civil wedding – the registry office was right next to her apartment and the clinic – and then in a church ceremony in Zepernick, just to the north of Berlin, where her parents lived. Ernst was the only one of the Himmler family who thought about going, but then decided against it because he was in the middle of his final examinations for his diploma in electrical engineering. The witnesses were Marga's father, a former estate-owner in Torun (the German Thorn, since 1919 part of Poland), and her brother Hellmut. Eleven years later the Reichsführer SS was to be made a freeman of the small town of Zepernick. Ironically, the correspondence concerning the award was conducted by Heinrich's secretary and mistress, Hedwig Potthast.

In her last letter to Heinrich before the wedding, Marga had written, 'Darling, make sure we're not surprised by visitors during the first fortnight. Also that we

don't need to go into town to see your family.' She was
well aware that the happy life with just the two of them
together, which she repeatedly invoked ('then we will be
together for always' – 'I have only you, you are my sole
joy'), would not last long, since Heinrich would soon be
away on the campaign trail. On the other hand, she was
understandably afraid of closer acquaintance with the
people who were to be her new family. She clearly did
not feel confident in her ability to win over her parents-
in-law. Consequently her contact with Heinrich's family
remained sparse.

Marga, who joined the NSDAP immediately after they
got married, was by herself in Waldtrudering most of the
time. Heinrich constructed the henhouses, then he was off
again, for days or even weeks on end. So she had all the
work, but it brought in no money, since the hens hardly
laid any eggs. Visitors seldom made the long journey out
of the city. On 28 September 'Ernsti' came to see her and
brought supplies with him, above all puzzle magazines.
She must have found the solitude hard to bear. After nine
months of marriage, now pregnant, she complained in a
letter to Heinrich of moods of depression: 'What's happening to me? . . . I don't ask any questions. I don't even
think any thoughts.'

Their daughter Gudrun was born on 8 August 1929.
It was a Caesarian birth and Marga had to stay in
hospital with the baby for three weeks. When she came
home Heinrich took leave in order to look after his wife
and child before setting out on his travels again. A few
days after he left, her parents-in-law rang to see how
Marga and the baby were. The Himmlers loved their

granddaughter and always asked with great concern how their 'Püppi' was doing. They also came out to see them occasionally.

The social status he had worked so hard to achieve mattered a great deal to Gebhard Himmler senior, especially since December 1925 when the Ministry of Education had accorded him the title of *Geheimer Studienrat* (privy education councillor), the highest he could aspire to. Heinrich's unconventional choice of profession, his commitment to a fringe political party, his marriage to an older, divorced woman – all this his father must have seen as confirmation of his fear that his son was incapable of fulfilling the family's ambitious expectations – indeed, might even endanger the Himmlers' social position. Relations with his family only improved when Heinrich became a member of the Reichstag after the Party's success in the elections of 14 September 1930, which must have meant a huge rise for him in his parents' esteem. His father began to keep files with all the newspaper cuttings in which he was mentioned. 'From our d[ear] son Heinrich's political life,' he inscribed on the covers of the files, which contained predominantly cuttings from the *Völkischer Beobachter*. The idea of my cultured great-grandparents reading that primitive, rabble-rousing rag still surprises me, even though during 1929–30 in order to appeal to broader sections of the electorate the racial and anti-Semitic tirades were cut back in this main Party organ, as well as in Hitler's great campaign speeches. And the ploy was successful.

Heinrich's career in the Reichstag was the result of the sharp increase in the NSDAP's share of the vote from 2.6 per cent at the 1928 election to 18.3 per cent in September

1930. With this it became the second-largest party after the Social Democrats, and now made every effort to get rid of its image as a gang of thugs. Until then people in the mainly Catholic areas had had strong reservations about the Nazis, while in mainly Protestant areas a considerable number of their voters already came from the upper classes.

It is no coincidence that at this time, even though he had worked with 'the good Captain Röhm', Heinrich, middle-class as he was, was more interested in the elitist SS than in the SA, notorious for its 'hooliganism' which conservative sections of the population found repugnant. Heinrich had a good nose for the way the wind was blowing. In 1927 he had been appointed deputy leader of the organization and in January 1929 leader, Reichsführer SS. From the very beginning his aim was to build up a racial elite within the National Socialist movement, with minimum height and Nordic looks. By the end of the year he had turned Hitler's tiny bodyguard squad providing secuirty at public meetings into a thousand-strong organization that was attracting more and more ex-officers and men from the nobility, among them many former members of the Freikorps. By April 1931, with over three thousand members, the SS had become an integral part of the Nazi movement, even if it was still very small compared with the SA. Hitler gave it the motto: 'Thy honour is loyalty.' In August that year Himmler commissioned Reinhard Heydrich, a discharged naval intelligence officer, with setting up the SS's own security service. In the summer of 1932 it became commonly known as the SD (*Sicherheitsdienst*, Security Service) and in May 1934 the sole intelligence agency of the Nazi Party – a decisive step towards Henrich Himmler's ambition of making the SS the Party elite.

Heinrich's nurturing of an elite corps of guards whose loyalty was to the Führer also gave his parents a sense of belonging to the elite once more – a new elite – as it did for his brothers who, around 1930, began to associate themselves more and more with the Nazis. Gebhard was teaching in Munich and, despite his lack of pedagogical training, seems to have been a good teacher. 'Teaching can't be learnt, you have to be born to it,' he once told his eldest daughter. His own assessment seems to be confirmed by the consistently positive appraisals of his superiors. Thus an official report of 1929 acknowledged his 'remarkable skill in teaching and training', adding that he was also reliable and meticulous. The appraisal of 1931 is similar, commending him both for his good relations with the pupils and for his discipline and 'precision'.

On 16 October 1930 Gebhard and Hilde's second daughter was born. At some point during this time Gebhard became a member of the Bavarian Federation of Technical Colleges, where he soon played a leading role. He also joined the *Verein für das Deutschtum im Ausland* (Association for Germans Abroad), an organization that went back to 1880, when its forerunner, the German School Association, was founded. According to the statutes of the association, 'Germanness' was to be protected irrespective of national frontiers, and German minorities supported all over the world. In its ideological orientation as well as in its practical politics, the association was part of the nationalist movement. Its name was changed to Association for Germans Abroad in 1908. Its main task was the foundation and promotion of German schools abroad and, during the First World War, looking after the interests of German nationals living abroad.

How did Gebhard come to join this association? One influence may have been the close family contact with Marianne Nässl, who was active in promoting German interests in Brazil. In 1935 their father sent an extract from one of Marianne's letters on to Heinrich – 'She sends her most affectionate greetings. She is a brave German lass in a foreign country.' In the letter Marianne expressed her fury at a German theatre company that had had the cheek to perform plays by 'of all people, our worst enemies . . . The Germans, treated with contempt all over the world, eagerly study the plays of their enemies and then go and perform them abroad, as if the German nation was short of plays.' She asked Geheimrat Himmler to pass the message on to the Propaganda Ministry so that they could put a stop to it. Himmler immediately informed his son, who replied by return of post that his personal assistant was passing the message on to the Ministry.

One year later in Rio de Janeiro 'Mariandl' married Philipp Freiherr von Lützelburg, a botanist. In May 1938 Heinrich Himmler sent a telegram to Rio offering the fifty-eight-year-old baron the post of head of the new botanical section that was to be set up within the SS, the *Ahnenerbe* (a group carrying out research into and teaching on heredity), at a monthly salary of six hundred marks. Lützelburg accepted and immediately joined the Party, of which his wife and been a member since 1930. They moved to Berlin, where von Lützelburg, on the direct orders of the Reichsführer SS, cultivated a plant that supposedly cured cancer, the effectiveness of which he would test out on human beings in Dachau together with the concentration camp doctor Rascher. Later on Rascher denied this, but the suspicion remained. In 1942 von Lützelburg's research institute employed people in nine different locations in the Reich, including Dachau concentration camp.

Gebhard's eldest daughter still remembers well the Lützelburgs' apartment in Berlin-Wilmersdorf, filled with masks, snakes and other exotic decor, and the exciting stories about Brazil that Uncle Philipp used to tell the children. However, he was 'not particularly happy' in the *Ahnenerbe*, she claimed. But that was hardly likely to be due to latent political opposition to the Nazi regime, as was the story perpetuated within the family, but rather to his lack of recognition as a scientist in the dubious research outfit, which did not even enjoy particular importance within the SS. The Lützelburgs were convinced Nazis who, after years in Brazil, had returned to Germany to be part of the 'national renascence' of the German Reich. My grandmother must have been very fond of Philipp von Lützelburg; for years she kept a photo of him with a dedication to 'my dear Paula'. She also remained in contact with Marianne after 1945.

Ernst graduated in the summer of 1928. He had done various stretches of work experience during the vacations – in 1925 at the instrument works of the Munich section of the Reich Postal Ministry, for instance, and in that same year at the Municipal Electricity Works there; then, in 1927, he had worked as an electrician and motor mechanic at the Post Office garage. He was not yet twenty-three when he completed his diploma – with very good grades – and went to Berlin. Moving to the capital, particularly as traditionally there was little love lost between Bavaria and Prussia, must have meant a great change for him. Except for the time his father had spent in St Petersburg, the family had always lived in Bavaria. Was it the poor employment prospects for engineers at the end of the twenties that forced him to look further afield? Was he attracted by a new challenge? Or did he simply want to get away from the care and control of the parental home, which he had so far never left?

On 3 September 1928 Ernst started work at the central laboratories of Siemens & Halske AG in the Siemensdorf district of Berlin. His experience with Siemens was to be of use to him later when he worked for the Reich Broadcasting Company. He was involved in the development of broadcasting equipment and in 'working on patents in the field of high-frequency measurement technology, broadcasting technology and audio-frequency technology'. High-frequency technology was concerned with waveband range, the development of aerials and the optimization of transmitters and receivers at very high frequencies.

Even though he was earning his own living in Berlin, Ernst received a ceaseless supply of parcels from his mother in Munich, as had his brothers before him. These not only contained cakes and other treats; she was also sending 'baskets of clothes' to him in Berlin, which presumably meant he was still having his worn shirts and underwear mended by her. Would it not have been cheaper and easier to get it done in Berlin? On 10 May

1930 Ernst sent an express letter for Mother's Day to Munich. After he had thanked his mother effusively for two parcels, he asked after his parents' health with the phrase that had become standard in the family, 'and Daddy should take things easy now!!' – their father had retired in July of that year. He went on, 'There's no need to get worked up about Paula B. I always think over things like that very carefully. For me the basic question with any woman, if she is to be evaluated at all as such [sic!], is: what will children with her look like? That's the way things are, unless I'm completely obsessed, bowled over or whatever.'

This letter records the start of his relationship with the woman who was to become my grandmother. Where they met is unclear. My father thinks it was in Bayreuth, which would account for the B. after Paula. Paula completed her training as a milliner in Bayreuth on 21 October 1929. My aunt, on the other hand, believes Ernst and Paula became acquainted through a mutual friend in Berlin, a very beautiful woman, 'one of Mummy's old school-friends', with whom Ernst had had a liaison.

In his Mother's Day letter Ernst was clearly trying to reassure his parents, who must have heard something about his relationship with Paula, by presenting himself as calm and discriminating in his dealings with women – unless he happened to be 'completely obsessed, bowled over or whatever', which was evidently not unknown. He seems to have made a clear distinction between a woman one could have a good time with and a woman he was prepared to 'evaluate at all as such'. For the latter, suitability as a mother was essential. Amongst other requirements, she had to be attractive and healthy; perhaps, also, she had to correspond to concepts of Nordic racial appearance ('what will children with her look like?'). And indeed, my grandmother was tall, blonde, blue-eyed and a beautiful woman.

The letter will certainly not have helped reassure his parents. They were probably worried that Ernst might make as unsuitable a choice as Heinrich had with Marga. Unlike Marga, however, Paula was single, Catholic and barely a year older than her future husband.

Gertrud Paula Melters was born on 29 March 1905. Her father, Carl Melters, had a painting and decorating business with a shop attached in Dinslaken on the Lower Rhine. She was one of four daughters; the longed-for son, Walter, was eventually born in 1913. Paula's mother was a strict Catholic who brought up her daughters – Paula was the second – in the same belief. Paula spent three years at the Catholic primary school, then seven at a 'school for young ladies' run by nuns. There she was taught the standard subjects of the time for girls from the middle classes: a little English, a bit of French, probably a lot of religion and, above all, domestic economy. She left school in 1920, at the age of fifteen. She was the only one of the daughters to take her father's advice not simply to wait for an eligible bachelor, but to learn a trade, a decision that was to enable her to support herself and her four children after the war.

In those days millinery was considered an acceptable occupation for women. To learn the trade Paula went to Cologne, where some relatives lived; there she learnt everything about making hats, from the strenuous shaping of the basic felt form to the decoration of the finished object. In 1922 she passed the first part of her diploma with a grade of 'very good'. She spent the traditional 'journeyman years' travelling around various south German towns, among them Pforzheim and Bayreuth, where she completed her diploma as a 'master craftsman' in October 1929. Then, for unknown reasons, she ended up in Angermünde in the Uckermark, to the north-east of Berlin. Why such an out-of-the-way place? If she was determined to go to provincial Prussia, why not to Guben, a town which, at the time, was a leading hatmaking centre? Perhaps because Angermünde was closer to Berlin? By this time Paula had got to know Ernst and there was a direct railway connection to the capital – the journey took less than two hours.

Shortly afterwards she managed to find work in Berlin. Starting in January 1931, she was employed as manageress in the millinery department of a firm called Janke, at 120 marks a month. There are pictures from the three years Paula and Ernst knew each other before they got married showing them either by themselves or with friends, mostly during excursions on the River Havel in their canoe or on a largish sailing-boat belonging to friends. Her son remembers that after the war Paula used to go on about these canoe trips she and Ernst still undertook even when they had two children.

Given the economic situation, during the year Ernst first met Paula there were presumably many rumours about likely redundancies at Siemens, for in 1930 Ernst was looking around for other possible employment – with the Berlin firms of Mix & Genest and C. Lorenz-AG amongst others, as well as with the Reich Post Office where he had done work experience as a student in Munich. His father made great but ultimately unsuccessful efforts to use his influence to find him a post there. Ernst's attempts to find a position with the broadcasting company in Munich or with the city's schools department, where he enquired about a possible post as teacher in a technical college, were equally vain. He doubtless possessed 'all the qualities necessary for a teacher at a technical college', the reply he received says, 'but there is no prospect of us needing an electrical engineer in the immediate future'. It looks as if Ernst was not particularly happy in Berlin; for a long time he seems to have dreamt of returning to Munich.

In 1931, when the economic crisis was at its height, Siemens was obliged 'for reasons of economy' to abandon its own projects in the fields of broadcasting and electro-acoustics and hand them over to Telefunken. On 29 August Ernst, together with many of his colleagues, was given his no doubt long-expected notice, with effect from 30 September. His testimonial of 21 September certifies that he had 'done extremely good work' for the firm and had always been a 'conscientious colleague and very pleasant to work with'.

Despite the unemployment rate of 30 per cent among engineers, he very quickly, after all his attempts, found a new position. On 7 October 1931 Ernst took up his post as assistant engineer in the low-voltage department of the Vereinigung der Elektrizitätswerke (VDE – Consortium of Power Companies). There, as he wrote in a later curriculum vitae, he was involved in 'experiments in the reduction of interference and the measurement of signal strength' and developed 'a new instrument for measuring signal strength in order to determine usable signal strength and the strength of interference'.

On 1 November, one month after joining the VDE and a year after the Reichstag elections at which the Nazis had made such huge gains, Ernst became a member of the Party. His membership card was made out in Munich under his parents' address. After his father had retired in the summer of 1930 they had moved out of the school apartment and were now living at 19 Jägerstrasse.

How did Ernst come to join the Nazi Party? Was his relatively early membership an expression of the desire of the generation that had been mere observers during the First World War and the subsequent revolution to become actively involved themselves in a time of radical change? And what political influence had his brother Heinrich had on him? He was, after all, a member of the Reichstag, representing the increasingly successful NSDAP, and the two of them probably met fairly frequently in Berlin when Heinrich came to attend Parliament. My father is convinced that it was Heinrich who persuaded Ernst to join the Party. Paula, he said, often told her children how difficult Ernst found it to liberate himself from Heinrich, who always felt very responsible for his younger brother, but also often used to boss him around as if he were still a child. But bossing around takes two, and by then Ernst was no longer a child.

At that time, however, Berlin, unlike Munich and Nuremberg, was anything but a Nazi stronghold. Even at the Reichstag elections of 5 March 1933, at which both Ernst and Paula voted for the Nazis, Hitler's party received 'only' 34.6 per cent of the vote in Berlin, in contrast to 44 per cent over the whole of Germany. The conservatives hated Berlin. The centre of modernity and cosmopolitanism was, in their eyes, a hotbed of immorality and decadence. For the Nazis Berlin was the embodiment of the 'Weimar Jew Republic'. Was one of the reasons why Ernst wanted to return to Munich to be where it felt as if things were happening and to be part of the 'national revolution'?

9

'Finally Got a Foothold in the Fortress': The Seizure of Power

The short interlude of German democracy that character-ized the Weimar Republic was marked by constant govern-mental crises, the break-up of coalitions and new elections, none of which exactly boosted the electorate's confidence in the parliamentary system. Government by emergency decree transferred more and more power to President Hin-denburg, who had been a field marshal under Kaiser Wil-helm II. On 27 March 1930 the last coalition between the Social Democrats, the Centre Party and the two liberal parties collapsed, initiating the phase of presidential dic-tatorships, at first under the Centre Chancellor Heinrich Brüning, then, from May 1932, under Franz von Papen of the right wing of the Centre Party.

The astronomical increase in unemployment figures and the destitution of whole sections of the population led to increasing panic, as people feared the loss of their jobs would mean social degradation and poverty. The blame for the catastrophic situation was put on the Weimar 'system'. For many, only the National Socialists with their strong, charismatic Führer seemed to possess the determination necessary to overcome the crisis.

No one knew better than Hitler how to attract to himself people's yearning for a strong man, yearnings by no means restricted to right-wingers alone. The National Socialists also profited from the epidemic of elections in the years before 1933 in which they could exploit to the full their greatest strength: political agitation. The vagueness and ambiguity of their programme was hardly seen as a disadvantage. The growing use of terror tactics accompanying their campaigns, to which hundreds of Communist and socialist opponents, but also almost as many Nazi 'martyrs', fell victim, did nothing to lessen the increasing admiration.

In the July 1932 elections the National Socialists had become the largest single party in the Reichstag, with 37.3 per cent of the vote. While many voters had cast their vote less *for* the Nazis' programme than *against* the prevailing conditions, the Party members – by then already numbering over eight hundred thousand – were fascinated by the Party's youthful dynamism, its determination to bring about change and its sense of belonging. But with the 40 per cent mark it seemed to have reached the limit of its potential. Despite intensive propaganda, its number of votes dropped slightly in the September 1932 election.

Since the summer Gregor Strasser had been arguing for participation in a coalition; Hitler, on the other hand, supported by Göring and Goebbels, stuck by his insistence on assuming power alone. This was what led to the break with Strasser, who resigned all his Party offices. Franz von Papen tried to persuade Hindenburg to appoint Hitler as Chancellor; Papen himself was willing to be his deputy. And this time he found the senile President, who had long refused to accept Hitler, open to persuasion.

On 30 January 1933 Hindenburg agreed to the appointment of Hitler as Chancellor. In Berlin the SA battalions marched in a long torchlit procession through the Brandenburg Gate. The painter Max Liebermann, whose apartment was on Pariser Platz right next to it, watched the procession from his window and commented, 'I can't eat as much as I'd like to spew up!' Many others, by contrast – and probably including my grandfather Ernst – lined the streets and cheered fervently. On the day after Hitler's appointment Gebhard Himmler senior wrote to his son Heinrich:

> *Dear Heinrich,*
>   *You too – we have just written to the Chancellor – should receive our heartiest and most sincere congratulations on the Movement's success and victory, to which you have made such a great contribution. So you've finally got a foothold in the fortress. May you, surrounded by countless enemies and some false friends, succeed in maintaining and extending your position and may Heaven also grant you, my d. son, the continued good health you need, and your work its well-earned success and reward.*

He fully understood, he added, that because of the work awaiting him they would presumably not see Heinrich for some time. He concluded with an affectionate 'best wishes and kisses'.

Heinrich's mother also wrote to him that day:

> *My dear Heinrich,*
>   *Filled with joy, I too would like to congratulate you on the fulfilment of what you and all of us have yearned for and on the long-fought victory your*

*Führer has gained. May he continue to enjoy fortune
and God's blessing . . . We were tremendously
pleased to receive your card from Lippe with Hitler's
signature, which we have so long desired. I hope you
were in Berlin for the day of victory. It must have
been wonderful, that show of homage! My thoughts
are always with you. With loving devotion.*

These and other letters to Heinrich from 1933
onwards show how inordinately proud of their son his
parents were. Not only had he, after all, achieved something in life, but despite their long-held reservations it
looked as if he had backed the right horse from the very
beginning and was now reaping the reward ('you've
finally got a foothold in the fortress'). Looking back, they
must have been impressed by Heinrich's unshakeable
belief, which for so many years had been idealistic and
untainted by opportunism, and which now through his
tenacity had finally brought him success. 'We are *so*
delighted at every picture of you, *my* dear Heinrich, and
at the reports on the radio and in the newspapers,' his
mother wrote two months later. And a year afterwards
a signed portrait of the Führer 'sent her into ecstasies'.

By this time my great-grandparents had become keen
supporters of Hitler. In October 1933 they applied for
Party membership which, with Heinrich's help, they were
eventually granted, despite the block on new members
that had been announced in the meantime. They delighted
in the influence Heinrich enjoyed, through which they too
once more came into proximity with power, even with
the state's new first man. They congratulated Hitler personally and treated a card with his signature as if it were
the relic of a saint.

At the beginning of 1933 Heinrich and Marga sold their house in Waldtrudering and moved, in February, with their four-year-old daughter into a spacious apartment in Prinzregentenstrasse, to the east of Munich city centre – the street in which Adolf Hitler also lived. Although they were so close to the centre, Heinrich's parents did not visit them even once during the year they lived there. According to Gebhard, Heinrich often attended their regular Sunday lunches, at which the family gathered in Jägerstrasse, but alone or with his daughter. The Himmlers, Gebhard said, had never been able to overcome their reserve towards their daughter-in-law. But Marga, too, 'a cool, hard woman with extremely delicate nerves who radiated no warmth at all and spent too much time moaning', had played her part. She was, however, a model housewife, 'simple, clean, not giving herself airs', who always stood by her husband. He and Hilde, Gebhard added, had never really got on with her either.

The new Chancellor persuaded President Hindenburg to dissolve the Reichstag again on 1 February. The elections were set for 5 March. The Nazis used the intervening weeks effectively to dismantle the legal system. The 'Decree for the Protection of the People and the State', which, with Hindenburg's signature, was promulgated immediately after the Reichstag fire, was the start of a permanent state of emergency. Fundamental basic rights, such as the freedom of the press, of speech and assembly, as well as the privacy of the post and telephone, were abrogated, and 'preventive detention' was introduced to allow political opponents to be arrested; this was immediately used against Communist Party officials and deputies. In addition, the decree shifted responsibility for the state of emergency from the President to the Chancellor and his Minister of the Interior, Wilhelm Frick. Despite the massive use of violence against their opponents, the National Socialists, with 43.9 per cent of the votes, did not achieve an absolute majority on 5 March.

Immediately after the Reichstag election, on the pretext of the threat of unrest and of 'Communist acts of violence endangering the state' – and contrary to the constitution – Reich commissioners were installed in the individual states to annul the power of the regional governments. The minority government in Bavaria (the second-largest state after Prussia), under Heinrich Held of the Bavarian People's Party, initially refused to yield to the pressure exerted by SA march-pasts and the installation on 9 March of Ritter von Epp as Reich Commissioner; but eventually, on the 16th, it resigned as the last of the regional state governments. With the Enabling Act that was passed on the 23rd the Reichstag eliminated itself. In the following months, one party after another dissolved itself, last of all the Catholic parties: the Bavarian People's Party and the Centre Party.

As soon as he arrived, on the night of 9 March, the new Bavarian Reich Commissioner appointed the Gauleiter of Munich and Upper Bavaria, Adolf Wagner, as acting Minister of the Interior; Ernst Röhm, Chief of Staff of the SA, as State Commissioner without portfolio; and the Reichstag deputy Heinrich Himmler as chief of the Munich police. The latter appeared to have been fobbed off with a relatively unimportant post. In fact, however, it gave him the opportunity of building up a very effective power structure, which, implemented first of all on a small scale, would form the basis for the takeover of the political police in other regional states, and ultimately in the whole of Germany.

From 10 March, the elimination of opposition organizations in Bavaria was carried out under the direction of Adolf Wagner; it was organized by Heinrich Himmler.

Himmler immediately went to work with a will, setting up a prison in which political opponents were interrogated and tortured. It was situated behind the building housing the Bavarian Political Police in Briennerstrasse, the genteel street where he had once lived as a student. At a press conference on the 20th Himmler announced the setting-up of the first 'concentration camp for political prisoners' in Germany, in Dachau to the north of Munich. There, too, political opponents were taken into indefinite 'preventive detention', against which there was no right of appeal. In April and May 1933 alone, twelve prisoners were murdered by the SS in Dachau.

Heinrich's new post also provided a new occupation for his father. As early as 13 March he was writing to Heinrich: 'It's Father again, you'll be thinking. And indeed, if you stay for long in your present post I'll have to open an office for people in need of assistance. Yesterday two came to see me.' One of these cases, he said, was very urgent, that of 'my d. friend Dr Weber of the Theresiengymnasium, my successor as chairman of the Bavarian Association of Headteachers'. Himmler senior asked Heinrich to see this man and 'give a *sympathetic* hearing to his paternal concern'. He had always been a true nationalist, but his eldest son had 'gone off the rails', and had – perhaps out of necessity, but certainly misled by his 'half-crazy wife' – defended Communists in his role as a lawyer. Now the son was suspected of being a Communist himself and had been arrested; his parents' house had been searched several times. 'Since I cannot imagine you bother with small fry,' Heinrich's father went on, 'unless Weber's got up to something as a Communist, I beg you at least to do what's possible for this well-respected family.'

Again and again during the next few years his parents were to find themselves in a similar dilemma, when family friends and acquaintances were caught up in their son's 'purges'. They had no objection to the persecution of Communists and other political opponents, but they were concerned about the reputation of a respected family – more than about the fate of the son. Another time Heinrich's father passed on a 'pitiful letter' from an old friend of his wife from Ingolstadt whose husband had been sent to Dachau. Heinrich's mother, Gebhard senior said in his letter to Heinrich of 15 November 1934, had been 'terribly affected' by the letter, and he went on to complain that 'hardly a day goes by without similar mail'. Heinrich reassured him by return of post that their acquaintance had already been released from preventive detention.

After his appointment as chief of police in Munich, Heinrich received many congratulations – from his parents and from countless relatives and friends. His father wrote that the first visitor on the morning of 10 March had been his former teacher, Hudezeck, followed shortly by Kätha Zahler and others. Paula, who was in Dinslaken at the time, also sent her warmest congratulations through his parents. Ernst wrote to his brother from

Berlin about his new position: 'The enthusiasm and solemn dedication in Munich must have been tremendous! It's really good that the Bavarian People's Party gang were chucked out. They must have had to be prised out of their seats.'

My grandfather was obviously very pleased at the violent end to democracy, or at least at the end to the People's Party administration in Bavaria. And then, the purges carried out by the Nazi leaders opened up new professional prospects for others. Ernst scented his chance of getting into radio, by which he was increasingly fascinated, especially when a colleague at the VDE encouraged him to make use of his contacts: 'My immediate superior, Dr Dennhardt, said to me – and in a very nice way – "I advise you if possible to get your brother to get you a post somewhere, you've got ability, you're no fool and you've got something to show on the measurement of signal strength among other things . . ." '

Alfred Dennhardt was a physicist and electrical engineer, and had gone around the country in 1923–4 making election speeches for the extreme nationalist movement. In 1930 he joined the VDE, which later became the Electricity Supply Group in Berlin-Moabit, as a scientist; he was made head of the telephone engineering section at the beginning of 1933, where, as Ernst's boss, he came to appreciate his abilities. Ernst must have been aware of the nepotism inherent in his enquiry to Heinrich – otherwise, he would not have felt the need to put his self-praise into the mouth of another person. But he also knew he could rely on his brother when it came to using his influence to help his family and friends. One of Heinrich's particular strengths lay in the cultivation of personal contacts and their exploitation by loyal allies and subordinates. Heinrich first of all approached the Bavarian Broadcasting Company for his brother, since Ernst would have preferred to return to Munich. There, however, he met with a rebuff, so he mobilized his influential contacts in Berlin, where Ernst started work on 1 June 1933 as an engineer with the Reich Broadcasting Company.

Ernst had put his request to Heinrich at an opportune moment. The Nazis had immediately occupied the premises of the broadcasting companies on the day they assumed power, and had gradually taken control of programming. The most important positions – and, little by little, all other posts – were filled by reliable Party members, political opponents dismissed. These efforts were intensified after 13 March, when broadcasting was placed under the aegis of the newly founded Ministry for Public Enlightenment and Propaganda and the Minister, Joseph Goebbels.

In his very first speech to the directors of the broadcasting companies Goebbels, who was in charge of personnel and programming – technical matters remained the responsibility of the Minister for Postal Services – announced the new line. For him, radio was a weapon that was just as important for arming the Reich as bombers and tanks. And he knew something about propaganda. He urged the directors: 'Never get boring. Never let things drag. Never give the listener the message on a plate. Never imagine the best way to serve the national government is to play rousing marches evening after evening.' The new way of thinking had to be presented to the masses in a way that was 'modern, up-to-the-minute, interesting; informing them without lecturing them'. The appropriate medium was radio, the 'most modern and most important instrument for influencing the masses' there was.

On 1 May 1934 Eugen Hadamovsky, the National Programming Director, made their task clear to the staff of the Broadcasting Company: 'In our work we are all fully aware that today and in the future radio is the vanguard of the National Socialist revolution . . .' In this relatively new medium the feeling of a new departure was intense. 'Be bold,' Hadamovsky encouraged his staff on 2 July 1935: 'We are fresh, we are young, we are lively, we have no truck with tradition, we rely on our own healthy instinct, we can experiment, we can be bold. This is the great opportunity facing National Socialist broadcasting.' My grandfather probably also found this pioneer approach inspiring when he started work as an engineer with the Company, where he met many young colleagues who were all gripped by a wonderful feeling of actively helping to shape a new age.

In order to get blanket coverage for his propaganda instrument, Goebbels pushed ahead with the development of a cheap and reliable radio for all, the so-called *Volksempfänger* (people's receiver), which in future was to be in every living-room, in bars and places of work. The new model – which became popularly known as the *Goebbelsschnauze* (Goebbelsgob) – was presented to the public at the Tenth German Radio Exhibition in August 1933. At seventy-six Reichmarks it was much cheaper than its predecessors, which had cost between two hundred and four hundred marks and were still considered luxury items. Two years later, 1,300,000 *Volksempfänger* had been sold; at the outbreak of war the figure was around 3,500,000. An appeal issued by the National Socialist Chamber of Broadcasting in October 1933 states, 'In these times, when a powerful affirmation of the dignity, honour and unity of the German nation must be made to the whole world, there should be no German home without a radio ready to put every member of the national community, at any time, in direct contact with the Führer and his comrades-in-arms in the Party.'

Two years later, Ernst Himmler and his former boss Alfred Dennhardt were to dampen this euphoria a little. They published a *Manual for Suppressing Interference in Broadcasting* in which they bemoaned the fact that radio broadcasting had spread at such a furious pace that the supporting technology was still in its infancy, which had resulted in the fact that standards had been neglected in the installation of receivers, leaving them liable to interference. Their manual was to serve as a 'guide to technicians', whose task it was to investigate and suppress interference, and thus to contribute to the creation of 'a sure foundation for high-quality broadcasting'.

On 8 July 1933 Paula and Ernst were married. Before the wedding Paula had been summoned to Munich, where for a month she was initiated into the secrets of running a household, especially *haute cuisine*. Her prospective mother-in-law particularly wanted her to learn to prepare her son's favourite dishes, especially Bavarian pastries. But there was probably more to it than that. Paula came from a tradesman's family. Presumably one purpose of her stay in the Himmler household was to give her the necessary polish to take her place at the side of her future husband.

The wedding was held in Dinslaken, Paula's home town. Heinrich was best man. Paula's cousin said that the bride's strict Catholic mother was 'not exactly delighted' with her new son-in-law, but at least her daughter was marrying into a respected and – thanks to Heinrich Himmler – influential family. Walter, the young son and favourite of the Melters family, seems to have had no problem with his two new relations. On the contrary, in 1935 Heinrich was to make it possible for him to join the SS. Later, Walter took part in the Russian campaign as an SS *Sturmmann* (lance corporal) and war correspondent. He fell on 4 September 1941. Heinrich was the first to hear of his death.

Heinrich arranged a honeymoon for the young couple at the Hotel Dreesen, Hitler's favourite hotel, near Bad Godesberg on the Rhine. On their return Ernst and Paula thanked him effusively; Heinrich had probably paid for it as well, perhaps as a wedding present. The couple were so taken with this romantic part of the Rhine valley that they returned there several times.

From the very beginning at the Reich Broadcasting Company Ernst worked closely with his boss, Dr Klaus Hubmann, and soon became his right-hand man. Hubmann was another who had profited from the posts made vacant by the Nazis' purge immediately after assuming power. On 1 April 1933 he was appointed Chief Engineer and Technical Director of the Broadcasting Company. It is very probable that he was Heinrich's contact, through whom Ernst got his position. Hubmann was an old acquaintance. After serving in the First World War he had studied at the Technical University in Munich, joined Epp's Freikorps in 1919 and taken part in the overthrow of the *Räterepublik* there. After that he joined Epp's Rifle Brigade 21, of which Gebhard and Heinrich were also members. In November 1921 he had been a candidate, as a member of a duelling fraternity, for the student parliament and on the same 'fraternity list' as Heinrich, who at the time described him in his diary as a 'polite, enthusiastic and definitely good young man'. In 1923 and 1924 Hubmann was a member of the Oberland League. He took part in Hitler's Beer Hall Putsch, during which he was wounded and later awarded the *Blutorden* (Order of Blood). In August 1924 he started work in the laboratory for high-frequency and mechanical engineering at the firm of C. Lorenz in Berlin-Tempelhof, which I had come across during my first study of the file on Ernst Himmler in the Federal Archives. In August 1928 Hubmann moved to the Reich Central Post Office, where he was employed until April 1933 as a scientific assistant in the field of wireless telegraphy and telephone engineering.

At the end of 1931 Hubmann joined the National Socialist Party and in the same year began 'secret work for the SS', initially without being an SS member. This was stated by Heinrich Himmler in a letter of 1934 to the SS *Oberabschnitt Ost* (Eastern Division) to which Hubmann was attached. It probably meant that Hubmann had worked for the SD. He joined the SS together with Ernst Himmler on the day my grandfather started work with the Broadcasting Company. In October 1933 both became part of the SS *Nachrichtensturm* (intelligence unit) 2N23, to which Hubmann gave lectures on oscillation and high-frequency engineering. At the beginning of the next year he was made leader of a 'half-platoon, mainly composed of SS leaders with technical qualifications', with which he was to 'work on a special task assigned personally to him by the Reichsführer SS'. SS Mann Himmler II – Private Ernst Himmler – was also a member of this half-platoon. In August 1935 Ernst and Klaus Hubmann transferred to the SS *Nachrichten-Sturmbann* (intelligence battalion) 8, of which Alfred Dennhardt had been technical leader since April that year.

What was Heinrich Himmler's purpose in building up units of telecommunications specialists at the SS Central Office when he already had Heydrich's security service? What was concealed behind all this secrecy, behind this 'special task' for Hubmann? Was there any connection between this and the 'interesting information' Ernst had been sending his brother for months already? Ernst's letters to Heinrich contain only hints. In March 1933 he informed him that he had been able to give a Dr B. 'information about a gentleman in the RPZ' (presumably the Reich Central Post Office). 'The next time you're here I can give you a brief report . . .' And in July 1933, after he had started work with the Broadcasting Company, he wrote, 'for today just a brief report on the assignment: very nice people. Can I see you to give you more details? There's various interesting things I'd like to tell you about.' And a repeated request: 'Please give me a ring.' Clearly they had some agreement that Ernst would report on the political reliability of his colleagues, perhaps also on people whose skills Heinrich was interested in for his telecommunications plans.

During the next few months Heinrich was working

single-mindedly towards taking over the political police in the individual states; the last was the largest, Prussia, where the *Geheime Staatspolizei* (the Gestapo, Secret State Police) came under the Prime Minister, Hermann Göring. On 20 April 1934 Heinrich was appointed Inspector of the Prussian Secret State Police Department; Reinhard Heydrich was made Chief of the Secret Police Department in Berlin.

Formally, the SS was still subject to the SA Chief of Staff, Ernst Röhm. In the power struggle that ensued during the following months, Heinrich had no compunction about eliminating his former mentor, 'the good Captain Röhm'. Conditions were in his favour. Röhm and other SA leaders were increasingly unhappy with the line Hitler was taking. The usefulness of street violence was now past and Hitler had decided on a new phase of allying himself with the traditional elites, especially the Army. On 30 June 1934 the SD and the Gestapo put out a report of an imminent putsch by the SA in which Hitler's predecessor as Chancellor, General Schleicher, and the Party's former Head of Organization Gregor Strasser, were supposed to be involved. During that night, not only senior SA leaders but also other opponents who were regarded as a nuisance were arrested and murdered. During the next two days around two hundred people fell victim to the SS purge, including Röhm, Strasser, Schleicher and Kahr, the former Prime Minister of Bavaria.

There was widespread relief that the Führer had finally taken vigorous action against the arrogant and violent SA. Neither the Army nor the Church made any comment on the murderous operation, even though highly placed individuals from both organizations were killed in the

massacre. After it, Hitler's power was more firmly established than ever. On 1 August, shortly before Hindenburg's death, he went to see the aged President and got
his agreement to a law abolishing the office of president.
Hitler now took over all these functions himself in his
capacity as Führer and Chancellor. From that point on,
soldiers and officials, including government ministers,
no longer swore an oath to the constitution, but to the
'Führer of the German Reich and people'.

After the bloody purge, the political police no longer
came under Frick's Ministry of the Interior, but were
nominally independent, at first under Hermann Göring.
But Heinrich Himmler immediately set about installing in
Berlin the Central Office of the Commander of the Political Police of the individual states, in order to concentrate
his own powers. In November 1934 Göring transferred
the operations of the Prussian Gestapo to him, making
Himmler the head of the whole Secret State Police long
before that office was officially created in the summer of
1936.

10

'National Socialist Reliability':
The Brothers' Rise

Ernst had found somewhere for himself and Paula to live on Biedermeierweg, in the 'railwaymen's estate' in the quiet Berlin suburb of Ruhleben. The estate had been built in 1927–8 and until 1933 had belonged to the railwaymen's union. The small semi-detached houses with their relatively large gardens had mostly been rented by ordinary white-collar workers, plus some union secretaries and the occasional graduate.

On 2 May 1933, a day after the Nazis had taken over the traditional socialist Labour Day with their May Day celebrations, SA squads and units from the Nazi *Betriebszellenorganisation* (Workplace Cells Organization) stormed the buildings and offices of the trade union movement, seized its available assets and arrested its officials. A few days later the members of the *Allgemeiner Deutscher Gewerkschaftsbund* (General German Trade Union Association) were compulsorily integrated into the *Deutsche Arbeitsfront* (German Labour Front) set up on 10 May under Robert Ley.

The Nazi workplace cells were created in the years preceding the takeover of power at the suggestion of the

Party's head of propaganda, Joseph Goebbels, in the hope of infiltrating large concerns, in particular, with Nazis, and giving them something to set against the essentially Social Democratic works councils. Ernst, too, was a member of the Workplace Cells Organization. The earliest documentary evidence I can find is for 1934, but the likelihood is that he belonged before that, and I cannot exclude the possibility that he was involved in the 'raiding parties' of May 1933. At least as a member of the organization he would have heard about the operation and could have worked out for himself that the whole estate, after it had been cleared, would become the property of the Labour Front – of which he was a member – and that a home would become available for a young couple who were in the right place at the right time. I wonder whether Ernst gave even a moment's thought to the criminal way in which the Labour Front had acquired the houses. I suspect he was just happy to have found the ideal district for himself and his bride; quiet, leafy and only three stops on the underground from his new place of work in Masurenallee. On top of that was the prospect of soon being able to buy a house of his own on the estate.

On 17 May 1934, the birthday of Ernst's father, Ernst and Paula had a daughter. When they moved into a more spacious house on the estate a few months later, Paula was once more pregnant. There, on Brombeerweg, Ernst's boss Klaus Hubmann had been living with his family since the beginning of the year. The neighbouring semi-detached house, where previously a union secretary, an artist and a civil engineer had lived, had become 'free' and Ernst and Paula had moved in. What can have been the fate of the former inhabitants?

I know my grandparents' house from an old photo and from the few memories my father has of it, above all of the garden and the street where he played as a child. One day I set off from Ruhleben underground station to walk through the estate with its little semi-detached houses and – for Berlin – large gardens. I had the feeling I was in an oasis of calm. Birds chirruping instead of traffic noise, sunflowers in bloom and knotgrass among the old pines. Finally I was outside the house where my father had spent the first years of his life. He had always described it as very small, claiming his parents had to extend it to make room for the family. To me the house did not seem small at all.

I rang. The owners were in. When, hesitantly, I explained who I was, the oldish couple who had opened the door seemed almost frightened. I didn't really know what I was doing there myself. Was I merely curious to see who lived there now? Embarrassed, I said that I had seen old photos of the garden, and could I perhaps have a look at it? I was taken round the house and was amazed at the size of the plot. It must have been a paradise for children.

It turned out that the present owners knew very well who I was, and at first had feared I had come to demand the return of the property. When they bought it, they told me, they had been informed by the local planning department and the owner, the railway company, that the houses had been expropriated in 1934 and rented or sold to members of the Nazi Party. There, I was astonished to learn, not only countless Party officials had lived, but also SS leaders. This did not really fit in with what my father had told me. No one important had lived here, he had assured me, only 'little Nazis', in houses that were 'very cramped' and with no room at all for servants.

None of these family stories was true. Undoubtedly none of the top-drawer Nazis had lived here – their villas were in the select districts, in Grunewald or Dahlem – but with its modern houses and generous gardens the area had definitely proved attractive to Party members and to middle-ranking officers of the SS, to whom the Labour Front gradually sold off the property. My aunt remembered that Ernst and Paula had always had a maid living in the attic room with the mansard window, usually a girl doing her compulsory one year's community service. When one was as well paid as the respectable middle-class Chief Engineer Ernst Himmler, then it went without saying that one had a helping hand in the house. And during those years the 'help' was not always voluntary. Sometimes my grandparents, like their neighbours the Behrends, had a young girl from the Ukraine – it was forced labour. When one day the Behrends' girl ran off and disappeared it was the number-one topic of conversation between the two families for days on end.

By this time Ernst's brother Gebhard was often in Berlin in his capacity as an officer of the National Socialist Teachers' Association, attending national conferences of technical colleges as well as sessions of the Professional Association of Teachers at Vocational and Technical Colleges. Sometime before 1933 Gebhard had already become head of the Bavarian Federation of Technical Colleges. When, that year, this became part of the NS

Teachers' Association and thus affiliated to the Nazi Party, Gebhard was initially appointed deputy head, then head, of the professional body for the *Gau* (administrative region) of Upper Bavaria. He joined the Party in May 1933. His wife Hilde had joined one year earlier, as a substitute for her husband. At least, that was what Gebhard maintained a few years later when he suspected the late date of his Party membership was affecting his promotion chances, claiming that as he was working for the public education service he had been barred from that kind of political activity before 1933, which was why his wife had had to deputize for him: 'Because I had an official position teaching at a technical college in Munich, it was not possible for me to join the Party before the seizure of power, so my wife acquired party membership in my place on 1 May 1932.' The point was to show that long before he actually joined the Party he had 'supported it in every way, especially by fighting to enlist the support of my colleagues for the cause'.

In January 1935 Gebhard applied to the Party's Central Office to be allowed to take over the lower membership number of his wife. He did so on the basis of a regulation that had been brought in for officials who were 'disadvantaged' before 1933. At first after the seizure of power, Gebhard wrote, he had rejected this procedure, 'since I had the feeling, if I did so, that I could be accused of trying to procure advantage from the Party'. Now, however, he went on, he had decided, upon mature reflection, to submit this request to the Central Office, because 'he had again and again been undeservedly held back' in his work for the National Socialist Teachers' Association through his being counted a 'March violet'.

'March violet' was the mocking name for those Party members who had joined only after the elections of 5 March 1933. Even at that point the proportion of officials and teachers in the Party was above average. According to the official statistics of 1 January 1935, 7.3 per cent of those in employment were Party members. Professions with above average Party membership were office workers with 12 per cent, officials with 20 per cent and teachers with 30 per cent.

It may well not have been easy for Gebhard to make his mark without constantly being regarded as a protégé of his brother. On the other hand, when his career depended on it he clearly had no compunction about exploiting his brother's influence. In 1935 the special arrangement for 'disadvantaged officials' was applied only 'in exceptional circumstances', so that in Gebhard's case his request was only granted with the help of Heinrich, whose signature adorns the application to the regional administrative office in Munich. It was approved that March.

The gibes from his colleagues at conferences and training days of the National Socialist Teachers' Association were not the only reason for Gebhard's desire to have his early commitment to the Party publicly recognized retrospectively. He was ambitious, and a membership card with an early enrolment date in his personal details definitely looked better for his plans for professional advancement.

In March 1935, against the terms of the Treaty of Versailles, Hitler reintroduced military service, thus starting to build up the Army. Gebhard had immediately enlisted for voluntary training as an officer of the reserve, which began that same summer. He had to take part in military exercises twice a year, which meant two months' absence from teaching and from his family. One year later he was a lieutenant of the reserve in the new Army.

For the next step in his career he put out feelers during his frequent sessions in Berlin. At the beginning of March Bernhard Rust, the Reich Minister of Science and Education, requested that 'the personal files of the technical college teacher Gebhard Himmler be sent as soon as possible'. Bauer, the relevant schools inspector in Munich, was asked for an assessment of Gebhard's suitability for the educational administration service. Bauer expressed his regret at the prospect of losing Gebhard Himmler, but welcomed Rust's presumed intention 'to appoint him to a post in your Ministry'. His 'National Socialist reliability' went without saying, he wrote; after all, Gebhard was the brother of the Reichsführer SS and his father, a former head teacher, had 'always been known for his nationalist views'.

In expectation of his forthcoming promotion Gebhard urged Heinrich, at a meeting at the end of June 1935, to promote him to *Oberscharführer* (quartermaster sergeant) in the SS. In July he attended a one-week 'course for education leaders' organized by the Labour Front. Finally, at the beginning of August, his acceptance by the Ministry of Education came through, though now, strangely enough, the Munich schools inspector who had initially praised Gebhard to the skies started to back-pedal a little. Gebhard, he declared, was 'certainly suitable material for the schools inspectorate or management', but his training as a mechanical engineer meant that 'without specialized pedagogical training the area in which he could be used would be restricted to technical schools'. One possibility would be a 'senior managerial post in a vocational college'. Clearly Bauer felt the Ministry was going too far in its readiness to accept Gebhard. Did he suspect backstairs influence?

On 1 November Gebhard was indeed put in charge of a vocational college when he became principal of the Oskar von Miller Polytechnic, an engineering college in Munich. A mere six months later he was promoted to senior principal, earning the for those days handsome salary of 1,000 marks a month. Alongside his administrative duties, he taught drawing and cultural history. An appraisal written at the time emphasizes that he took over the latter 'ideological' subject out of conviction, the political education of young people being 'one of his particular concerns'. It was obviously what he had learnt in the NS Teachers' Association, plus his membership of the nationalistic Association for Germans Abroad, that qualified him to teach that subject.

The training courses of the Teachers' Association, which Gebhard attended in the evening and at weekends and later organized himself, were intended to 'round out' the participants' professional training 'in the spirit of National Socialism', through political indoctrination, physical exercise and a strictly controlled system of instruction.

That summer the older Himmlers, now grandparents five times over, made frequent excursions out into the countryside to the north of the Alps, for which Heinrich, as in the previous year, put an official car together with a driver at their disposal. Anna especially, who had never been a particularly good walker, enjoyed these trips immensely and sent her son grateful postcards ('it was really most enjoyable, and I do like being driven anyway'). In the spring of 1935 she went for the first and only time to the distant capital. They probably stayed with Ernst and Paula. They made plans for Himmler senior's forthcoming seventieth birthday and for a summer holiday together in the Alps. For the birthday, on 17 May, Heinrich took Ernst and his little daughter in his aeroplane, a Ju 52, with him to Munich. Paula stayed in Berlin; two weeks earlier her second daughter had been born surprisingly prematurely. The birthday in Munich was a great event. Many people came to congratulate Gebhard senior and another of the traditional family photos was taken. Grandfather Himmler proudly wore his Party badge.

Whether Marga and her daughter attended the family celebration is not clear, but the following day the grandparents went to visit them in Gmund on the Tegernsee, where Heinrich and Marga had bought a house called 'Lindenfycht' from the proceeds of the sale of their house in Munich. Heinrich had set up an office for a section of his Personal Staff there, though he himself was mostly in Berlin, where he had an apartment provided by the Party. In the meantime Heinrich and Marga's family had grown by the addition of a foster-son (the son of a member of the SS who had died), and one year older than their daughter. The idea probably came from Heinrich rather than Marga, who appeared little enamoured of the boy, frequently complaining in her diary about Gerhard's 'bad manners' and his 'criminal character' while rejoicing that her Püppi was so 'sweet and good'. The grandparents seem to have ignored the boy; they always sent greetings to Püppi alone, never to him. Just once, in a letter from Ernst and Paula, I found 'special greetings' to both children.

In September virtually the whole family was together in Nuremberg for the Party rally, the annual climax of the stage management of its own image. The three brothers had all been there the previous year and Ernst had made a 35mm film of the march-past of Heinrich's SS. It was at the Nuremberg rallies that the members of the Nazi movement swore their oath of allegiance to Adolf Hitler. The participants had to listen to the Führer speaking for hours on end while the various sections of the Party and their associated organizations, the SA and the SS, endlessly processed; in 1935 the Army marched past the rostrum and stands for the first time. That year the Himmlers' father also wanted to experience the occasion. Heinrich did everything he could to make it comfortable for him, sending a car with a chauffeur to his hotel in the mornings, and Ernst accompanied him to the various events when he was not needed elsewhere.

The Party's 'Freedom Rally' lasted from 10 to 16 September 1935. On the penultimate day the notorious Nuremberg Laws were proclaimed. The anti-Jewish agitation and ready violence of that summer had aroused the displeasure of many conservative circles. The Nuremberg racial laws now legalized the gradual exclusion of German Jews from society. Widespread disapproval was not to be expected. The majority of Germans abhorred the violent methods, but not the goal of the policies towards the Jews, which was to expel the Jews first of all from society and then from Germany itself.

On 17 June 1936 Heinrich Himmler was made 'Head of the German Police in the Reich Ministry of the Interior'. He had thus successfully resisted Frick's attempt to get the Gestapo incorporated into his Ministry and made part of the state apparatus. Instead, the entire police force was put under the control of the SS leadership. Taking the police out of the traditional framework of state institutions created an organization with enormously increased powers in the continuing state of emergency decreed after the Reichstag fire, and one that eventually became the main instrument of terror.

Heinrich's parents and brothers seem to have had no reservations about the all-powerful position of the SS and the police. On the contrary. In their letters his parents express their admiration for the 'magnificent black columns that are your creation', as his father wrote on the occasion of the SS parade on 9 November in memory of the fallen 'heroes' of the Beer Hall Putsch. Heinrich had secured seats for them for both the 1934 and the 1935 ceremonies. Gebhard and Ernst used meetings with Heinrich to put the case for their own further promotion within the SS. And they too, thanks to their brother, had the opportunity now and then to meet those who wielded the power in the Reich.

On 2 July 1936 the grandiose ceremony to commemorate the thousandth anniversary of the death of King Henry I was held in Quedlinburg Cathedral. Since the nineteenth century there had been countless myths connected with that king: for chauvinistic German nationalists – especially the leader of the early-nineteenth-century gymnastic movement Friedrich Ludwig Jahn and the writer Ernst Moritz Arndt – Henry I, also known as Henry the Fowler, was the founding father of the German Empire. He had, so they believed, opened up the 'road to the east' to enable the Teutons to subjugate the Slav peoples, 'the most contemptible dregs of humanity', who lived there. The achievements imputed to the king – curbing the influence of the Church on politics, introducing the principle of unconditional allegiance, the creation of a Greater German Empire – made Heinrich, who had a mystical side to him and pursued similar aims, see himself as a reincarnation of the king he so much admired.

The notables of Nazi Germany, among them guests of honour such as Robert Ley, the head of Party organization, Wilhelm Frick, the Minister of the Interior, and Hans Frank, at that time Minister without Portfolio, gathered round the King's tomb in the cathedral crypt for the ritual ceremony – with an SS guard of honour, a bombastic speech from Heinrich Himmler, candles and wreaths of oak leaves. Gebhard played the organ. At Heinrich's request he improvised so as to give appropriate continuous musical backing to the lavish spectacle, which lasted several hours. Heinrich did not trust a professional pianist to undertake the task.

In the folder his parents kept of Heinrich's political life, the report of the ceremony is the last article his father cut out of the *Völkischer Beobachter* and filed. Shortly afterwards he fell ill. Heinrich and Ernst were so busy that summer that it was only very late on that they realized how serious their father's condition was.

On 29 August Gebhard Himmler senior wrote his last 'business letter' to Heinrich. It was the first to contain a complaint: '. . . I long for the moment when you can appoint an intermediary to relieve me of at least some of the drudgery of all these petitions, which weighs heavily on an old man in the shadow of your position.' And his mother added, 'I am worried that your father's health is still not good.' A most definite reproach was her comment that 'many, many people have sent their best wishes' to his father on his name-day two days previously – 'only your wishes, dear Heinrich, were missing.'

His mother's reproach had its effect. Heinrich, pricked by a guilty conscience because he had neglected his parents, urged his father to see a homoeopath and sent him gingerbread from the Party rally in Nuremberg: 'Taken in small portions, even a sick stomach can tolerate it.' He got an old friend of his, Professor Karl Gebhardt, a surgeon at Hohenlychen Clinic, to contact his father's doctor Professor Bauer, and was told at the end of September that the problem was cancer of the pancreas, and at an advanced stage. In consultation with Bauer, Professor Gebhardt concluded that 'where life is fading away like this . . . any surgical experiments' were to be avoided.

Geheimrat Gebhard Himmler died on 29 October 1936. The funeral took place two days later, perfectly organized by Heinrich Himmler and with all the trappings of a state funeral. SS guards lined the route in Munich's Southern Cemetery all the way from the main road to the chapel and from there to the grave. The Führer himself had sent a large wreath, as had his deputy Rudolf Hess, Prime Minister Göring and many others. A guard of honour of SS leaders marched at the head of the funeral procession, then the wreath-bearers followed by the priest, the coffin with further SS leaders, the family and, finally, representatives of the Party, the state and the Army: 'a huge funeral procession' as the *Völkischer Beobachter* wrote the following day. Lots of VIPs had come, amongst others three *Reichsleiter*, Martin Bormann, Franz Ritter von Epp and Karl Fiehler, the Mayor of Munich; senior officers of the SS including Reinhard Heydrich and August Heissmeyer; and Ludwig Siebert, the Prime Minister of Bavaria. An SS music platoon softly sang chorales. In his funeral oration, the *Völkischer Beobachter* wrote, the priest emphasized that during his life the deceased had 'always remained true to his blood, to his family, to his profession, to his Fatherland and to his Lord God'. Gebhard junior's eldest daughter, on the other hand, claims to remember that the priest, in his speech at the grave, spoke about Himmler senior's displeasure at the career of his son Heinrich. Not only does the enthusiasm both parents openly showed for the SS make that unlikely, it would have taken literally suicidal courage to make such a comment face to face with the assembled Nazi bigwigs.

At this period Heinrich, who suffered from stomach trouble, had a worse attack than he had had for a long time, and on 12 November he went with Marga to Wiesbaden to take the waters. They divided their days between hydrotherapeutic treatment and excursions; Heinrich took English lessons as well. At first they went out every evening – to the theatre, to the cinema or to play bridge; later they often spent their evenings in the hotel and Heinrich would read to Marga.

1 Soon after this photo of Gebhard and Anna Himmler with their sons was taken, Gebhard Himmler went on a long voyage. Before he left he wrote letters of farewell to his family setting out what was to happen if he should die: the reduction of the household, the wage rises for the servants and their sons' future choices of career. 'It will be better if they don't become Classical scholars or officers,' he cautioned his wife, 'and, I beg you, don't let them study theology.'

2 Gebhard Himmler, shown here around the time of his marriage, was just eight when his father, a former customs officer, died. The harsh material circumstances in which he grew up was something he never forgot.

3 On 22 July 1897, Gebhard Himmler married Anna Heyder. The wedding breakfast was held in the Silver Room at the elegant Café Luitpold in Briennerstrasses Munich – a street where Heinrich Himmler later set up the SS's own prison for political opponents of the Nazi regime.

4 Gebhard, the eldest of the Himmlers' three sons
– here as a five-year-old – found everything easy.

5 Heinrich, the middle brother – here with his father –
was prone to illness from an early age.

6 The youngest, 'Ernsti', 'Bubi' or 'Mizzi' as he was called by the family, was a happy and self-assured child, his parents' 'little ray of sunshine' and a model pupil, technically minded like Gebhard, non-musical and non-sporting like Heinrich.

7 Heinrich with his class, in his second year at the Wilhelmsgymnasium
(second row, second from right). In the front row (third from left) is his best
and lifelong friend, Falk Zipperer, who would join the SS; to the left of him is
their Jewish classmate George Hallgarten, who emigrated with his family and
later became an eminemt historian. In his memoirs, Hallgarten describes how
Heinrich's 'determination to do well at sport made one feel sorry for him'.

8 Every year the Himmler family went to the mountains for their summer holidays. Activities included bathing, excursions and sightseeing, but their father also saw to it that they continued their studies during the holidays and kept diaries, which he checked every day. Above are the three brothers in the summer of 1914 in Tittmoning, with the daughters of friends. That year the family had to break off their holiday prematurely on the outbreak of the First World War.

9 On the far left here is Ernst; at the top right, Heinrich; and between them, Lu Zahler. The Zahlers were distant relations and close friends of the Himmlers. Lu and his two sisters, Mariele and Pepperl, also in the photo, spent a lot of time together with the Himmler brothers. While at university in Munich, Heinrich, Lu and Gebhard saw each other almost every day – in the family circle in the Pension Loritz, but also for the military exercises of Rifle Brigade 21, a successor organization to the Freikorps Epp, which they all joined together.

10 Professor Gebhard Himmler was proud of his father's military past.
He himself had been classed as 'permanently unfit for service' because of
extreme shortsightedness. Despite this, at the outbreak of the First World
War he, like many educated middle-class Germans, dreamt of Germany's
'national greatness' and celebrated the capture of Warsaw in August 1915
with fireworks. He believed so firmly that Germany would win that
he invested a considerable sum of money in war loans.

11 For Heinrich and Gebhard the training in the use of firearms and close
combat in the volunteer Cadet Corps after the outbreak of the First World
War was not military enough – too much fun, they said. They couldn't wait
for a chance to 'prove themselves in combat'. When Gebhard joined the
Landsturm (the reserve army), Heinrich, who was fourteen, sighed enviously,
'Oh, if only I were that old too, I'd have been out there ages ago.'
Finally, on 1 January 1918, he proudly went off for officer training.

12 Gebhard received his posting in April 1918.
After fighting in the front line (only '65km to Paris!') his unit was
withdrawn to a position near the Belgian town of Ypres, which the months
of trench warfare had turned into a desolate lunar landscape.

13 While Gebhard, returning from the war battle-hardened and decorated with the Iron Cross, could go straight on to university, Heinrich (front row, second from left) had to return unwillingly to school. And, of all people, it was his father (the right-hand of the two teachers) who took this 'special class for men returning from the war'.

14 The Wittelsbacher Gymnasium in Munich, of which Gebhard Himmler senior was head from 1922 until he retired in 1930 – the hard-won culmination of an unrelenting career.

16 (above) Heinrich Himmler with a unit of the Reichskriegsflagge under Captain Röhm early in the morning of 9 November 1923, outside the occupied Bavarian Divisional Army Headquarters, 'the flag on his arm', as a university friend, Mariele Rauschmeyer, later wrote. 'One could see from the flag how safe and secure it felt, and how proud he was.' On the evening of 8 November, Adolf Hitler had proclaimed the revolution throughout Germany and given Röhm the order to occupy the former Ministry of War in Munich.
The putsch was defeated the very next day.

15 (opposite) As a nine-year-old, Heinrich was required, by his father, to keep a diary. From then on he was to keep a record of everything to do with the family – meals, excursions, piano lessons, bathing expeditions, the weather. His entries were checked by his father, corrected and amended. Even later there was no room for emotions in these dry-as-dust notes. It was only his great longing to be a soldier that could extract emotion from Heinrich: 'Soldiers marched past. Oh my God!'

17 Heinrich admitted to his brother that he would rather 'clear a hall of a thousand Communists on his own' than confess his relationship with Marga Siegroth to his parents. She was seven years older than him, a Protestant and, to cap it all, divorced. In the family she was looked on as 'a woman with extremely delicate nerves who spent too much time moaning'.

18 Generally Heinrich and Marga saw very little of each other and, according to Gebhard, a coolness developed between them soon after the marriage. A stay at the spa near Wiesbaden in November 1936 seems to have bought them slightly closer together again.

19 Both Marga and Heinrich were extremely fond of their daughter Gudrun, known as 'Püppi'. Marga was delighted that her daughter was so 'sweet and good'; on the other hand, she had not a good word to say about their foster-son, a 'criminal character', whom they had taken on in 1934. In 1936, Hedwig Potthast, known as 'Häschen', became Heinrich's private secretary, then two years later his mistress. He had two children by her. Their relationship had to remain a secret and Hedwig suffered for it. Her letters to Heinrich always ended: 'Do not forget me. Your X.'

20 Heinrich and Marga dreamt of keeping chickens, and growing vegetables and herbs. Himmler's father sought out 'dirt cheap' properties on the market. Marga sold her share in the private clinic she owned jointly with a gynaecologist ('That Hauschildt! Those Jews are all the same!'), and Heinrich used the money to buy this house in Waldtrudering, to the east of Munich; he made the henhouses himself. There were repeated quarrels about money: 'I'm at my wits' end how we're going to pay for all this,' Marga lamented.

21 From the proceeds of the sale of the house in Waldtrudering, Heinrich and Marga bought 'Lindenfycht' in Gmund on the Tegernsee in 1934. Marga and Püppi lived there permanently after 1940; Heinrich was mostly in Berlin, though he had set up an office in Gmund. When he was working there he was often accompanied by his private secretary and mistress, Hedwig Potthast, for whom, after the birth of their two children, he bought a house called 'Schneewinkellehen' close to Schönau in Berchtesgaden with a loan from Party funds.

22 On 2 July 1936, the grandiose ceremony for the thousandth anniversary
of the death of Henry I was held at the King's tomb in the crypt of
Quedlinburg Cathedral. As early as the nineteenth century, Henry I was
venerated by German nationalists; according to them he had opened up the
'road to the east' for the Teutons to subjugate the 'racially inferior' peoples
there and had pursued the vision of a Greater German Empire. Heinrich
Himmler saw himself as a reincarnation of the king. The ceremony, at which
Himmler made a bombastic candle-lit speech, was attended by the notables
of Nazi Germany including Robert Ley, head of Party administration, Wilhelm
Frick, Minister of the Interior, and Hans Frank, Minister without Portfolio.
His brother Gebhard played the organ – he was the only person Heinrich
trusted to improvise musical backing to the lavish spectacle,
which lasted several hours.

23 In July 1933, Ernst and Paula were married in Dinslaken. They had first met in the spring of 1930. He wrote to his parents, who were worried he might be entering into as unsuitable a relationship as Heinrich's, 'There's no need to get worked up about Paula B. I always think over things like this very carefully. For me the basic question with any woman is: what will children with her look like?' Before the wedding Paula was summoned to Ernst's parents' house, where for a few weeks she was to learn to cook her future husband's favourite dishes and was initiated into the ways of polite society.

24 My grandmother Paula came from a craftsman's family in the Rhineland, was brought up as a Catholic and was the only daughter to follow her father's advice to learn a trade. She completed her diploma as a milliner and worked until her marriage as manageress of the millinery department of a small firm in Berlin. Her marriage to Ernst was a step up the social ladder, bringing a comfortable life with their own house, servants and holidays every year. After the war, when she was thrown back on her own resources with her children, her trade helped her, and them, to survive.

25 Heinrich Himmler's attendance as best man at Ernst and Paula's wedding caused something of a stir in the small town of Dinslaken. Here he is posing in his uniform of Reichsführer SS. Paula's mother was said to be 'not exactly delighted' with her new son-in-law, his brother or his politics. Paula's younger brother Walter, however, who was twenty at the time, got on well with Heinrich, who found a post for him in the SS. Paula was soon on familiar terms with her brother-in-law, calling him 'dear Heini'. Shortly before the wedding, he found Ernst a position with good prospects in the Reich Broadcasting Company in Berlin, and over the next few years helped him in both his professional and his private life. In return, Ernst supplied information and did favours for Heinrich's Security Service.

26 Ernst with three of his children. After they were married Ernst and Paula moved to the Berlin suburb of Ruhleben. This former trade-union estate had been expropriated after the seizure of power by the Nazis and handed over to the German Labour Front, which sold off the semi-detached houses with their large gardens to Party members. High-ranking SS leaders also lived there, among them Hermann Behrends who, from 1933 onwards, was head of the Berlin SS Security Service and later became Senior SS and Police Commander in Serbia. The Behrendses, who were friends of Ernst and Paula, in 1937 bought adjoining semi-detached houses on the estate together – with a loan from the Reichsführer SS. The neighbouring house belonged to Klaus Hubmann, Ernst's boss at the Broadcasting Company and likewise a good friend.

27 Ernst in the garden with his eldest daughter and, behind them, Hubmann.

28 Through Heinrich and with help from Hubmann, who had been 'secretly working for the SS' since 1931, Ernst obtained a position with the Reich Broadcasting Company. He soon became Hubmann's 'right hand'. The two of them often went on business trips together – as in the photo (probably from 1938), to the Königsberg broadcasting station. Together Hubmann and Ernst organized – all without a hitch – the broadcasts of the Nuremberg Party rallies, the 1936 Olympics and the Anschluss of the Sudeten Germans after the German invasion of Czechoslovakia. Hubmann, a fervent Nazi but not a man to mince his words, was dismissed without notice by Goebbels in the summer of 1942. Ernst, unofficially his successor, clearly took the dismissal as a warning; contact with the Hubmanns was broken off.

29 With the help of Fritz Todt, Superintendent General of the construction industry, Gebhard transferred in 1939 from his post as head of an engineering college in Munich to the Education Ministry in Berlin. In his double function as the official responsible for engineering issues and head of section in the Central Office for Technology of the Nazi Party, he was the man within the Ministry who successfully pushed through the aim of Todt's Central Office to force German engineers either to join the 'racial community', thereby controlling them, or to exclude them from it on 'racial' grounds and thus refuse them the professional title of engineer. In 1944, Gebhard was promoted to head of department in the Ministry; in addition, during the final years of the war he took on the post of inspector of the Waffen SS.

30 Richard Wendler had known the eldest of the Himmler brothers since 1919, from the student fraternity in Munich; seven years later Gebhard married Wendler's sister Hilde. In 1939, Wendler went with Hans Frank to the 'Government General' of Poland, where, as Governor of Cracow and Lublin, he worked 'smoothly' with the SS on the deportation of Jews and the resettlement of Poles. He rose in the SS to the rank of Gruppenführer and got on very well with Heinrich, supplying him with inside information on Frank and other officials. After the war, Wendler went underground for a while; later he fought obstinately to reduce his classification as a 'major offender' until he was rehabilitated and eventually able to practise as a lawyer again.

31a and b In May 1945, Gebhard was interned by the English in the
camp at Neumünster, where his sister-in-law Paula smuggled a letter to
him hidden in a cake. He spent the next three years in internment camps,
where he kept coming across 'old comrades'. He made sketchbooks of his
time in the camps and wrote poems, in which he portrayed himself and
others as innocents led astray by Hitler. On his release in August 1948,
his daughter was waiting to greet him at the camp gate in Ungerstrasse in
Munich. Later Gebhard found a modest post and successfully fought to
have his pension rights as a senior civil servant restored.

Generally, though, the two saw very little of each other and, according to what Gebhard later said, a coolness had developed between them soon after the marriage. The stay at the spa seems to have brought them slightly closer together again. A few months afterwards they bought a house in the Dahlem district of Berlin, where the family spent the next few years. At the end of 1937 Marga accompanied her husband on a four-week trip around Italy, which Heinrich undertook through his good contacts with the Italian Chief of Police. Otherwise she was rarely with him on official occasions and mostly not even named on the few press photos in which she appeared.

At New Year 1936, after he had returned from the spa, Heinrich received a letter from Ernst and Paula. Ernst thanked his brother for the best wishes he had sent on his birthday and, above all, for 'the magnificent picture – it has been hung in a particularly fine place in our living-room'. Paula added a few lines at the end: 'Dear Heini, You should see the way our two are rampaging round, I'm sure you'd love it . . . Just at the moment it's getting more and more difficult to write. I.'s bawling for all she's worth and they're both tugging at my chair as hard as they can. Will the two of you come and see us sometime in January?' I wonder how long this familiarity between them had existed, the natural way Paula calls her brother-in-law 'Heini', which even Ernst did not do in that personal letter.

My grandmother also told Heinrich that ' "little Siegfried" hasn't announced his presence yet'. Clearly, Heinrich had enquired hopefully whether a male heir was on the way. Paula and Ernst's son kept them waiting for another two years; and when he arrived it wasn't as Siegfried, though he was, like his sisters, given a Teutonic-German name, followed by that of his godfather Heinrich. Was it important for Heinrich that there was a male descendant in the family at last? All three brothers loved their daughters dearly. And yet something seems to have been missing. When my father, the first boy in the Himmler family, was born in February 1939, Paula wrote an enthusiastic letter, while she was still in hospital, to her elder sister asking after *her* son, who had been born three weeks previously, adding that she hoped that their youngest sister, who already had two daughters, would also have a son now. Paula and Ernst also joyfully recorded the birth of their 'healthy son and heir' in the SS house magazine *Black Corps*.

By now the couple were doing well financially; at thirty-two they were the proud owners of a house and had a maid and a car – even if only a small DKW, called the DKWobble-you 'because it used to judder so much', their daughter said. The family photos of the period show happy parents and beaming children. Paula's clothes are strikingly chic and elegant. Her daughter believes that her father used to spoil Paula a lot: 'He didn't even let her cut the bread, he always did it himself.' He hardly let her do anything at all, she said; only later did Paula have to learn 'to knuckle down and deal with things herself'.

The price Paula had to pay for her 'spoilt' existence was that Ernst made the decisions on all important matters affecting their life together. My father remembers his mother complaining, for example, of his insistence that the house be always immaculately clean and tidy, which suggests that the husband Paula later more and more idealized had a definite tyrannical side to him. And he appears to have insisted, also, on his stricter methods of bringing up children against her more liberal ideas. His children remember him punishing them: he would make them stand motionless with their faces to the wall and feel ashamed of themselves, or send them to bed without their supper or lock them in a dark cupboard. But they also have memories of a father who loved playing and fooling around with them. There are photos showing this side where they are all happily bathing or going sledging together.

The few letters from Ernst to his wife that have survived reveal how much he missed her when he was away. He was convinced, he assured her in a letter of 22 April 1937, that not the least reason for his successful rise was their solid marriage and the fact that his wife looked after him 'really' well, 'so that my mind's really free for work and that after work I look forward to going home instead of being afraid to'.

Unusually, this letter was not written during a business trip:

> Today you are going to get a beautiful, typed letter from your husband. Even though he isn't away on a journey. But you must be able to write just as well soon, so that you can send me a letter like this too. And not only that, but so that you can type my work with the ten-finger system as well. Then we'll buy one of those marvellous Erika portables with a tabulator to make it easy to type tables and columns of figures. In the meantime I've more or less familiarized myself with the ten-finger system again, so you can see that the whole business can be learnt pretty quickly. But

one thing above all: don't start writing before you've mastered the positions of the Mercedes ten-finger system properly. Once you've done that, you'll be even more competent than you already are. I really oughtn't to say that because, you never know, you might get bigheaded.

What did he mean by 'my work'? Did Ernst want to take a doctorate and was my grandmother to help him by typing out his thesis? In fact, he doesn't seem to have published anything after 1935 – probably because he didn't have the time, given his increasing responsibilities with the Broadcasting Company and his growing family.

On the one hand I find it touching that my grandfather should send his wife a letter from work without any specific reason; on the other I find the patronizing tone he suddenly adopts repugnant, going against the romantic intention of the letter. It is full of the sense of his own ability, ambition and delight in what he had achieved; delight at the career he had made for himself already and satisfaction at their standard of living, but also satisfaction with himself, since it was through his hard work that he had got that far. Perhaps it was because he had grown up in privileged circumstances, making his way always with the support of others, that he failed to see that it was not through his own efforts alone that he had come so far.

In the letter quoted above my grandfather seemed suddenly to remember that he actually wanted to write a nice letter to his wife, for he goes on: 'But now we can look forward to our holidays. Let's hope we have some decent weather. And we're going to enjoy it. We deserve it! There's still a lot of work and learning to do this year. Things have gone very well so far.' The holiday planned in April 1937 was spent on the Baltic coast, as was the next year's. In July 1938 Paula sent a postcard to her elder sister and her husband. 'We've ended up in Müritz again and are having a lovely time. The kids love going in the water and really splash about.' Then, expressing her surprise, she asks her sister, 'Aren't you going away for a holiday?' She seems to have adjusted to her new standard of living very quickly.

Paula and Ernst also regularly went to a spa for their health, most often to the Felke Spa Sobernheim in the Rhineland, established by Emmanuel Felke, the nineteenth-century naturopath. Paula had heart trouble and Ernst clearly suffered from stomach pains as frequently as his brother Heinrich. Ernst was also very short-sighted. My father recalls that after a long course of special training Ernst no longer needed to wear glasses. Hardly surprising, then, that he became an enthusiastic fan of Felke's methods. But paddling in cold water, taking alternating hot and cold baths and running barefoot were not restricted to their stays at the spa; whenever possible they did all this at home as well.

In the years before the war, the Nazi regime received wide support. Anyone who belonged to the German racial community could enjoy the improvements in conditions and the feeling of being part of a tremendous surge forward in exciting times. And this was particularly true of people who, like Gebhard and Ernst, were closer to those in power than the average German. One of the things that contributed to the improvement in Germany's standing abroad, as well, was the Olympic Games of 1936, with which Ernst was heavily involved.

The decision to hold the Games in Berlin had been taken in 1931, before the Nazis came to power, and the International Olympic Committee was unwilling to change it despite international protests. Hitler, for his part, recognized the opportunity it gave him to present himself to the world as a peace-loving host. He had all the telltale anti-Semitic signs removed from the capital.

During the 1936 summer Olympics television pictures were transmitted for the first time, for eight hours a day, to twenty-five public television parlours in Berlin and in other cities. In my grandparents' living-room there was also a television set, at that time doubtless a sensation that the children regarded with a mixture of awe and admiration. Those early sets were huge pieces of furniture with tiny screens. The story went in my family that Klaus Hubmann and my grandfather had played a major part in the technical development of television; in Hubmann's SS file there is a short note that he 'made a major contribution' in the field. At the time it was only those who were doing such work who had a personal set. But the part Hubmann and my grandfather played was far from being as significant as our family tradition made out. The real father of television development was a young physicist called Manfred Baron von Ardenne, who, in Berlin at the end of 1930, was the first to succeed in transmitting fully electronic images using a Braun tube. The electronic transmission of images took time to establish itself, however, only gradually supplanting the mechanical system with Nipkow discs favoured by the directorate of the German Postal Service under its Minister Walter Ohnesorge. Since 1929 the Postal Service had had a television department in the Berlin-Tempelhof district, where Hubmann was working at the time, and later a television studio in Charlottenburg.

From the spring of 1934 onwards, the Broadcasting Company began to compete with the Postal Service. It set up its own television laboratory, directed for the next two years by the physicist Friedrich Kirschstein. His initially very small staff was part of the engineering section and therefore came under Hubmann. He and Kirschstein had studied electrical engineering together in Munich and from 1929 to 1933 had been colleagues in the television department of the Postal Service. On 22 March 1935 the Postal Service and the Broadcasting Company started operating an experimental television transmitter with regular programmes, including sound films and a newsreel; two weeks later the Postal Service opened the first television parlour for communal viewing. The quality of the pictures left a great deal to be desired, however. The Broadcasting Company's head of programming, Carl Heinz Boese, did not mince his words when he wrote, 'After a time watching the programmes on the television receiver makes one's eyes ache . . . so-called good reception is a matter of luck.'

During the next few years the Broadcasting Company persistently tried to make itself independent of the Postal Service in the development of television, but in this they were deluding themselves because the transmission and reception installations were the responsibility of the Postal Service, which frequently made difficulties when the Broadcasting Company wanted them for its broadcasts.

In the final analysis, however, neither of them got anywhere with their plans because Hitler was not really interested in the civilian use of television, being exclusively concerned with its military applications.

The militarization of television after the start of the war was clearly due to the ambitions of the Minister for Postal Services, Ohnesorge, who used the considerable surpluses from the Post Office's monopoly to finance weapons for Hitler's wars. Very early on he was active in promoting the development of new, remote-controlled weapons, what he called 'seeing bombs'. The idea was that these bombs would be controlled by means of a minicamera installed in them, which would transmit television pictures in order to increase the percentage of hits during air-raids. The necessary technology did not develop quickly enough to influence the course of the war in Germany's favour, but it did make enough progress for the Allies to use the research of German scientists after their victory.

After he had been made Hubmann's deputy in 1935/6, Ernst was often away on official business. At rallies and parades he organized and supervised the radio broadcast, sometimes together with Hubmann, sometimes on his own. In addition, he frequently visited the broadcasting studios of the various federal states, presumably not just to discuss the coordination of the various stations but also to consolidate the overriding authority of the central Broadcasting Company. In March 1938, immediately after the *Anschluss* – the 'joining-together', as the Germans euphemistically called the annexation of Austria – he was in Vienna in order to supervise the technical aspects of the linkage of Austrian radio to the German

Reich. In recognition of his 'special services' rendered during the 'reunification of Austria with the German Reich' he was awarded a medal. And by the autumn of that year he had already gained his second decoration, together with Hubmann, following a trip 'on official business' to another annexed country – the Sudetenland. This time it was for 'special services' in the 'overall direction of and responsibility for the technical deployment of broadcasting since the beginning of the Sudeten crisis'.

11

Educating People to Make Sacrifices for the Community: Gebhard – a Civil Servant's Career

Since his appointment as head of the technical college, Gebhard had been conspicuous by his absence from the institution. The main reason was his numerous voluntary activities. Beside his work running the college, his officer training and his participation in the NS Teachers' Association, at the beginning of 1936 he became involved on a voluntary basis with the Party's *Hauptamt für Technik* (Central Office for Technology) and the *NS Bund Deutscher Technik* (NSBDT, the Association for German Technology) that was affiliated to it. Both were run by Fritz Todt, who gave Gebhard great support during his next career moves.

By 1938 the NSBDT had swallowed up almost all of the technological and scientific organizations, including the Federation of German Engineers through which Gebhard had arrived at the Association for Technology. The aim of this centralization was to ensure that the 'efforts of German technology were in line with the requirements of the people and the state'. Since the announcement of the four-year plan in the autumn of 1936, the Nazi regime had placed increased emphasis on technological innovation, above all in order to increase the production of goods that were important for warfare. Germany was to be armed and capable of waging war within four years.

Initially many engineers were sceptical about this course. The profession had gone through a severe crisis during the last years of the Weimar Republic. The poor employment situation meant their numbers had declined steadily and they continued to do so at first under the Nazis. This was soon to have serious consequences, as the push for increased production in the construction industry and armament technology turned the former surplus of engineers into an acute shortage. But even this did not mean that older engineers, who had often been unemployed during the final years of the Weimar Republic, found work again. In an article published in the *Rundschau Deutscher Technik* (Review of German Technology) of 23 March 1939 Gebhard, in his function as coordinator of the 'Bounden Duty Campaign', appealed to German industry to consider older engineers when making new appointments, since they had mostly become unemployed through no fault of their own during the earlier 'years of decline' – under the 'regime of Jews and Freemasons', as he added in the October 1942 issue of the magazine *Reich und Geist* (Reich and Spirit).

The artificially created boom meant that engineers were now in demand and their work was more and more highly regarded. In the period running up to the war there was a growing rapprochement between National Socialism, with its nationalistic, racial ethos, and technology.

In January 1938 Gebhard attended a one-week 'national training course' run by the NSBDT in Plassenburg Castle in the north of Bavaria. He was responding

to a 'call-up order of the National Socialist Party' – failure
to attend 'without good reason' would result in 'a sum-
mons before the Party court or other disciplinary consequences'. A leaflet sent out in advance gave those
attending precise instructions: 'Participants in the training
course will march as a unit from Kulmbach station to the
Castle.' It was essential they bring a brown shirt so that
the whole camp was in uniform. In his accompanying
letter for Gebhard's course, Todt wrote that 'the men
from a technical background have also to comply with
the spirit of Plassenburg Castle'. The course was probably
a prerequisite for a senior position in the NSBDT. In the
November Gebhard was made responsible for the 'section
dealing with professional matters in the Central Office for
Technology of the National Socialist Party' and at the
same time took up a similar position (*Reichsberufswalter*)
in the NSBDT. In this double function he was responsible
for the internal memoranda of the NSBDT, but above all
he was the one who decided, following the guidelines
drawn up by Todt, who was allowed to use the title of
engineer and who not. Not the least of the requirements
was 'absolute political reliability'.

During that same year, Gebhard was also called up for
various military exercises. His Army commitments were
becoming ever more frequent. In March he took part in
the invasion of Austria as a platoon commander, in the
summer there was a two-week compulsory exercise as
platoon and company commander, in October a three-
week 'mobilization exercise' as company commander in
the Sudetenland. Three days before that, on 1 October,
the Germans had invaded Czechoslovakia and annexed
the Sudetenland.

Immediately after his return, Gebhard applied to take leave of absence on 'official business': in November he wanted to take part in a propaganda trip about 'German technology in the Sudetenland'. He obviously felt drawn to the Sudetenland. It seems clear that his repeated applications for leave to fulfil these and other obligations were granted without exception; nowhere in the files can I find any suggestion of misgivings or objections to his frequent absences on the part of the education department.

During the November trip Gebhard must have made a deep impression on Todt, for in a letter of 12 December 1938 he asked the Mayor of Munich, Reichsleiter Fiehler, to pass on to Gebhard his 'heartfelt thanks and appreciation' for 'the exemplary way in which he had carried out his duties'. But that was not the end of the story. In a letter of 16 January 1939 to the staff office of the Reichsführer SS he suggested that 'Party member Himmler be considered for promotion to the next higher rank'.

Gebhard presumably knew nothing about this letter for, at an SS 'midwinter celebration' in Dachau a few weeks previously he had complained to the head of the SS Business Administrative Department, Gruppenführer (Lieutenant-General) Oswald Pohl, about his 'high-and-mighty brother' who wasn't promoting him quickly enough. Pohl passed on Gebhard's complaint to the head of the SS Personnel Department, Gruppenführer Schmitt.

Gebhard's daughter recalls that her father sometimes used to complain about how hard Heinrich was on his brothers in order to avoid giving the impression that members of his family received preferential treatment. Eventually, she said, Gebhard had got fed up with being mocked by others all the time because of his 'very low rank' and had made his dissatisfaction clear to Heinrich. On 30 January 1939 he was made *Sturmbannführer*, which corresponded to a major in the Army. In fact, he appears to have neither been given preferential treatment, nor held back; his promotions came at the usual intervals of twelve to eighteen months.

Six months after his trip to the Sudetenland Gebhard received another invitation from Todt. This time it was 'to participate in the Nordic journey of German technology from 10 to 16 May on the steamship *Robert Ley*'. For the members of the NSBDT it was 'official business, since there would be important meetings taking place during the journey'. This time Hilde accompanied him. The trip was something special for both of them, since neither had ever been abroad. They were enraptured by the beautiful Norwegian scenery – and probably also by the luxurious conditions on board. There were six meals a day and the food was not merely ample, it was also good: cod in white wine, ham in burgundy, for instance. Very few people enjoyed such privileges and the members of the NSBDT were clearly among them. But the 'business trip' was also a pleasant way of convincing the passengers of the merits of the organization and of securing their further – often voluntary – commitment. During the journey Gebhard would also have had plentiful opportunity to develop his friendly relations with his superior, Todt, whom he much admired.

Fritz Todt, a member of the Nazi Party since 1922, had been made Inspector General of German roads in 1933 and from 1934 on was head of the Party's Central Office for Technology and of the Association for German Technology; in addition, in December 1938 he was made

Superintendent General of the German construction industry. He was thus responsible both for Germany's autobahns and for military fortifications, for example the construction of the *Westwall* (generally known in English as the Siegfried Line). In 1938 the 'Todt Organization' was set up with the specific purpose of building large-scale military installations, for which concentration camp prisoners and other forced labour were put at its disposal. During the war, in March 1940, Todt would be made Minister for Armaments and Munitions. The Central Office for Technology, of which he remained head, was to take over the 'mobilization of the arms industry'. With this 'special commission from the Führer' the future organization of military equipment was finally handed over to engineers and industry, to whom Hitler gave precedence over the Army.

It was Hitler's wish that Todt should use the departments of the Central Office for Technology as well as the engineers belonging to the NSBDT to carry out his projects. This did not mean an end to the arguments with the Army about who was in charge of armaments planning, since the military did not relinquish the sole responsibility it had so far enjoyed without a fight. But the technical experts had Hitler's backing and thus the long-desired opportunity to organize their work themselves.

For Gebhard, Todt was the epitome of the engineer. A few years later he was to celebrate him, in the article in *Reich und Geist* already mentioned, in his bombastic German, as the 'greatest National Socialist engineer', who had given German engineers that 'professional ethos' which enabled them 'to match up to the immense tasks awaiting them [in the] present life-and-death struggle of the German people'. Taking their rightful place in the German racial community, Gebhard wrote, German engineers had assumed a new responsibility to do 'great service for the community'. Thus their work no longer merely served the 'rational, practical purposes of civilization' but had become 'a vital, integral part of our culture!' '[This] young blood and new spirit,' he went on, would 'give birth to something new that will seize hold of us like a clear, fresh mountain wind rushing forth from mysterious valleys and sweeping all before it!' Technology had to let itself be guided by this 'stance and conviction of the reawakened German soul' on its way into 'the bright sunlight of a great German future'.

With what amounted to religious fervour Gebhard believed in this 'higher unity', the awareness of which was to be instilled into every level of the hierarchy and transmitted to the next in celebration of the 'greatest teacher of the German people, Adolf Hitler'. Like Heinrich, who was very pleased with the article and recommended it be included in Gebhard's file, Gebhard felt he had a mission from the Führer to educate others. As he saw it, each person had a specific educational task of his own to perform, alongside his particular contribution to building up the country. Engineers, especially teachers at technical colleges, officials, lecturers, should inculcate in the new generation of technologists a sense of their great historical mission.

In 1939 Gebhard wrote to the publishers of the *Völkischer Beobachter* reminding them that they should ensure that adverts for technical positions used the correct, standardized titles. It sounded banal, but behind it was a comprehensive plan devised by the Central Office for a 'great campaign of public enlightenment' to counteract the 'boundless chaos [of the] system years' – that is, the Weimar Republic. The standardization of the award of the title of engineer was not the only key element in this campaign of public enlightenment: it also included the long-term aim of the NSBDT, which was affiliated to the Central Office, to take over sole responsibility for granting the qualification. And Gebhard played a substantial role in promoting its monopoly of the engineering profession and imposing compulsory membership of the Association for German Technology on everyone who in future wanted the right to call himself an engineer. How important the control and supervision of engineers was for him can be seen in a working paper of 20 February 1941. It is a survey of 'problems of technology' which had to be dealt with 'in the interests of the Reich' and includes a handwritten note from Gebhard to the effect that Heydrich, the head of the Reich's Central Security Department, had to be involved in the discussions.

In an official communication of 1941 to his brother Ernst, Gebhard said that he could only agree to the granting of the title of engineer to longstanding sound engineers at the Broadcasting Company on condition that they 'become part of the National Socialist community of engineers. I have linked the award of the title to membership [of the NSBDT] because there are so many cases where men come to the Association or the Central Office for Technology just because they need something from them, only to slip away quietly afterwards.' It was clearly the case that many engineers were extremely suspicious of the attempts to direct and control the profession and tried to wriggle out of any more binding contact with

Reichsberufswalter Gebhard as quickly as possible. Gebhard seems to have found it very difficult to get his counterparts in the various administrative regions to adopt his approach. Again and again in the files I came across letters expressing their dissatisfaction with his instructions. Many of them were unwilling to be forced to step into line politically. But this only seems to have strengthened Gebhard's determination.

When a *Gauberufswalter*, a regional offical dealing with professional matters, from Vienna wrote in October 1940 firmly rejecting 'compulsory membership', the *Reichsberufswalter* took his time to reply. It was not until three months later that Gebhard gave the reasons for his instructions. There had been an increasing number of cases, he wrote, 'in which the applicant has only come to the NSBDT for the advantage he could gain. I do not see why we should grant such individuals the professional title, which is certainly useful for them, when they, as engineers, cannot show sufficient community spirit to want to be part of the Party's organization for furthering German technology.' His instruction was 'far from amounting to compulsion', but if the person in question did not want to join the National Socialist Association for German Technology, then 'his application simply will not be not processed'. The prerequisite for this was the willingness to make a 'sacrifice for the community' in joining the NSBDT.

Despite Gebhard's attempts to thwart such 'exploitation', the habit among engineers of resigning from the NSBDT as soon as the title of engineer had been awarded them seems, if anything, to have increased over the next few years – which only spurred him on to pursue such cases 'with all the means at my disposal'. Those who dug their heels in were sent a letter; W., a *Gauberufswalter*, received this in March 1940:

> Dear Party Member W.,
>
> In your letter you have once more talked of reservations regarding the award of the professional title of 'engineer' by the Association's central Reich administration. We suggest it would be advisable not to be the only one constantly expressing 'reservations'. We know exactly what we must do or not do in this area. In the meantime you will have received our communication of 19 December 1939 with the announcement of my appointment to the Reich Education Ministry with responsibility for colleges of engineering, in a capacity, therefore, which will enable me when the time comes to make a decisive contribution to the discussion regarding the legal protection of the professional title of 'engineer'.

Gebhard was indeed now working at the Reich Ministry of Education. At the end of 1939 Todt had put his name forward for a head-of-section post that had become vacant. He had been impressed not only by Gebhard's conscientiousness, but also by his 'impeccable convictions'. Todt's recommendation was not entirely selfless. He hoped that placing a loyal and reliable colleague in the Ministry would decide the struggle with the German Labour Front over responsibility for colleges of engineering in favour of the NSBDT. Formally, the Central Office for Technology came under Robert Ley as head of the Party's political organization; the Office for Technical Sciences, also run by Todt, came under the head of the German Labour Front – again, Robert Ley. Todt and Ley were clearly engaged in a bitter struggle for control of a profession the significance of which had risen enormously since the build-up of armaments technology.

In addition, Todt's Central Office for Technology was pursuing plans of its own to extend its area of responsibility. The University of Technology planned for Munich was to have a Fritz Todt Institute attached, in which the technologists intended to try to integrate scientific research and thus remove it from the sole responsibility of the Reich Education Ministry. Gebhard seems to have been Todt's Trojan horse, with the purpose of trying to break the Ministry's monopoly of scientific research. Todt obviously believed him capable of carrying out these difficult and varied tasks, and Gebhard was not to disappoint him.

By the summer of 1939 Gebhard was a member not only of the NS People's Welfare Organization, the Association for Germans Abroad, the NS Teachers' Association and the NS Association for German Technology; over the years he had become a member of a number of other organizations – the Reich Association of German Civil Servants, the Air-Raid Protection Association, the NS Association of Former Students, the German Red Cross, the NS Reich Soldiers' Association and the Reich Colonial League.

The latter had been founded only in 1936, as a successor to the German Colonial Society which had been compulsorily wound up. It was run by Franz Ritter von Epp, who had been acquainted with the two elder Himmler brothers since their Freikorps days. In 1934 Epp had been appointed head of the Party's Office for Colonial Policy. During 1904–6 he had been an officer in the

German colony of South West Africa and had been involved in the genocide of the Herero people who had rebelled against German rule. Until 1943 Epp was still dreaming of conquering colonies for Germany, but then the Colonial League was ordered to cease its activities by the Führer, who had long since opted for the colonization of the eastern territories instead.

At first, after the victory over France, things looked different. Then, all the leading executive organs of the system, from the Office for Colonial Policy to Heydrich's Central Security Department, showed a keen interest in France's colonial possessions. Imperialist ambitions to flex their muscles in 'colonial technology' were aroused in the Central Office for Technology as well, first and foremost at the Federation of German Engineers – Gebhard's stepping-stone to the NSBDT in 1936 – which organized a first 'conference on technology in the tropics and colonies' in December 1940. In April 1941 Todt himself, who a month earlier had been made Armaments Minister in addition to his other offices, was assuming that 'colonial responsibilities' would come his way in the future.

After 1933 the Association for Germans Abroad under its director Hans Steinacher, an officer and a recognized expert on ethnic and cultural questions, had not only seen a massive increase in membership, it had also made great efforts to preserve its independence of the Party. Its annual meetings in particular, perfectly organized mass gatherings, were an increasing cause of concern to the Party leadership because they upstaged their own events. In addition the Association, despite its acceptance of the authoritarian leadership principle and nationalist, anti-Semitic opinions, rejected the ideology of a 'master race' and consequently all attempts to assimilate, drive out or resettle other ethnic groups. This did not fit in with the expansionist plans of the Party leadership. In mid-1938 the Association was compelled to accept its subordination to the Ethnic German Assistance Office (*Volksdeutsche Mittelstelle*, VoMi), and therefore to the SS, and shortly afterwards Todt and Gebhard Himmler sought, through the NS Central Office for Technology, to play a part in the repressive ethnic policies of the VoMi in the Sudetenland.

On 1 August 1939 Gebhard was called up, and from then on was on standby with his company in the Protectorate of Bohemia and Moravia, close to the Polish frontier, ready to take part in the invasion of Poland on 1 September. 'I soon became very attached to my motorized unit; it was a splendid group of comrades I had under my command,' he wrote in his 'Reminiscences' more than three decades later. 'With my front-line experience in the First World War, I managed to come through this episode [the invasion of Poland], despite some of the daredevil strokes we pulled off during the headlong advance, with only two wounded men and one damaged vehicle.'

Even thirty years later, for him the invasion of Poland seems to have remained first and foremost a great adventure that he came through with flying colours. At the very beginning the Army High Command had distributed a leaflet warning the troops about Polish 'duplicity' and 'cruelty'. The overheated expectations of encountering snipers and *francs-tireurs* that this propaganda aroused were a welcome justification for laying waste to the country and shooting hostages, prisoners, Jews and civilians. The generally accepted view that Poles and East European Jews were inferior races and at the same time, as guerrillas, represented a threat to the German troops, seemed to justify this course of action. Gebhard did not have a word to say about the dead he and his unit left behind them on their 'headlong advance'. Given this, I am not very convinced by his claim to have been annoyed by a card from the head of the Personal Staff of the Reichsführer SS, Karl Wolff, who wrote something along the lines of, 'What a jolly war your company commander exercise has turned into!' Gebhard's daughter recalled that, even years afterwards, he still got worked up about it. But there is no great difference between Wolff's jocular postcard and Gebhard's own 'Reminiscences', in which a country was simply overrun by his unit of 'splendid comrades'.

Gebhard's Infantry Regiment 19 from Munich was part of the 14th Army; he was presumably in an anti-tank unit, since they were the only motorized units in the regiment. At the conclusion of hostilities on 16/17 September the regiment was just outside Lviv (Russian Lvov, German Lemberg), but at the beginning of October his unit was transferred to the Lower Rhine in preparation for the forthcoming attack on France and the Benelux countries. It was there in December that the news of his appointment to the Ministry of Education reached him; he was transferred to a reserved occupation with immediate effect.

The Reich Ministry for Science and Education had been established in 1934 under Bernhard Rust. Rust, a former teacher, was not considered an ideological fanatic, but he faithfully carried out the 'racial purging' of the universities. He was seen as not very good at promoting the interests of the Ministry against rival institutions or politicians such as the Ministry for Public Enlightenment and Propaganda, the office of the editor of the *Völkischer Beobachter*, Alfred Rosenberg, or the Third Reich's youth leader, or even against the Reich student leadership and the NS University Lecturers' Association.

That same month Gebhard started work in Department E IV of the Ministry, which was responsible for vocational and professional training. Initially he lodged with Ernst and Paula, while Hilde stayed with the children in Munich where they had rented a house only two years previously. At the time she was seven months pregnant. For six months Gebhard saw his family only on weekend visits. Their third daughter was born on 13 March 1940. It was a difficult birth and Hilde, who had just turned forty-one, recovered only slowly and with the assistance of a wet-nurse. It was not until July that the whole family moved to Berlin – in Heinrich's plane, since he thought such a long train journey was too much for a baby.

Their departure must have been particularly hard for Anna Himmler, for now none of her sons was in Munich any more. But the move to Berlin was also difficult for Gebhard's children. Their father spent the summer holidays exploring the city with the two older girls on the urban railway so as to help them learn to find their way around themselves. They did not get on well with the Berliners and their rough and ready manners; at school they were mocked by their new classmates as 'Bavarian bumpkins'. One comfort was that they felt happy at home. They had a large apartment in the suburb of Friedenau; Gebhard and his eldest daughter regularly went out for walks at six in the morning; and in the evening when their father came home, the family read aloud to each other and made music. Through Gebhard's colleagues at the Ministry the parents at least soon found a circle of friends that met regularly.

Yet initially there had been much opposition within the Ministry to Gebhard's appointment, one of his daughters recalls. They didn't want a brother of Heinrich Himmler in the department. Gebhard made great efforts to allay his new colleagues' distrust. In this he was helped by the fact that immediately after he took up his duties he won a 'victory' over the Labour Front: he succeeded in 'outmanoeuvring the Labour Front and thwarting their expansionist designs' so that 'we could work freely and undisturbed'. Continuing at breakneck speed, he then proceeded to establish good relations with his superior and head of department, one Professor Heering, who had the reputation of being 'difficult': 'I soon got on well with him, especially once my success in the so far fruitless struggle between the Labour Front and the weak – because of Rust – Ministry became apparent.'

On 20 May 1940, following a suggestion from Gebhard, Heering decreed that in future engineers seeking recognition of qualifications that came from technical colleges outside the Reich would have to provide evidence both of their Aryan descent and their political past. Applicants would have to demonstrate their political reliability via an examination on the subject of 'National Political Studies'. In fact, this tiresome exam was in practice very quickly abandoned and such applicants simply rejected, as can be seen from a letter of June 1941 written by one of Gebhard's assistants. Citing Gebhard by name, he rejected an applicant from Pilsen with the curt explanation that 'the title of "engineer" is not granted to graduates of Czech colleges'. When the local *Gauberufswalter* persisted, pointing out that the applicant was, after all, a German citizen, Gebhard's assistant responded, in accordance with his boss's views, with a tart question of his own: 'Why did this "German citizen" attend the Czech technical college in Pilsen when there was also, as we are well aware, a German college there.'

A letter of July 1941 from Gebhard to the Vienna *Gauberufswalter* makes this racial, nationalistic criterion even clearer. Applications for the title of engineer, he wrote, were 'naturally' only to be processed when the applicant was German. And, he went on, previous experience suggested that these German inhabitants of the 'Protectorate' (Bohemia and Moravia) should be subjected to a particularly thorough examination – for example 'when there are doubts about the college attended or when a German has even attended a Czech instead of a German college. This procedure has proved successful in Upper Silesia, now attached to the Reich, since it prevents Germans who previously denied their German identity and attended foreign colleges from being granted professional recognition.'

With these questions Gebhard was pursuing a rigid racialist policy. Interestingly, in this point he diverged not only from the previous policy of the Association for Germans Abroad, but also from that followed by Heinrich, whose view was that ethnic Germans should be recognized as such as long as they had 'the right blood'. Even if they had not actively asserted their German identity previously, he still regarded them as 'educable'.

Gebhard's honorary activities at the NS Central Office for Technology were certainly not simply an expression of his devotion to duty and readiness to sacrifice his time to the Party. The decisive motivation seems to have been his urge to form minds, the opportunity to be involved in the spread of the ruling ideology. It was his habit to back up his arguments with a strict interpretation of his superiors' guidelines in order to 'stop the unregulated use of the title of engineer', and to use the authority of the Party to 'impose order in some particular area'. At the same time he was equally firm in ignoring or brusquely rejecting suggestions and criticisms from subordinates that he did not like, telling them it was none of their business. Suddenly the comradeship he liked to go on about so much seemed forgotten.

Todt's death in a plane crash in January 1942 must have been a heavy blow for Gebhard. On the day of the accident itself Albert Speer, in addition his other duties, took over the direction of the Central Office for Technology and all of Todt's other functions. Unlike his predecessor, Speer's main interest in the Party organization – especially after he became Minister for Armaments and War Production a month later – centred on its effectiveness in increasing the supply of armaments. Gebhard seems to have coped well with this new policy. He not only continued his honorary activities for the Central Office, but was promoted in 1943 (though this did not change his responsibilities).

In May 1941 Gebhard was taken on by the Luftwaffe as a reserve staff flight technician, thus giving up his position as an Army reserve officer. The purpose of this transfer was a further honorary post, this time as 'Adviser for the Technical Colleges of the Armed Forces Sections'. Less than a year later, in March 1942, he transferred to the Waffen SS, the SS's fully militarized combat formations, where he worked, again in an honorary capacity, as an inspector. Six months later he was awarded the 'Military Cross 2nd Class, without Swords' for services 'important for the war effort' as adviser and inspector of the colleges of the Army and the Waffen SS. Then, in January 1944, when almost the only people to be promoted were full-time SS officials and members of the Waffen SS fighting in the field – but hardly any reserve officers, such as Gebhard – he was made a *Standartenführer* (corresponding to the rank of colonel) of the Waffen SS.

At the military colleges associated with the Waffen SS special technical units for tank divisions, artillery, intelligence and so on were trained. When Gebhard announced an inspection visit at one of these establishments and arrived with his adjutants, all the units had to fall in to greet him. Reports were presented and later the recruits had to demonstrate what they had learnt; the visit ended with a banquet. In his role as an inspector Gebhard must have felt like a king.

When his superior, Heering, retired in 1944, Gebhard was to take over his post and become head of department in the Ministry of Education with the rank of *Ministerialdirigent* (equivalent to assistant secretary). Years later he was still regretting that this promotion came 'too late . . . the progressive destruction by the enemy air attacks' had made 'systematic and successful work impossible'.

12

'Keep Marching. Keep Fighting. Keep Working': Ernst and His Friends

Ernst and Paula's neighbours were the Behrends. They lived next door to them in Ruhleben, and together they applied for a loan to purchase the two adjoining houses – not, however, to a bank, but to the Personal Staff of the Reichsführer SS. Ten days later the application was passed on to a Staff official with the note: 'Speedy appraisal requested'; only three weeks after that Bruno Galke, head of the SS Savings Collective, sent a positive response, with 'SECRET' stamped on it: 'The Reichsführer SS has approved your application for a loan.'

The Behrends, only a little younger than my grand-parents, were among their best friends. They celebrated New Year's Eve together, their children played together in the garden, and 'Granny Behrends' sometimes looked after Ernst and Paula's children. Once Paula must have helped save their neighbours' marriage. This, at least, is what is suggested by a letter Ernst sent her from Vienna in 1938: 'I'm glad that things are OK with the Behrends again, give them my best wishes. God forbid that something like that should ever happen to us, but if it did, then may He grant us the friends to bring us joyfully back together again.'

Unfortunately, neither my father nor my aunt could say how the Himmlers and the Behrends had become acquainted; Paula never mentioned it to her children, even though she remained on friendly terms with Frau Behrends and her daughter until the end of her life. That their neighbour was not simply a 'minor Nazi', as my father had believed, was something he only learnt through my researches.

Hermann Behrends, a man with fearful scars on his left cheek from his duelling days – as a student in Marburg he had belonged to a duelling fraternity – was a lawyer. He joined the Nazi Party in January 1932 and the SS one month later in Wilhelmshaven, where he immediately took command of a platoon. In the course of the next year he qualified as a gunnery leader at the Coastal Artillery School.

Behrends obviously displayed promising leadership qualities – and had the right contacts for getting on. In 1932, after his appointment as head of Himmler's Security Service, Reinhard Heydrich managed to persuade his boss that Behrends was the right man to take over the direction of the new department of the SD that had been set up in Berlin. It is possible that Behrends and Heydrich knew each other from the time when Heydrich had been stationed with the Navy in Wilhelmshaven, where Behrends's father had an inn which, according to the former *Spiegel* journalist Heinz Höhne, Heydrich used to frequent.

In December 1933, one week after taking his final examinations, Behrends was sent to Munich and trained as an SD leader. It must have been a crash course, since on 13 January 1934 he started as head of the SD Berlin office. Three months later he married his fiancée, Hertha Hörger from Rüstringen in East Frisia, where he too came from. Initially the Behrends lived in Westend in Charlottenburg, Berlin, but moved, probably at the end of that year, at the same time as my parents, to the house in Ruhleben, where they had three sons in quick succession followed some time later by a daughter.

Behrends quickly worked his way up in the SD. He was ideally suited for the SS headquarters, where many young graduates with the right ideological convictions made their way. At first, as Heydrich's protégé, he was in charge of a special section that had been given the task of collecting incriminating evidence against the SA prior to the bloody purge of June 1934, and then of seeing through the follow-up to the operation. Afterwards, with the rank of *Standartenführer*, he took charge of Central Department II.1 Ideological Evaluation within the SD home affairs division. The task of this department, according to a directive circulated by Heydrich in December 1934, was to maintain surveillance on 'the enemies of the National Socialist idea' and to bring pressure to bear on the 'police authorities to combat and counter them'.

Behrends had four departments under him: 'Ideologies', 'Jews' (which included Adolf Eichmann's section), 'Political Religion' and 'Political Opponents'; the other large central department within the SD home affairs division, II.2 Evaluation of Living Areas, was run by Reinhard Höhn. In the spring of 1937 Franz Six, a former university lecturer in journalism, took charge of Behrends's and Höhn's departments, thus becoming de facto head of the SD home affairs division. By this time Behrends already had another post with good career opportunities.

In 1937 the Führer's deputy Rudolf Hess had set up, at Hitler's instigation, the VoMi, the Ethnic German Assistance Office, to bring together under one umbrella all the Party and government offices dealing with questions concerning ethnic Germans. Its head was SS Obergruppenführer (equivalent to the rank of general) and General of Police Werner Lorenz. Behrends was made his deputy, responsible for the administration and for liaison between the SD and the VoMi. As head of the VoMi staff, Behrends had access to the files of the German Foreign Office and the Armed Forces Ministry, and in November 1937 he offered to borrow this material regularly to be photocopied for the SD Central Security Department. The VoMi and the SD worked closely together – for instance in initiating unrest in the Sudetenland in 1938, which provided Hitler with his excuse to invade.

In July 1938 the two most important movements for ethnic Germans, the Association for Germans Abroad, of which Gebhard Himmler was also a member, and the League for the German East, were brought under the VoMi; after this process of *Gleichschaltung* (coordination under the Reich), Lorenz and Behrends took over the running of these organizations.

When in October 1939 he was appointed Reich Commissioner for the Consolidation of the German Nation, Heinrich Himmler worked closely with the VoMi to resettle thousands of ethnic Germans and continued to do so during the war years. Behrends was given responsibility for the organization of mass resettlement operations in Russia, Bessarabia, Galicia, Romania and the Baltic states. He had ultimate responsibility for the resettlement units, which were subordinate to and trained by the SS. Parallel to this, and in close cooperation with the VoMi's resettlement of Germans, ran the programme for the 'removal of Jews and Poles from the new eastern provinces' carried out by Heydrich's Central Security Department from November 1939 onwards.

After Heydrich, who was also Protector of Bohemia and Moravia, died on 4 June 1942 following an assassination attempt, Heinrich Himmler took over his functions himself. In January 1943 he appointed the Senior SS and Police Commander of the Danube/Vienna section, Ernst Kaltenbrunner, head of the Central Security Department. When on 13 December 1942 Himmler had asked Kaltenbrunner to suggest someone to replace him in Vienna, he had proposed Behrends, a suggestion that Himmler, however, rejected. He wrote to Lorenz on 16 December:

> *My dear Werner,*
> *I am writing to you personally because of my concern about the development of SS Brigadeführer [Major General] Dr Behrends. I have known Behrends for many years. On a personal level he is decent, competent and bold in action. He is married to a nice woman and has nice children. All qualities and things that count in his favour. However, the man has one basic fault – that is his corrosive, unhealthy ambition.*

Himmler was convinced that Kaltenbrunner's recommendation was the result of Behrends's own initiative, and he did not like that. The man, he went on, was clearly forgetting the 'almost incredible career' he had already made for himself at thirty-four and which he owed entirely to his – Himmler's – and Heydrich's support. Himmler suspected that Behrends had even dreamt of becoming Heydrich's successor. He requested Lorenz to inform his deputy 'that he will only move from his present post to a more senior one when I am convinced his character has matured'. He assumed it was Frau Behrends who was the driving force behind his ambition: 'If this should be the case, then Herr Behrends should be told that, for all his love for his wife, he should start to take command of his marriage.' Quite the strict but just patriarch, Himmler's final advice – through Lorenz – to Behrends was 'to put his trust in the old tradition, which has done nothing but good for the whole of the SS': as far as promotion was concerned, 'an able SS man [had] no better advocate than the Reichsführer SS himself'. It was therefore not necessary for individual members to draw attention to themselves – his attention would be drawn to them by their performance and character.

Himmler gave Lorenz express permission to show the letter to Behrends. He was duly angry and defended himself in a letter of 29 December to the Reichsführer. He had never, he insisted, spoken to Kaltenbrunner; he was the 'Reichsführer's man through and through'.

It was clearly not the first time Behrends had been criticized for pushing himself forward, since he felt obliged to stress that, as a member of the SS, he had much more often held back and had done so with the intention 'of providing evidence to counter the criticism that his personal ambition was too great'. By that time Kaltenbrunner had already spoken up for him and emphasized, in a letter to the Reichsführer of 23 December, that his only reason for suggesting Behrends was because he had come to his notice as 'a skilled expert familiar with questions of racial policy'.

Himmler, however, considered it advisable to allow Behrends to prove his abilities in the front line. He was called up once more and commanded several different tank divisions, at first in Wunsdorf near Berlin, then, among others, the Mountain Division in Croatia. From April to October 1944 he was Senior Police Commander of Serbia and Montenegro and the Reich's representative there. This appears to have been his reward for his successful fight against the partisans and the swift evacu- ation of the privileged ethnic German minority. Having collaborated with the German occupying forces, they feared the vengeance of the Yugoslav population at the end of the war.

The partisans had caused great problems for the hated German occupying forces. As early as 1942 Heinrich Himmler had ordered that, in order to deter them, these 'bandits' were to be executed on the spot, likewise their male relatives; their women were to be deported to con- centration camps and their children to the Reich, where they would be interned in the VoMi camps.

During the last months of the war Behrends was Senior SS and Police Commander for the Eastern Territories and North Russia. At the end of the war he fled to Flensburg, then disappeared; he was arrested on 5 July 1945. At first he was sent to a special camp for high-ranking Nazi officers in Neuengamme, then to the Islandfarm camp in England, until Yugoslavia demanded his extradition as a war criminal in February 1947. He was condemned to death and executed.

At the trial of Werner Lorenz in Nuremberg in 1947–8 many of his former colleagues in the VoMi made Behrends the scapegoat, building him up into the diabolical force behind Lorenz, the man who wielded the real power in the VoMi. Lorenz, who was sentenced to twenty years' imprisonment in March 1948 but released from Landsberg six years later, was obviously much more popular than his deputy.

For the rest of her life my grandmother kept up her friendship with Frau Behrends and her daughter, unlike that with the Hubmanns, which did not continue after the war. This is possibly connected with Hubmann's sudden dismissal in 1942 from his post as Technical Director of the Broadcasting Company. Klaus Hubmann, for years my grandfather's boss, was obstinate and self-assured, a man who, according to Paula's children, 'never minced his words' and was therefore always getting into trouble with his superiors. He often disagreed with guidelines issued by Goebbels's Propaganda Ministry and expressed his opinion on them in what he himself called his 'vigorous Bavarian manner'. He was several times given a severe dressing-down for this by various senior Ministry officials – given a taste of his own medicine, so to speak – though it appears to have been like water off a duck's back.

As early as 1936 he had vehemently criticized the Propaganda Ministry's policy as regards personnel. They were trying, he claimed, 'to yoke contrary forces together', but anyone who thought they could yoke 'a

Bolshevist and a reactionary' together should not be surprised if it did not produce 'National Socialist thinking'. He vigorously defended the independence of the Technical Department against the encroachment of the Commercial Department, refusing to accept the latter's superiority in financial matters because he thought Voss, its director, was completely incompetent. He threatened to resign if he was compelled to accept Voss's decisions. In a personal letter to Goebbels he explained, with his usual self-assurance, that he was only prepared to withdraw his threat of resignation if he was authorized to run the technical group as he saw fit. His only aim was to 'place at your disposal for Germany broadcasting technology that is always on the ball yet works economically, and that is a world leader'. This was possible only as long as he was not 'subject to restrictions placed on him by sections that were technically incompetent', he wrote to Goebbels on 12 March that year.

The disputes and arguments about responsibilities among the various departments in the Broadcasting Company continued over the next few years and did not stop when the Director General, Heinrich Glasmeier, centralized power in 1937. After he assumed office Glasmeier saw to it that Hubmann was finally given parity in financial matters with the other directors. In return, Hubmann and my grandfather clearly helped him to consolidate his new position – presumably not just because Glasmeier had the confidence of Heinrich Himmler, but because they hoped this alliance would strengthen their own positions vis-à-vis the administration and the production department. However, according to Hubmann's statement, these initially friendly relations later turned into the opposite, presumably because at some point Glasmeier asserted his higher authority.

Hubmann must have been very sure that his universally acknowledged technical expertise would save him from more serious consequences. He was nonetheless dismissed in the summer of 1942 on Goebbels' instructions, clearly after he had been denounced by a colleague. Hubmann, who was an ardent Nazi, seems to have disastrously underestimated the possibility – almost a matter of course at the time – that he was being spied on.

After a meeting on 9 June 1942 he had sat together with a few colleagues late into the night over a bottle of wine. Earlier on, he said, he had 'done all he could, together with Herr Himmler, to help Dr Glasmeier'. But once the latter 'felt safe in the saddle' he had not shown the least gratitude but had, to put it briefly, 'treated them like shit'. For that reason he – Hubmann – would not rest until Glasmeier had been removed from his post. On the 22nd one of those present reported Hubmann's comments to the Propaganda Ministry and the two other participants in the nocturnal episode confirmed them when asked. Only a few weeks previously the Permanent Secretary at the Propaganda Ministry, Leopold Gutterer, had explicitly reminded all senior broadcasting staff at a meeting that it was the last time 'the constant carping would be dealt with in a round-table discussion'. The logical consequence was that Gutterer demanded Goebbels have Hubmann dismissed on the spot; it was, he said, the only way 'of finally getting some peace in the Reich Broadcasting Company'. The very next day Goebbels ordered Hubmann's dismissal, pointing out that for years he had made great efforts 'to establish the harmonious labour relations that are urgently needed in German broadcasting'; now, though, Hubmann had once more 'put these seriously at risk and at the same time defied both my instructions and the authority of his superior, the Director General'.

One of those who had initially confirmed Hubmann's comments, Joachim von Braunmühl, an engineer who was a friend and neighbour of both Ernst Himmler and Hubmann, tried – too late – to make his statement less damaging. My grandfather, too, tried to avert the inevitable. That same evening he telephoned his brother in his headquarters at Hegewald, close to the Führer's headquarters in East Prussia, and Heinrich's secretary, Brandt, arranged a meeting between Ernst and Werner Naumann, the head of Goebbels's office in the Propaganda Ministry. The dismissal without notice remained in force, however, which meant that Hubmann lost his pension rights for the nine years he had worked for the Reich Broadcasting Company.

The evening he received the telephone call from Ernst, the Reichsführer SS offered to take Hubmann on in his own organization at the same salary. Hubmann, however, does not seem to have been interested. Instead, he doggedly pursued negotiations with Goebbels until he got him to agree to continue paying his salary for eight months.

In a testimonial for him, his successor Herbert Dominik, head of the broadcasting department in the Propaganda Ministry, attested that in 1933 Hubmann had swiftly reorganized the technical side, thus providing the technical basis for the large-scale exploitation of broadcasting during the following years. In addition he had introduced various technical innovations. Pieces of equipment developed under his direction, Dominik wrote, had 'given such excellent service that they have been adopted by almost the whole of European broadcasting and other bodies'. Moreover, Hubmann's 'exemplary organization' of the Reich Broadcasting Company's technical laboratories had made it possible to support the Army, especially its 'propaganda companies'. He had concerned himself with the development of a new generation of technical staff, encouraging especially gifted engineers; but also, when the war meant there were fewer and fewer young men available, he had instigated the setting-up of a technical school for broadcasting to train men disabled in the war, plus female assistants.

From 1 April 1943 Hubmann was working for his old employer again, the German Post Office, which seconded him to the German Administrative Staff of Philips, the electronics firm, where he dealt with questions relating to the manufacture of appliances in the various affiliated companies.

The Hubmanns continued to live on Brombeerweg. The Propaganda Ministry had insisted on filling Hubmann's post with someone from the Ministry, but Herbert Dominik was only rarely to be seen in the broadcasting building since he retained his post in the Ministry. This meant that in practice Ernst, who had been Hubmann's deputy for years, took over the duties of Technical Director and Chief Engineer; as Hubmann's closest colleague he was, anyway, the person best acquainted with the work in hand. In the long run this cannot have helped his relationship with Hubmann, especially since Ernst would surely have seen his dismissal as a warning.

On 9 August 1942 Paula and Ernst had their fourth child, a daughter. Like her brother, she was named – so my grandmother told me later – after one of the founders of Naumburg Cathedral whose statues had so impressed Ernst and Paula when they visited it before the war. It is certainly not mere chance that all four children were given warlike Teutonic names. In his letters my grandfather never called his wife 'Paula' but 'my Gertraudmaiden'. The name Gertraud means 'spear-might', suggesting something akin to a Valkyrie; its combination with 'maiden' possibly expresses Ernst's ambivalent view of women: his partner was to be strong and full of fighting spirit, but at the same time remain his 'maiden'.

In 1942 the massive air-raids on German cities by American and British bombers began. The central districts of Berlin suffered severe damage from the night raids, including Hähnelstrasse in Friedenau where Gebhard and his family lived. When, in the spring of 1943, more and more of the neighbouring houses had been hit by bombs and they had to spend more and more nights in the cellars, Gebhard urged his wife to take the children back to Bavaria, where things were still peaceful. Heinrich put one of the SS apartments on his estate in Gmund at their disposal.

Paula and the children stayed in Berlin until the summer, when the order was given to evacuate all children of school age. By this time Ruhleben was no longer an idyllic retreat. My aunt recalls the constant alerts and the air-raid shelter in the garden, which they often reached at the last moment, while the missiles were already whining overhead. My father was a four-year-old toddler at the time and his favourite game, my aunt said, was to lie under the table playing at soldiers and firing his 'machine-gun'. He has forgotten that himself, but what he can remember clearly is his fear when the air-raid siren sounded at night.

In Heinrich Himmler's handwritten notes on his telephone calls, which are difficult to decipher, there is an entry for 30 July: '7.15 p.m., Paula Himmler Berlin, resettlement in Warthegau', indicating that in August Paula and the children left the city, relying on Heinrich Himmler's help. It was presumably Gottlob Berger, head of the SS Central Office and, since July 1942, SS Liaison Officer with the Ministry for the Occupied Eastern Territories, who found them suitable accommodation. Berger was devoted to the Reichsführer SS and always willing to oblige him. A small estate was 'free' close to his farm near Szrem (German Schrimm) in the Warthegau, so sometime in August Paula and her four children moved to nearby Torse, due south of Poznan. My grandmother must soon have become friendly with her new neighbour, Berger, since she stayed in contact with him after the war.

My father thinks he can recall a 'small, very modest manor house with a working estate'; his eldest sister, however, remembers that the manor house was 'almost like a little castle'. The house of the steward across the courtyard, on the other hand, was 'tiny . . . you could hardly stand up in it'. The houses in the village too were low cottages, she said, but anyway the children were forbidden to enter them. However, they found plenty to occupy them on the farm: they could watch the pigs being fed or soap being boiled up in a cauldron, or play with bales of straw and conkers.

The previous Polish owners had long since been expelled, victims of Heinrich Himmler's brutal 'resettlement plans'. The house was so spacious that there was room for Paula's youngest sister from the Ruhr and her three daughters as well. During the week the older girls boarded in the school hostel in Szrem. There, my aunt said, 'they were very strict'. She also remembers joining the junior section of the German Girls' League, where they had to look after smaller children and were sent out gathering herbs.

Ernst came from Berlin to see them, at most once every four weeks. But then he took the children skiing to the nearby River Warta, which was frozen over. Both children recall 'fantastic winter scenes' as they lay with their father 'stretched out flat' on the frozen flooded meadows and 'gouged out air-holes in the ice'. One of these merry expeditions came to an abrupt end, however, at least for my father. He had been left a long way behind the others and suddenly started yelling. He urgently needed the toilet, but his father did not realize this and, irritated, sent him home. 'You go back then,' he barked at him, 'and I'll go on with the girls alone.' So the little boy had to go back on his skis by himself and arrived home distraught and having wet his trousers.

My father thinks he failed to match up to 'the idea people had in those days of what a boy should be like'. He was, he said, often called a 'softie' because of his frequent whining and moaning. My aunt suspects that

Ernst Himmler was harder on his son because he was a boy. That was why he expected him to be able to keep up with his two sisters when they were out skiing, even though they were four and five years older than him. It frightens me how much even today my father is prepared to accept the reproach of having been a 'whiny' boy.

During the last years of the war the family saw Ernst less and less frequently. In the autumn of 1942 for his work with the Broadcasting Company he was awarded the Military Cross 2nd Class, without Swords – that is, he was doing work that was important for the war effort without actually fighting. The proposal for the award was made to the Propaganda Ministry by Hubmann, two months before his dismissal. He praised Ernst Himmler's 'commitment and systematic endeavours', which alone had made it possible 'to meet the increased technical demands with the reduced technical personnel available' and for 'military as well as civil broadcasting to continue to function as impeccably as it has'.

In practice this probably meant that Ernst had been involved in establishing new radio communications with the units in the field and in facilitating both the rapid spread of the latest news from the front and the reception of German radio for all Army units. It must indeed have been an immense task since, after the invasion of Poland, Hitler occupied Denmark and Norway, the Benelux countries and France in quick succession from April 1940 onwards; supported his ally Italy in North Africa, Yugoslavia and Greece from the beginning of 1941; and in June 1941 invaded the Soviet Union. Up to December that year the territory occupied by Germany had been enlarged at breakneck speed. Just as swift was the provision of the delights of German radio's armed forces network for their soldiers from the Urals to the Libyan desert. After the summer of 1942, and especially after the destruction of the Sixth Army at Stalingrad the following winter, the German Army was on the retreat; the task of the radio technicians was therefore to relocate broadcasting stations as quickly as possible behind the new front lines and to cut off power supplies so that they could not be used by the enemy, the Soviet Army.

In 1942 the SS Security Service noted that 'with the continued duration of the war listeners feel the German news service is too monotonous and one-sided', and evidently obtained additional news from abroad in order to be able to make up their own minds about the situation. The censored news on German radio was not enough 'to satisfy their hunger for information'. In October 1942, when the situation for the Germans in Stalingrad became ever more desperate, the number of people informed on for listening to foreign radio stations increased; there was even a report that numerous relatives of soldiers reported missing had decided to listen to Radio Moscow 'until the German government provides information on the whereabouts of those reported missing'.

Such reports appear to have made little impression on Goebbels and those in charge of German radio. A meeting on programme planning was held every Wednesday, chaired by Hans Fritzsche, head of the broadcasting section in the Propaganda Ministry. The minutes that have survived for the meetings between 21 June 1944 and 7 March 1945 document the growing difficulty of maintaining anything like normal service as increasing numbers of staff were called up, even though Fritzsche kept repeating the slogan, 'Keep marching. Keep fighting. Keep working' to the very end. The fact that Goebbels constantly insisted on interfering in even minor details of programme planning did not make things any easier for the broadcasting staff. Their lord and master would make decisions regarding the choice of music and performers, the use of solo instruments and the order and length of the programmes, demanding that 'attention be paid particularly to tiny details'; for example, the announcers were not to emphasize the word 'and' so strongly.

My grandfather regularly spoke at these meetings, even occasionally opposing the wishes of Goebbels, whom Fritzsche represented. Thus Ernst repeatedly argued that the technical equipment from broadcasting stations should be removed in good time, as the Allies approached. Fritzsche, for his part, referred him to the Minister's directive that the stations were to continue working until the very last moment (meeting of 30 August 1944). When at the meeting of 23 August Ernst had pointed out that the use of two news announcers together 'produced a negative response, especially in light of the current campaign to cut posts', Fritzsche dismissed his argument with the comment that the pairing of announcers was following Goebbels's instructions. It is clear from these discussions that, for the Propaganda Ministry, maintaining the façade to the very end took precedence over everything else. In February 1944 Fritzsche, who for years had been one of the best-loved propaganda speakers in the Third Reich, regularly giving talks on 'enemy governments' and 'the Jews who serve them', suggested to Goebbels that they cease broadcasting. Goebbels rejected the suggestion.

Like his former boss Hubmann, Ernst had served the

regime as a willing technocrat. Now, however, as the system was collapsing, he attempted to save what could be saved for the time to come. He was outraged that women who had been trained as technicians by the Broadcasting Company were being sent to armaments factories, and in the autumn of 1944 he was concerned that their remaining staff might be withdrawn to join the Volkssturm (the 'Home Guard'). 'In response to an enquiry from Herr Himmler, the Assistant Secretary once more explained the situation regarding the Volkssturm' (meeting of 24 October). Doubtless, Ernst was afraid not only that broadcasting operations might collapse but that he, who so far had escaped the war, might be caught up in it.

During those last few months of the Third Reich, when the war had long since been lost and Germany was in ruins, Goebbels was happier than he had ever been with German radio. The minutes of 10 January 1945 noted, 'The Minister thinks our radio programmes have reached a higher level than ever before'; they were 'simply magnificent'. The reason, according to Fritzsche, was 'that the lighter tone we prefer in this crisis situation is exactly right'. Not all listeners shared his point of view. There were outraged reactions to excessively superficial light entertainment programmes, but there was also a protest in February that year from the leaders of the Party's women's section 'against unGerman dance music and light music'.

The discussions on such objections from outside sometimes give the minutes a touch of unintentional humour. Thus they recorded on 14 January that a particular soldiers' choir was not to be broadcast again, since shortly beforehand it had sung 'Lay Down Your Arms'. And on 24 January they note: 'Exceptionally, it happened that the Führer listened to the radio, to the programme "Something for Everyone". He liked it very much.'

In May 1944, when Ernst and Gebhard had been living together under one roof without their families for nine months, Ernst wrote the letter to Heinrich Himmler that I had found in his SS file in 1997, right at the beginning of my search for my grandfather. At the time all I could make of it was that Ernst must have been involved in performing some dubious service for Heinrich. I did not understand what it was about. When I read the letter again with greater distance and more background knowledge, I still found Ernst Himmler's language disturbing, what Victor Klemperer had called the *lingua tertii imperii*, the characteristic language of the Nazis that veiled some things and revealed others. My grandfather showed himself to be a master in its use to veil what he had to communicate to Heinrich.

Only now did I understand the purpose of the letter. Clearly, Heinrich had asked him for an expert appraisal of a Major Schmidt, who, in Ernst's opinion, 'was unfit to remain deputy manager of the firm of C. A. Lorenz AG'. Ernst had initially put this evaluation to SS Oberführer (brigadier) Walter Schellenberg and had obviously managed to convince him. At the time, Schellenberg was head of the foreign secret service at the Central Security Service of the Reich.

Ernst gave the reasons for his verdict to his brother in technocratic jargon that is difficult to understand. Up to

this point Major Schmidt had clearly enjoyed the protection of someone very high up, namely the Reichsführer
SS and Minister of the Interior himself, even though he
was Jewish – a so-called half-Jew. Criminal proceedings
against him had been suspended and Ernst, who had been
given the task of checking whether the man was still
worth protecting, gave him a negative report: Schmidt's
performance, he said, was unsatisfactory. 'It goes without
saying,' he conceded in his appraisal, 'that (irrespective of
the way such cases will be dealt with later on) every high-
calibre specialist, even non-Aryan ones, ought to be ruthlessly deployed in order to ensure our victory, even if that
means the sacrifice of a part of our ideological credit
among the people.' Albert Schmidt, he went on, was 'not
the technical man' he was made out to be, did not meet
the requirements noted above; 'consequently, the sacrifice
of ideological credit in the eyes of a large number of our
best intellectuals and of the broad mass of qualified
workers cannot in my opinion be justified'. In other
words, Major Schmidt did not deserve further protection.

The man who told the Reichsführer this must have
known that it probably represented a death sentence for
Schmidt, at the very least deportation to a concentration
camp. That Ernst was not only aware of the personal
consequences for the man, but that he also approved of
them, can be seen in his cryptic remark, 'irrespective of
the way such cases will be dealt with later on'.

Neither my grandfather's callous decision nor his
language, steeped in Nazi ideology – even making allow-
ances for the fact that it was an official letter – were those
of some non-political hanger-on. He had made a decision
determining a man's fate that he did not have to make.

He could have written a report that would have enabled Major Schmidt to retain his relatively safe post. Was Ernst, by recommending that the deputy manager be dismissed and therefore sent to a certain death, trying to prove his ideological reliability to his brother? Even if he had written a positive report and the suspicion had been voiced that he was trying to shield someone, my grandfather, as the brother of the Reichsführer SS, would not have had to fear any serious consequences.

Various things about this letter remain a mystery. Why, for example, was Standartenführer Bender, the senior SS judge and magistrate on the Reichsführer SS's staff, present at the discussion on the future of Major Schmidt? He was brought in only for cases under the SS's own jurisdiction. Schmidt was certainly not a member of the SS; if he had been, my grandfather would have used his SS rank, as he did for everyone else he mentions in his letter. Above all, it is unclear how Ernst came to take on this task at all. What is, however, undeniable, is that he made every effort to convince Heinrich that the major he had been protecting was not worth the preferential treatment. Even if, at that point, he was not yet fully aware of his brother's murderous activities, it must at least have been clear to him that he was destroying someone's livelihood and that his decision placed the person in question in danger of his life.

It took me six years finally to face up to this letter and the uneasy feelings it aroused in me – and that despite the fact that I had not even known Ernst Himmler personally. During those years I had become increasingly prepared to ask awkward questions, but at the same time dealing with my grandparents' lives had brought them closer to me.

The letter made it difficult to maintain the cautious empathy with my unknown grandfather, which had grown in the course of my researches.

In the letter Ernst enthused about the fact that in his conversation with Schellenberg he had had the opportunity to discuss with him 'the fundamental importance of the deployment of technology in our Reich'. By now I had come to see that it was quite plausible that my grandfather would discuss that with Schellenberg. As head of Section VI, the foreign security service of the Central Security Department, he had amongst other things been responsible for the construction of a powerful radio communications station, known as the Havel Institute, that had several transmission and reception units. In his letter to Heinrich, Ernst also expressed the hope that, 'on some evening when we would be disturbed as little as possible', he and Gebhard might have the opportunity to present to their brother 'the full extent of the things that concern us most deeply with regard to the present war and the expected competition between the great powers over the next twenty years'. To that end they, the two 'technological brothers', had, he said, already 'done extensive preliminary work in separate discussions'.

What can the two of them have been discussing, one year before the final collapse of the Reich? I can hardly believe that, surrounded by bombed-out cities, seemingly endless streams of refugees and widespread destruction, they were capable of making plans for 'the next twenty years'! Did they genuinely believe their Reich would be one of those participating in the 'competition between the great powers'? Gebhard's daughter recalls that after the war her father repeatedly stated that Ernst was the most intelligent of them all. In their adult lives, Gebhard had never been particularly close to his youngest brother, so he presumably reached this assessment during the last two years of the war when the two grass-widowers lived together in Ruhleben, drawing up utopian visions of Germany's splendid future while all around them the bombs were reducing everything to rubble.

That they wished to present their plans for the future to Heinrich was not without good reason. Hitler had always wanted the SS to be a high-technology corps, and during the final years of the war Heinrich made great efforts to incorporate armaments technology and innovative research in high-frequency technology in his steadily growing SS empire. He visited the rocket test site in Peenemünde on the Baltic several times in 1943, where he had extensive discussions with the scientist in charge of the development of the V2, Walter Dornberger, who was impressed by his 'rare gift for attentive listening'. Dornberger admired the Reichsführer SS's ability to grasp the essential points very quickly and 'to sum up difficult problems in a few words that were both generally understandable and got to the crux of the matter'.

Between 1939 and 1943 a complex of buildings strictly screened off from the outside world had grown up in Kleinmachnow, to the south of Berlin. This was the Hakeburg, a research institute of the German Postal Service. The Minister for Postal Services, Walter Ohnesorge, used the Service's research institutes to develop weapons technologies which it was hoped would win the war. The main areas of research were high-frequency technology, television, radar and atomic physics. The Postal Service worked closely together with the SS; in

March 1942 the protection of the Service was placed under the SS and run by the head of the SS Central Office, Gottlob Berger. Ohnesorge welcomed the close cooperation and regularly informed Himmler about progress in high-frequency technology; he also several times transferred sums amounting to millions to the SS budget and provided 'front-line support' for the Waffen SS from the Postal Service's personnel and vehicles.

Could the Reichsführer SS's 'secret commission' to develop broadcasting, on which Hubmann, my grandfather and other engineers had worked during the 1930s, have been the groundwork for later research on radio surveillance carried out in the Hakeburg? I have not been able to find out whether Ernst and Gebhard knew about this project, or were even, perhaps, involved in it. I was unable to dig up anything more, in fact, than Ernst's remark about the plans for the future of the 'two technological brothers'.

It seems unlikely, though, that the meeting of the three brothers requested by Ernst ever took place. In addition to his other duties Heinrich, who had already taken over the Ministry of the Interior from Wilhelm Frick in 1943, was appointed Commander of the Replacement Army after the attempt on Hitler's life on 20 June 1944. Thus by the end of that year the power concentrated in his hands made him one of the leading figures of the Nazi regime; however, according to the editors of the *Dienstkalender Heinrich Himmler* (Heinrich Himmler's Appointments Book), it was power 'on an ever more fragile foundation'. From the end of 1944 Heinrich Himmler withdrew further and further, and in February 1945 he started his secret negotiations with the west. Heinrich had a perhaps more realistic view of the situation in the Reich than his brothers had. He had long since known that the end was near, but he could not break from Hitler and the oath of loyalty he had sworn to him until it was almost all over.

13

'Ever Your Faithful Richard':
Richard Wendler and His Brother-in-law

Among the family documents that Gebhard's eldest daughter keeps is a 'Party Badge in Gold' – from her Uncle Richard. After the war Richard Wendler, Hilde Himmler's elder brother, lived with his niece for some years. During the war, she told me, he had been sent to Poland to work in the 'civilian administration' of the Government-General (a term used to refer to the south-eastern part of Poland occupied by the Germans and sometimes to its administration). However, he had not been with the SS or the police and so 'quite definitely had nothing to do with the murder of the Jews'. On the contrary, he had helped Jews and Poles wherever he could, she insisted, using his connections with his brother-in-law Gebhard. After the war Wendler had to go into hiding for a while, because otherwise the Poles would 'most certainly have strung him up'. Later he did stand trial and several witnesses had spoken in his favour, she said, among them even a former rabbi who had been a member of the Jewish Council and who had come from the USA to testify. After that Wendler had worked as a lawyer again.

I was suspicious of Uncle Richard's 'harmlessness'. Had he really been a man who had used his rank and influence to help the persecuted? Why, then, did he have to go into hiding, afraid the Poles would have 'strung him up'?

Gebhard's daughter let me have a fat file containing personal papers of her uncle's. His meticulously documented curriculum vitae made it immediately clear that he had not been employed merely in the civilian administration, but had risen in the SS to the rank of Gruppenführer (lieutenant general). He had also documented his rehabilitation and second career after 1945. The denazification officials had been no more convinced of his innocence than were the public prosecutors of the Federal Republic charged with dealing with the Nazi past, who instituted proceedings against him as late as 1970. However, it could never be proved that he was directly involved in the murder of Jews.

I found supplementary information about Wendler and his activities in the appointments diary of the Governor-General of occupied Poland, Hans Frank, and in Wendler's SS file, as well as about his friendly relationship with Heinrich Himmler. He clearly shared the latter's distaste for the corruption that was rife among the leading officials of the Government-General, first and foremost Hans Frank, whom Wendler described as a 'corrupt swine'. He and Heinrich agreed that the confiscation of the assets of people who had been murdered and the economic exploitation of the country had to be carried out in a 'proper' manner, without individuals enriching themselves personally.

Who was this Richard Wendler?

He was born on 22 January 1898 in Oberdorf, near Bad Reichenhall in south-east Bavaria, where his father was a border official on the frontier with Austria. At twelve he was sent to the Ludwigsgymnasium in Munich, which was presumably where he got to know his later brother-in-law; they were in the same year. The cost of the school fees and of lodging in the Albertinum, a superior and strict hostel (similar in function to the houses at English public schools), was high, even though Richard was granted a 'three-quarters-free place' by the King of Bavaria; this was presumably the reason why Richard's sister could only attend the local girls' secondary school.

He left school in October 1916, six months before his *Abitur*, to join the Army; at the end of the war he was stationed in Nuremberg as a lance corporal in the reserve unit of the 3rd Signals Company. On the basis of a ministerial decree regarding servicemen, he was granted a school-leaving certificate in the summer of 1918, which enabled him to register as a law student at Munich University for the winter semester 1918/19. The following semester was cancelled, however, and Richard Wendler became a soldier again when he joined the fight against the Soviet-style *Räterepublik*. In April he volunteered for the Landsberg Freikorps – Heinrich joined the Reserve Battalion at the same time – and at the beginning of May marched off under its commander von Berg to 'liberate' Munich. From 1919 to 1920 he was a member of von Epp's Freikorps, a reservoir of future Nazi leaders. Despite his military activism, he was an outstanding student and passed a scholarship examination at the beginning of 1920 with distinction. Immediately afterwards, from 25 March to 25 April 1920, he was back in action with the 3rd Volunteer Company under Rittmeister von Rauscher, taking part in the 'Ruhr Expedition' to put down 'disturbances' caused by Communist workers.

After graduation, he settled in Deggendorf in eastern Bavaria, where he founded a local group of the Nazi Party in 1927. On 1 June 1928 he became an official Party member, joined the SA and was accepted into the SS in April 1933. In October of that year he was made Mayor of Hof in northern Bavaria, and in the same year was appointed to the Bavarian Political Police by the Reichsführer SS.

On 14 September 1939 Richard Wendler went to Poland with Hans Frank, when Frank was appointed head of the civilian administration there; at the time, the region was divided into the districts of Warsaw, Radom, Lublin and Cracow. It was his own decision. Wendler and Frank knew each other from their time in Munich; both had studied law there and Frank too had been a member of von Epp's Freikorps. Obviously, Wendler still got on well with Frank in 1939; his dislike only developed during the following years, when Frank began to rule in Poland with the ostentatious consumption of a Renaissance prince.

The fact that he had been Mayor of Hof meant that Wendler was one of the minority of officials who already had some experience of running an administration. This meant, in turn, that he rose rapidly in the Government-General. At first he was city commissioner for Kielce in Radom District; he was transferred in November 1939 to Czestochowa (German Tschenstochau) and in August 1941 back to Kielce. In February 1942 he was appointed Governor of Cracow District, then transferred in May

1943 to Lublin District, where he remained Governor until the town was taken by the Red Army in July 1944. The helpful Heinrich had a hand in Wendler's rapid rise as well.

On 7 October 1939, a few weeks after the German invasion of Poland, Heinrich Himmler was appointed Reich Commissioner for the Consolidation of the German Nation, charged with both the repatriation of ethnic Germans and the 'elimination of the harmful influence of foreign peoples'. Despite his multiplicity of offices, however, his authority in the occupied eastern territories did not go unchallenged. Every measure had to be coordinated with other bodies: the Party Chancellery, the office administering Göring's four-year-plan, Frank's civil administration, the Foreign Ministry. Competition between authorities – and there were constant power struggles between them in the Government-General – was one of Hitler's standard ploys to prevent any single institution from becoming too powerful.

From the very beginning of the war, Himmler and Heydrich planned to extend the powers of the police and the SS beyond the borders of the Reich. In proceeding with this they were assisted not only by Hitler's concept of ethnic cleansing but also by the Army's initial hesitancy about carrying out such a policy. Himmler and Heydrich exploited this unresolved situation to the full. By the end of 1939 a large part of the Polish intelligentsia and clergy had been either arrested or murdered by special SS units.

At that point there were still no clear guidelines as to what was to be done with the Jews. There were three million of them in Poland, and the German officials who ran the district and city administrations – with absolute powers and unlimited opportunities to intervene in local affairs – extorted horrendous sums from them in 'taxes' which went directly to support the German war economy. Richard Wendler, as city commissioner, also collected a set amount in taxes from the Jews and Poles of Czesto-chowa. After the war he attempted to justify his action in court by claiming that it had been an order from above and that the 'empty coffers' had made such a 'one-off' measure necessary. Moreover, he went on, the funds had gone back to the Jews and Poles, since, after all, 'benefits and other expenses had had to be paid for out of those sums'.

According to Hitler's plans, the Jews were to be gath-ered together in ghettos as quickly as possible, in order, as Heydrich explained on 21 September 1939 to the heads of section in the Central Security Department and the commanders of the special units, 'to have better control and the opportunity of moving them elsewhere later'. For the moment Polish and German Jews were to be concen-trated in specific areas of Poland.

On 17 October Hitler set out his guidelines for future policy on Poland to a small group of people. Present were Hans Frank, Heinrich Himmler, Rudolf Hess, Martin Bormann, Minister of the Interior Frick, Heinrich Lam-mers, the head of the state Chancellery, and General Keitel. The task of the Government-General, Hitler explained, was 'to clear the old and the new territory of the Reich of Jews, Polacks and riff-raff'. The Poles' living standard was to be kept low – 'All we want there is a reservoir of labour.'

With his 'Memorandum on the Treatment of People of Foreign Race in the East' Heinrich Himmler provided the programmatic basis for Hitler's policy in Poland; the Führer expressly authorized the 'Memorandum' as an official guideline. In it the Reichsführer SS and Reich Commissioner for the Consolidation of the German Nation demanded that the 'hotchpotch of peoples in the Government-General' be cleared out, the population 'put through a racial sieve' and 'the racially valuable individuals fished out of the hotchpotch and sent to Germany to become assimilated'. For non-German children there was to be no education beyond the four primary school classes, where they were to learn to count up to five hundred and no further, to write their names and to understand that it 'is a divine commandment to be obedient to the Germans and to be honest, hardworking and well behaved. I do not consider reading necessary.'

During 1941 and 1942 Heinrich Himmler also succeeded in placing SS and police officers directly in key posts in the military and civil administration. The collaboration, however, was anything but smooth. The task of the civil administration was to run the territory as efficiently as possible and deliver its agricultural produce to the Reich. The SS, on the other hand, was constantly deporting more German Jews to the territory of the Government-General, at the same time driving out thousands of Poles with brutal terror tactics as part of the great resettlement plan. This could only exacerbate supply problems and endanger agricultural production.

Frank and his governors very quickly realized the pointlessness of trying to achieve the unrestrained exploitation of the labour force and agricultural production by brutal repression. The removal of the Poles and Ukrainians from Government-General territory, Frank argued at a meeting of administrators on 11 March 1942, would take decades as it was. For the time being they needed the Polish population as a labour force, which meant they had to ensure 'that it remained able to work to the fullest extent'. After the war had been won, they could 'make mincemeat of the Poles, the Ukrainians and the trash that is hanging about here'. At a meeting on 14 January 1944 Frank said that although he was 'no friend of the Poles . . . it is my responsibility to see that there is no rebellion in the rear of Germany's eastern front. If I give the Poles something to eat, let them keep their churches, give them schools, I do not do so as a friend of the Poles but as the politician with responsibility for this area.'

The Poles' resistance to the occupying power increased steadily, sabotage making things difficult for the officials. But Frank's attempt to persuade Hitler to modify his policy towards them for tactical reasons fell on deaf ears. In the summer of 1941, therefore, the officials hoped to solve the Government-General's problems of food and supply by using the Jews who were fit enough as forced labour and shifting the rest to the east, to the Russian marshlands.

Richard Wendler too, as commissioner for Czesto-chowa, set up a ghetto in the city on 9 April 1941. A few months later, on 23 August, the ghetto was sealed off after thousands of Jews from the surrounding area had been deported there, where they were crammed together in atrocious conditions. Wendler ordered the chairman of the Jewish council of elders immediately to place a precise number of Jewish workers at his disposal, for an armaments factory and other firms. In his defence after the war Wendler made much of his claim to have 'got on well' with Herr Kopinski of the council of elders and with the chairman of the Polish administration. At least Kopinski, he said, had always 'loyally carried out what was required of him'.

At one of his later trials Richard Wendler did indeed produce defence witnesses who attested that he gave a tailor's business employing several dozen Jewish workers in Czestochowa his 'unconditional support' and 'covered them against attempts at intrusion'; Jews as well as Poles, the court was told, were always treated in a friendly manner. It was on this basis that in 1952 the Württemberg-Baden Denazification Court, set up by the Allies, reduced his classification from 'major offender' to 'offender'. The judges were not entirely convinced of his proclaimed innocence, not least because of his high rank in both the SS and the civil administration, but they could prove nothing specific against him; and in mitigation they took into account that he appeared to be a 'decent Nazi' whose support for the cruel policies implemented by the Government-General had not been unreserved.

The SS and police units were actively supported by the civil administration in their murderous operations. Dr Bühler, the Permanent Secretary for the Government-General, and some other officials even pushed of their own accord for a rapid start to the 'final solution' because the Jews, as 'carriers of epidemic infection' and as 'those responsible for the black market', represented a great danger, and the majority were 'unfit for work' anyway. The officials were naturally well aware that the dramatic increase in cases of typhoid fever and dysentery was the result of conditions in the ghetto, which was unfit for human habitation. In their eyes, however, an improvement in the situation of the Jewish population was ruled out because of the 'general situation regarding the food supply and the war', so that to many of the officials the murder of the Jews seemed the obvious logical 'solution' to a multitude of problems.

At the beginning of 1942 Himmler, Bormann and other Party officials attempted to weaken Frank's position. Their pretext was his involvement in various cases of corruption, and Frank only managed to retain his position by agreeing to allow Senior SS and Police Commander Friedrich-Wilhelm Krüger a greater say in the running of the Government-General. On 13 March Himmler arrived in Cracow for the official appointment of Krüger as the new Secretary of State for Security. In his speech at the dinner Frank grudgingly allowed that they had successfully managed 'to achieve complete agreement on the cooperation between the police and the civil administration'.

In Himmler's private pocket diary – not in his official appointments book – a 'meeting with Governor Wendler' is noted, before the dinner. Wendler had risen to the position of Governor of Cracow on 1 February 1942, presumably as a result of pressure from Himmler, who hoped to receive a regular supply of incriminating material on the Governor-General from him.

The next day, 14 March, the Reichsführer SS flew on to Lublin, accompanied by Krüger and Wendler. That evening he invited several SS leaders for discussions; Wendler took part in these too. The SS and Police Commander of Lublin was Odilo Globocnik, a close associate of Himmler, who had stuck by him even when he had been dismissed as Gauleiter of Vienna in 1939 for illicit currency dealings. A few months after the Lublin discussions Globocnik, at Himmler's instigation, was put in charge of 'Operation Reinhard'. It was code – probably named after Reinhard Heydrich, who had died on 4 June following an assassination attempt – for the 'Jewish operation', the systematic murder of the Jews, which started in June 1942. Systematic mass killings in gas chambers with carbon monoxide from diesel engines had been taking place in the Belzec extermination camp near Lublin since March 1942. Sobibor extermination camp became operational in May, Treblinka by July; in these camps, as in Auschwitz, the murders were carried out using the pesticide Zyklon-B.

In an address to SS leaders in Kharkov on 24 April 1943 the Reichsführer SS would sum up progress so far:

> We are the first truly to translate the question of blood into action. By the question of blood we do not, of course, mean anti-Semitism. It is just like someone delousing himself as soon as he has the opportunity; but getting rid of the lice is not a question of ideology, it is a matter of cleanliness. In just the same way anti-Semitism . . . is a matter of cleanliness, and it will soon be over. We will soon be deloused; there are another twenty thousand lice and then it will be over and done with – in the whole of Germany.

At the beginning of May 1942, six weeks after the Lublin discussions, the civil administration and the police began a joint operation to register the Jews according to their ability to work; at the same time mass deportations from Wendler's district of Cracow to Belzec began. After two brutal operations, in June and October that year, the

Cracow ghetto was drastically reduced in size and the inhabitants categorized either as 'fit to work' or 'unfit to work'. As early as July Wendler could boast at a meeting that one whole section of his district had already been cleared of Jews. 'In the space of four days the twenty-two thousand Jews registered in the District,' he stated, had 'paid five million zloty in taxes, fines etc'. On the basis of this experience he planned, he went on, 'as far as possible to concentrate the Jews in the other sections in one or two places; they must definitely be cleared from the rural areas. The forced labour camps are proving exceptionally effective; a month's stay there works wonders.'

At a police meeting in Warsaw in January 1943 he praised the collaboration with the SS and police leaders. They had, he said, 'excelled' in carrying out their task; the 'Jewish operation' had 'gone off without any particular disturbances'. The Cracow ghetto was wound up two months later. The last Jews who were fit to work were taken to the nearby labour camp of Plaszczów; all of the rest were murdered by the SS or deported to Auschwitz.

According to Heinrich Himmler's order of July 1942, Jews who were important for the war effort were to be excluded from Operation Reinhard for the time being. However, the civil administration's interpretation of what was 'important for the war effort' differed from Himmler's. For Himmler, only those Jews counted who were directly involved in armaments production; not those making boots, coats and so forth for Army suppliers. By 1942 the civil administration, for whom initially the deportations could not happen quickly enough, were afraid that the economy of the Government-General would collapse completely if it lost its skilled Jewish workers too soon – that is, before replacements could be found for them. As early as 12 September 1940 Frank had reminded heads of department that the Jews in the Government-General territory were 'not simply tattered figures but craftsmen who were an essential part' of Polish society. They could not be replaced by Poles, since the latter possessed neither the energy nor the skills to take their place. 'Therefore we are compelled to allow these Jewish craftsmen to continue working.' But Himmler – with the help of his henchman Globocnik – had his way: by the end of July 1943 there were only 21,643 Jews left working in the armaments industry out of the three hundred thousand originally in the Government-General; by that time by far the greater majority of Polish Jews had already been systematically murdered.

In November 1942, after Operation Reinhard had largely been completed, Odilo Globocnik had, on Himmler's orders, started to expel the Poles from Lublin District. The mass expulsions and, above all, Globocnik's brutal methods provoked more and more resistance in the area. In April 1943 mass protests from the civil administration resulted – at Himmler's insistence – in the dismissal of the Governor of Lublin District, Ernst Zörner. He was at first succeeded by the Governor of Warsaw, Ludwig Fischer, but Globocnik put pressure on Himmler to appoint instead Richard Wendler, with whom he hoped he could expect better collaboration. Wendler was indeed appointed Governor, on 28 May, but clearly did not get on at all with Globocnik, and in June 1943, following massive protests from Wendler and Frank,

Globocnik was dismissed. But he remained in post temporarily, which led to constant friction between him and the head of the civil administration.

On 27 July that year Richard Wendler wrote a long letter to the Reichsführer SS:

> *Dear Heinrich,*
> *Above all I thank you for sorting things out as far as the Lublin SS and Police Commander are concerned and for having found alternative employment for Globocnik. It was the only possible, the only dignified solution. Now I must ask you to transfer SS Gruppenführer* [Lieutenant General] *Globocnik to his new position without delay. He is making use of the time he has left in order – contrary to your clear instructions – to push through things he has decided to do himself, and that with his notorious disregard for any agreements, even those made in the presence of the Obergruppenführer* [General Krüger, K.H.]*, without informing anyone or, at best, lying to them. Thus as part of the campaign to deal with the groups of bandits it was made quite clear in discussion that certain villages were to be evacuated and how they were then to be occupied.*

Despite detailed discussion amongst everyone involved in the operation, it was 'carried out by Globocnik in a different and much more radical manner, so that what we are left with can only be described as an unholy mess, with remnants of the population wandering to and fro. The situation has got to such a point that apparently even he and his men can no longer cope.'

It was above all the consequences that caused severe problems for Wendler, for 'the large-scale operation in the south of my district was a resounding failure. The number of attacks has not fallen, but risen. The bandits themselves are completely unaffected.' Therefore the method of combating the 'bandit' groups in Lublin District had to be 'placed on a fundamentally different footing'. However, Globocnik was not the right man for it. Wendler felt he would get on with his successor, Jakob Sporrenberg, 'if you make clear to him the way you want things done here and order him to stick to my instructions. I have spoken with him at great length.'

'To put him in the full picture,' Wendler went on to report to Himmler, 'our ruler is going round assuring people that he, Frank, has shot down Globocnik' and was boasting that in so doing he had 'achieved the greatest political victory of his life' over the Reichsführer SS.

In court after the war, Wendler managed to give the impression that he himself had engineered Globocnik's dismissal out of moral outrage at his brutality. Thus in 1952 the Denazification Court noted as a mitigating circumstance that 'even in cases in which particularly reprehensible actions by members of the SS, as for example by someone like Globotschnik [sic], had come to his knowledge, he was concerned to have such individuals removed'.

After the war Wendler spoke only about his first two years in Czestochowa and his last year in Lublin. He remained silent about the decisive phase of the mass deportations of the Polish Jews in which he was involved in Cracow. Only in a letter of 1959 to a former colleague, Friedrich W. Siebert, a lawyer who at the time had been head of internal administration in Cracow, did he make a clumsy attempt to present himself as a master of the double game, a heroic figure whose relationship with Heinrich Himmler had enabled him 'to get wind of quite a few things' and 'to stop quite a few things' that Krüger, as the senior SS leader in Cracow, had intended to do. Unfortunately, he did not give a single example.

This letter was presumably an attempt to secure Siebert's support. In 1959, four years after his dogged struggle had succeeded in reducing his classification to that of a mere 'follower' and Wendler was once more working as a lawyer in Munich, a threat emerged from another former colleague. Ludwig Losacker, President of the Central Office for Internal Administration during Wendler's time in Cracow and head of the German Industrial Institute after the war, accused him of collaborating with the SS in Cracow. But things only became really threatening after 1970, when for the first time proceedings were instituted against him on suspicion of his having been involved in the deportation of Jews. The proceedings were abandoned, however, out of consideration for Wendler's state of health.

His letter to Heinrich Himmler of 27 July 1943 makes it clear that Wendler's conflict with Globocnik was not a result of the latter's brutal methods in expelling people as part of the campaign against the 'bandits'; Wendler simply wanted the expulsions carried out in an orderly manner. Earlier, at a Government-General meeting on 7 December 1942, as Governor of Cracow he had already advised caution in responding to 'bandit' attacks, saying, as the minutes recorded, 'We always have to take into account that these bandits can only be kept in check with the help of the local population.' Clearly he had had some success with this strategy, for he was able to point out that 'the security situation is considerably better in Cracow District than in all other districts ... bandit troubles such as they have in Lublin or Warsaw District simply do not exist'. He must have been all the more outraged, then, that Globocnik undermined his efforts in Lublin to such an extent that he left the District in an 'unholy mess'.

The argument continued for some time. On 4 August Himmler summoned Globocnik for discussions and asked Wendler, in a letter of the same day, to remember that 'Globus', despite a number of 'overhasty and foolish actions', possessed 'an immense capacity for work, a dynamism which means that he, more than any other man, is made for the colonization of the east'. Only two days later Wendler was once more complaining to Himmler that Globocnik had no intention of changing anything, that he was lying to the two of them, and that under the circumstances he, Richard, simply could not 'accept the responsibility you have placed on me'. At this point Himmler requested that they solve the conflict themselves, leaving Globocnik in his post until September.

After Globocnik had been replaced, Wendler's first concern was to soothe the Poles. The relocation operations were halted and the starving population was allowed larger food rations – accompanied by the clear warning that any future support for the resistance movement would bring sharp retribution.

In September, SS and Police Commander Jakob Sporrenberg took over as head of police in Lublin. He and Richard Wendler not only got on well together, they now had the same SS rank; in June, when Himmler was planning to transfer Globocnik, he had promoted

Wendler to Gruppenführer. The only ones above this in the hierarchy were the Obergruppenführers and the Reichsführer himself. With reluctance Himmler agreed temporarily to proceed in a more measured manner, since the campaign against the 'bandits' was occupying too many SS men who were needed at the front. The 'moderate' Wendler was clearly the one who he believed possessed sufficient diplomatic skill to carry it through, and of whose loyalty he could be sure.

When, in February 1944, the civil administration was planning to allow Polish secondary schools again, Himmler had his secretary, Brandt, telegraph a message to Wendler to the effect that he thought it was 'a good idea that *outwardly* we should *act* towards Poles with all seriousness in this matter' [K.H.'s italics]. Very soon Wendler – in agreement with Himmler and Sporrenberg, who was to take his orders from him, Wendler – had restored order in his district. In a letter to Heinrich of 30 August the same year he could proudly point to the fact that, before it was taken by the Red Army that July, his district of Lublin 'had sent almost 100 per cent of all its production to the west'; he closed with 'Heil Hitler! Ever your faithful Richard.' The population of Lublin District showed its gratitude for his efforts. According to several statements from Poles and Ukrainians, he was 'generally regarded as a moderate official to whom even those who had basically been deprived of their rights could turn with confidence'.

During the last months of the war Wendler and his administration were transferred to Oppeln in Silesia (now Opole in Poland). At the end he went underground in the American Zone and assumed a false identity because he was afraid of being handed over to the Poles and – considering the sentences passed on many of his former colleagues who, like him, had been 'only' civilian officials – given a certain death sentence.

14

'Do Not Forget Me. Your X':
Heinrich's Mistress, Hedwig Potthast

Heinrich and his brothers saw each other only rarely during the war. All three spent a lot of time travelling on official business and Heinrich stayed mainly in Hegewald, his operational quarters in East Prussia, close to Hitler's headquarters in the Wolfsschanze.

Anna Himmler died on 10 September 1941. The three brothers met in Munich for one last time, to bury their mother and wind up their parents' affairs. At the funeral, Gebhard told us later, Heinrich shook hands with his brothers over the coffin in a solemn vow that they would always stick together.

One year afterwards Heinrich noted in his appointments book a dinner with Gebhard and Ernst, for which he made himself free for several hours. Such an extended social occasion had long become a fairly unusual event for a man with countless official functions. Ernst's eldest daughter recalls a visit from 'Uncle Heini' to Torse, when he sat by her sickbed. Otherwise during that year Heinrich kept in contact by telephone or through his adjutant's office. By now his rare free time had to be divided between two families.

In an interview Gebhard gave the journalist Heinz Höhne in 1966, he assured him that his brother had kept his relationship with Hedwig Potthast, his former secretary, and their two children so secret that even he had only heard about it after the war. It seems to me highly unlikely that not even Heinrich's elder brother knew about it. And Gebhard's daughter recalls her father telling her that he several times urged Heinrich to sort out his personal situation once and for all – that is, to settle for one of the two women, for Marga or for Hedwig.

Hedwig Potthast, Gebhard said, was quite different from Marga, much younger than Heinrich, very pretty, sentimental and 'soft-hearted, perhaps too soft-hearted'. Eleven years younger than Heinrich, she came from a Cologne business family. After attending school in Trier she had spent some time in England and then, at the age of twenty, attended classes at the senior commercial college in Mannheim, where she studied economics for a few semesters but mainly learnt shorthand and typing. In 1934 she went to Koblenz, then in 1935 took a job as a secretary at the Central Security Department in Berlin. She had lodgings in Steglitz, was a member of the German Girls' League and the gymnastics association, did rowing and gained her Reich Sports Award in the same year.

Perhaps she went to Berlin because she dreamt of a sophisticated lifestyle. In a letter from Prerow on the Baltic where she was spending her summer holidays in 1936, her elder sister Thilde, clearly getting at Hedwig, wrote that the nearby artists' village of Ahrenshoop, 'the resort for the supposedly fashionable set', would presumably be just the right place for Hedwig. There was 'a bar there with film actors and other artistes, mostly tarted up'. In the same letter she expressed herself shocked at what she called an 'Amazonian letter' Hedwig had sent to their mother. 'Here [in Prerow] people would perhaps have been less horrified,' she added in another dig at her sister, for there were many people on the lonely beach 'quite happily playing at Adam and Eve in Paradise'. As a girl, Hedwig seems to have rebelled against a home that she found too conservative and prudish.

In January 1936 she started work as the Reichsführer SS's private secretary, at the same time assisting Erika Lorenz, a sister of Werner Lorenz, the head of the Ethnic German Assistance Office (VoMi), in the time-consuming organization of the punctual distribution of presents to the Reichsführer SS's many godchildren; they also had to keep track of what presents each had already been sent. One of the lists she kept contained the birthday and Christmas presents my father received from 'Uncle Heini'. From the very beginning she was in close contact with her boss Heinrich Himmler, since she also dealt with the extensive correspondence demanded by his certificate of ancestry, required to prove his Aryan descent.

Hedwig Potthast very quickly became popular with the Reichsführer SS's Personal Staff. In February 1937 she received a birthday telegram signed by Heinrich Himmler, Karl Wolff, Rudolf Brandt and a number of other colleagues. She clearly found in the SS the ideal of a different lifestyle she had been looking for. She frequently accompanied her boss to the office in Gmund on the Tegernsee in Bavaria, and the relationship between the two soon grew closer. At Christmas 1938, she wrote to her sister several years later, she and Heinrich had 'talked things through and confessed that we were hopelessly in love with each other'. In the two years that followed, she said, both of them had racked their brains 'to see if there was any honourable way we could come together'. For Heinrich a divorce was out of the question because 'it's not his wife's fault that she couldn't give him any more children'. Heinrich had, however, informed his wife 'that he would not accept the fact of not having [any more] children'. Now Hedwig and he had 'decided to have children' and since the summer, she wrote in autumn 1941, she had known for certain 'that our wish will be fulfilled'.

Following 'Teutonic customs', Heinrich Himmler was convinced that 'racially impeccable' SS men had the right to a second wife. According to his physician, the naturopath Felix Kersten, he considered monogamy a 'diabolical invention' of the Catholic Church. Himmler thought it 'unreasonable' to expect a normal man to spend his life with just one woman. Moreover, he hoped that 'in a bigamous marriage the one wife would be a stimulus for the other' and that the competition would force the first wife to 'curb her henpecking'. However, the first wife was to be honoured with the title of 'Domina', giving her special privileges over the second.

Hitler and other Party members were also considering the idea of bigamous marriage, though in their case only for the future and above all out of concern that, with so many fallen 'heroes', many women would be left without a husband and not have children. Himmler and other SS leaders, however, did not want to put off the introduction of bigamous marriage until after the war. The SS's *Sippengemeinschaft* (clan community) had its own lifestyle with which it consciously set itself apart from currently accepted social norms. And many SS wives appear to have tolerated having to share their husbands with a second wife. Possibly they felt that belonging to the elite of the future 'Greater German Empire' was sufficient compensation.

The 'first lady' of the *Sippengemeinschaft* was Marga Himmler. However, she was not popular, nor was she ever recognized as the *Reichsführerin SS* (the SS women's leader). In 1950 Lina Heydrich, Reinhard Heydrich's wife, described in an article in the news magazine *Der Spiegel* her first meeting with Marga: 'The first time I saw her I was flabbergasted. And this narrow-minded, agoraphobic blonde, with no sense of humour but constant facial tics, dominated her husband until 1936 at least and was the sole influence on him. Her house in Dahlem was furnished in a style that was as petty-bourgeois as she was herself.'

Marga Himmler seems to have made great efforts to assert her influence over the other SS wives as well as over her husband. When, at the 1938 Party conference, she tried to impose a binding programme on them, they protested; their husbands also objected to her demand to be treated as Reichsführerin SS. Heinrich Himmler's response to these criticisms of his wife is said to have been a resigned shrug.

In contrast to Marga, Lina Heydrich found Hedwig Potthast a woman with whom she could get on well:

When she started to have an effect on Himmler's way of life and thinking, [she developed] a breadth of vision that amazed us . . . Only then did he achieve true stature. That woman was neither a narrow-minded petty-bourgeoise, nor an eccentric, nor one of your SS sophisticates; she was an intelligent woman characterized by warmheartedness. Reinhard [Heydrich] once said you could warm your hands and feet on her.

Hedwig Potthast gave her only interview, at the age of seventy-five, to the journalist Peter-Ferdinand Koch. Koch maintains that she had not only been Heinrich's lover and the mother of his children, but also 'his sole confidante, the only person with whom – when he was particularly beset with troubles – he could talk without fear at any time and on any subject'. In November 1944, for example, in Brückenthin in north Brandenburg, the two of them had spoken openly with Oswald Pohl, head of SS administration, and his wife Eleonore about the fact that the war could no longer be won.

Initially it was only those working on the Reichsführer SS's staff who knew about his lover; they looked after Häschen (bunny, a common term of endearment), as she was called by both Heinrich and her brother Walter, with touching care after she gave up working in the Central Security Office in the summer of 1941. Hedwig, however, was afraid her family would disapprove – a fear that was confirmed as far as her parents were concerned.

Her brother and sister clearly knew about the secret liaison from fairly early on. Walter appears to have got to know Heinrich personally and to have supported the relationship. Dr Walter Potthast was a lawyer, at that time an officer on active service in France, then from July 1941 in the Soviet Union. Hedwig kept him supplied with cigarettes, which she no doubt got through Heinrich, in return for which Walter sent her detailed descriptions of the country and its people. Thus he wrote on 7 July, shortly after the invasion of the Soviet Union, 'The inhabitants of the USSR are incredibly friendly. The whole day they've been bringing in chickens and eggs. They absolutely refuse to accept money. They seem to be glad that the Reds have left, above all because of the church, which they're going to reopen.' It was not long, however, before his prejudices took over from his astonishment that the population did not correspond to what he had expected. Only two weeks later he was writing to his sister, 'The people here are terribly primitive and really have no idea what war is about. Under the heaviest fire they stay calmly sitting in their wooden shacks and wait till they burn down. All they lose when that happens is a few rags and filthy pieces of deal furniture.'

The bitter poverty in which the people lived and their capacity for suffering, which the Germans encountered during their advance, were obviously beyond Walter Potthast's imagination. Even their hospitality he could see only as a cover for cunning and perfidy, or as the primitive nature of an 'inferior' race. Akin to this is the outrage he shared with many other officers: 'If only these fellows weren't so treacherous. When they shoot it's almost always as snipers,' he wrote on 13 July 1941.

Hedwig's unmarried sister, Thilde Potthast, worked as a teacher at a 'national political educational institute' (a secondary school seen as a training ground for future Nazi leaders) in Kolmar-Berg and lived not far from their parents. She was devastated by Hedwig's letter of autumn 1941 (quoted on p. 243). She replied on 7 November and then again, a week later, saying that she simply could not believe it – 'not because you're in love, I've known that for ages' – nor was she shocked by the baby, 'but that you have come up with *this* solution'. Hedwig's fear that her sister might possibly break with her was, however, unfounded. She would always be there for her, Thilde wrote, even if she found it difficult to approve of her decision to lead a life 'that is completely contrary to respectable norms'. But perhaps, she went on, trying to reassure herself, 'the people around you' might be imbued with honourable ideals. 'However, I also fear that neither of you quite lives in the real world – not just at this moment, but in general. And that makes me worry for you.'

Hedwig's son was born in Hohenlychen Clinic. Founded around the turn of the century as a TB sanatorium and set in the idyllic Brandenburg countryside with its woods and lakes, the splendid art nouveau buildings of Hohenlychen had become a clinic for the Nazi elite. Albert Speer was treated there in 1944 after a physical breakdown. From August 1942 to August 1943 the chief physician and senior SS clinician, Professor Dr Karl Gebhardt, a friend of Heinrich Himmler from their young days, carried out cruel 'medical' experiments on Polish prisoners in the nearby women's concentration camp of Ravensbrück, for which he was later condemned to death at Nuremberg and executed.

On 15 February 1942 Gebhardt assisted at the birth of Heinrich's son and became his godfather. It was a difficult forceps delivery, the baby weighing a strapping nine pounds. Hedwig was in a bad way both before and after the birth, since shortly beforehand she had heard that her brother had been killed. Both Hedwig's sister and her sister-in-law Hilde, Walter's wife, stuck by her. Hilde visited her and assured her in her letters that personally she could understand her decision; but she begged her to seek a different solution for her parents' sake: 'I don't know, Hedwig, if you can be completely happy if it ruins your parents' life.'

Hedwig's parents never came to terms with their daughter's decision. Initially they broke off contact with her, but eventually started sending parcels again; in the accompanying letters they behaved as if nothing had happened. They never asked after the baby; at most they expressed the hope that Hedwig and 'the little one' were well. But when, a year later, Hedwig wrote to her mother on Mother's Day and Himmler, who was always referred to by both sides simply as 'H.H.', sent flowers to his 'mother-in-law', her bitterness came to the surface and she replied, 'I still cannot understand how you could do this to me, Hedwig . . . I could be so content if you were married, and could rejoice with you in the birth of your baby. You have taken away the best thing that would have been left me after the bitter loss of Walter.'

How much Hedwig suffered from her parents' rejection can be seen from a letter of 23 September 1943 that she wrote to Hedwig H., an acquaintance of her mother's age who was also having difficulties with her daughter. Hedwig Potthast implored her not to break off contact with her daughter, who, she said, would certainly be suffering herself from having disappointed her mother. 'Write and tell your daughter how worried you are about her future. There will certainly come a time when you can talk to her about the past.'

Hedwig herself waited long and in vain for a sign of reconciliation from her parents, and was forced to look to others for understanding. It came from her landlady, her ex-colleagues on the Reichsführer SS's Personal Staff and a few tolerant SS wives. Apart from Lina Heydrich, she had made friends with Gerda Bormann, who wrote to her from Obersalzberg on 5 April 1943 to say she was delighted at the pictures of Hedwig's son; 'and his father is so proud and happy with him – I have never seen such relaxed pictures of him as these together with his son'. Bormann, too, had a second wife; Gerda had even congratulated him on acquiring her and had advised him to make sure that only one wife was pregnant at any one time, so that the other one was available. At that point she had already had nine children, and two more were to come.

At first Hedwig lived with her son in an apartment of her own in the Grunewald district of Berlin; in 1943 she moved to Brückenthin, close to Hohenlychen. Oswald Pohl and his wife and children lived not far away on the Comthurey estate. The two women became friendly. Eleonore Pohl also shared her husband with another woman: he had a son by his secretary.

And what was Marga's reaction to Heinrich's relationship with Hedwig? She was certainly bitter at his 'solution' to their marriage problems, but went along with it for the sake of her daughter. 'Nothing to look forward to, but I will, I must, put up with everything for the sake of my daughter,' she wrote in her diary on 6 September 1943. Marga was still attached to Heinrich, who continued to look after her and their daughter Püppi. She never spoke directly about his love affair in her diary, restricting herself to hints. 'This year . . . has brought much sadness . . . it cannot be changed. We poor women . . .' she had written on 22 December 1941. Three months later she described the bitterness of her own situation very clearly, when she talked of a Frau B. who was getting divorced: 'Her husband is to have children with another woman. That only occurs to men once they are rich & highly regarded. Otherwise, older women have to help to feed them or put up with them. What times we live in! Heinrich doesn't come in the evening at all now.' And again, a few months later in Berlin: 'So much lying and deceit all around me, I can't bear it any more . . . I can't cope with this world any more.'

Her work for the Red Cross at least provided some temporary distraction. Since the beginning of the war she had been travelling a lot as Field Commander of the German Red Cross, first of all in Poland in March 1940. Following that trip, she noted: 'This Jewish scum, the Polacks, most of them don't look like human beings at all, & the indescribable filth. Putting things in order there is an enormous task.' Soon afterwards she was working in Occupied France. She saw her work as a duty, as her contribution to the German victory, but she was also glad that the war gave her the opportunity of being actively employed again. 'Here [in Berlin] there is a lot to do in the Red Cross. But I find it completely satisfying. I couldn't stand being without work that took me out of the house during this war.'

She was unhappy, however, at having to leave her daughter with her sister in Gmund so often. Heinrich would not allow Marga to have Püppi with her in Berlin. Perhaps he thought it was too dangerous because of the air-raids. And Marga had a guilty conscience about leaving her child without her parents for weeks on end – it gave her stomach pains. Püppi was unhappy when her mother was in Berlin and her schoolwork suffered increasingly. She lived for the weeks when she had Marga to herself and for the rarer days when her father came to visit. When he came, it was usually for one night, but he did devote himself intensively to his daughter during the brief time available. Heinrich's appointments diary shows that he tried to make up for it by talking to her on the phone every two or three days.

The more Heinrich became estranged from Marga, the more Püppi became her sole comfort. 'We poor women, men have a much easier time of it. I have my child. That compensates for everything,' she noted in her diary on 5 July 1941. Over the years she had become more and more estranged from Heinrich's family. When Anna Himmler died, Püppi was sad that now she did not have a grandmother any more, and also that she was not allowed to go to the funeral. As with Grandfather Himmler's funeral some years before – Gebhard's eldest daughter had been the only child at that – Heinrich absolutely refused to allow Püppi to attend; it was 'no place for children' he said. For her part Marga was annoyed at the news of Anna Himmler's death because it meant she had to break off her holiday in Italy with her daughter and their friends, the Höfls from Apfeldorf. Her contact with her mother-in-law had long since been reduced to a minimum; latterly Anna's phone calls had mostly been taken by Püppi. It was only on Heinrich's insistence that Marga had visited his mother shortly before her death because the old woman was unwell.

Nor did Marga get on well with Gebhard's wife Hilde and their children, who had been living in Gmund since the spring of 1943. For Marga the extra occupants of the house were mostly just a nuisance, disturbing the peace and quiet that was so important to her; for her daughter they were more of a welcome change. Püppi must have been extremely lonely in Gmund, especially since Marga was away a lot as Red Cross Field Commander. The constant arguments with her sister-in-law meant that Marga restricted their contact to a minimum, much to the regret of Heinrich, who continued to get on well with Hilde. Püppi noted in her diary for 29 October that there was 'always trouble with the Himmlers upstairs, they're always giving themselves airs and taking decisions over our heads like nobody's business. We only have formal contact with them, they're invited round every other Saturday.' Püppi, who had very few playmates anyway, suffered from the conflict. On 15 July 1944 she noted that now she was going to school in Reichersbeuern together with her two cousins: 'I get on with them very well, but otherwise Auntie Hilde, Mummy and Auntie Lydia [a sister of Marga's who also lived there] ignore each other completely . . . I think it's a pity we don't see each other, it was very nice always to have someone to play with.' Of her mother she wrote that she 'can hardly bear to have anyone around her' at all.

Even more difficult was the relationship between Marga and her brother-in-law. On 16 January 1945 she noted:

> The Himmlers [Gebhard] came to see us. Then he wanted to talk to me alone. I suspected it was going to be bad. But not *that* bad, with him saying such nasty things about other people and talking about

Heinrich and his parents with that Cath. glance up to heaven, as if they were saints! I'll never understand. Despite that, I invited them, that was what he [Gebhard] wanted. I did it instinctively, so as not to be the one who broke with them. How I despise such people – and me, the soul of kindness.

Hedwig Potthast gave birth to a daughter at the beginning of June 1944, again in Hohenlychen. Shortly afterwards Heinrich Himmler got Bormann to give him a loan from Party funds with which in August he bought a house called 'Schneewinkellehen' near Schönau in Berchtesgaden. Gerda Bormann, who was living with her children in nearby Obersalzberg, made her first call there in September and wrote telling her husband how happy Hedwig was in her spacious new house.

Hedwig's relationship with Himmler had to be kept secret from the public, and visits by the father of her children were rare indeed. On 4 October 1944, Bormann wrote to his wife, 'Heinrich told me yesterday that he'd hung pictures and worked in the house and played with the children all day. He didn't take any telephone calls, but for once had a nice cosy day just with his family!' Both the Bormanns, however, had reservations about the way his son was being brought up. 'Uncle Heinrich is apparently quite content with the way Helge [his son] orders everyone around,' Bormann wrote to his wife on 18 February 1945. 'He regards it as a sure sign of a future leader. I, however, agree with you.'

All the same, Helge does not seem always to have lived up to the high expectations of his parents. His name had been selected from a list of 'first names charac-

teristic of the race' published by the Central Security
Department of the Reich, and it meant 'healthy, racially
pure and therefore happy'. But that is precisely what
he was not. He suffered from neurodermatitis and was
sickly throughout his life. He was shy with visitors as
well, and Hedwig found that embarrassing. It came out
clearly once when Eva Braun's sister dropped in (she
was married to Hitler's liaison officer, Hermann Fegelein,
whom Hitler had executed for 'desertion' as late as April
1945). After visiting Gerda Bormann, Hedwig wrote to
Heinrich, 'He was a model of good behaviour, but clung
on to me the whole time.' He was meant to be a 'proper
boy', but at the same time obedient to his parents. Hedwig's sister, the one who taught at the national political
educational institute, had warned her immediately after
he was born: 'If the boy should disturb you during the
night, then throw him out. Children have to feel a *firm
hand* from the very first day!'

However, when she visited Hedwig in January 1945,
she saw 'Helgi' in a different light. On this occasion
Hedwig's children were delighted with their aunt who,
for her part, thought Hedwig's daughter was 'unusually
well behaved' and was 'astonished at how obedient Helgi
was', as Hedwig wrote to Heinrich. Such reports about
his children's good behaviour were obviously important
for Heinrich – Marga also often wrote telling him how
well behaved her Püppi was.

The price Hedwig paid for her comfortable life was
loneliness. The few letters she wrote to Heinrich that have
survived all end with 'Do not forget me. Your X.' She
never signed her name, which was presumably part of
their agreement about keeping things secret. She clearly

found the secrecy a great burden and was genuinely afraid of being forgotten. But she must have retained a vestige of hope that after the war, sometime or other, she would have the opportunity to live openly with Heinrich Himmler.

15

'They Can't Take Our Happy Memories away from Us': The Brothers and the End of the Third Reich

At the end of January 1945 my grandmother Paula and the children had to leave the Warthegau before the relentless advance of the Red Army. Heinrich put a car at their disposal, then everything had to happen very quickly. Zilli, the Polish servant, took care of the youngest girl, while the older ones had to get their things together themselves. They were allowed to take only a few things with them. It was with a heavy heart that my father had to leave the handcart behind that his godfather Heinrich had given him for his birthday.

I try to imagine Paula and the children in their official SS car with chauffeur, driving past the long trails of refugees, many of whom had been travelling for weeks through the freezing January weather, on foot with handcarts or in horse-drawn carts. What kind of thoughts might have been going through her mind? One of those refugees was Anne-Margarete von K., eleven years old at the time, whose family set off from her parents' farm in Küstrin (now Gostyn in Poland), at first heading south and then, like Paula and her children, across the Oder towards Berlin. 'The roads were icy smooth' so that several 'carts got tangled up together'; everywhere there were 'wounded and dead horses. It was terrible, absolute hell.' They could make only slow progress in the intense cold, not least because of the frequent attacks by low-flying aircraft on the streams of refugees.

In their comfortable car Paula and the children drove first to Küstrin, only a little to the south of Szrem, where they were able to spend the night at a broadcasting station that had been evacuated. From there they made their way by a circuitous route to Breslau (now Wroclaw in Poland) and Berlin. The house in Ruhleben was still standing. Not only had Gebhard taken refuge there, but also the brother of one of Ernst's broadcasting colleagues. Paula did not stay in Berlin for long, but managed to make her way on to Westphalia. In an SS convalescent home at Horn, south of Detmold, she found refuge for herself and the two youngest children for two months; the two elder girls were housed at an inn in the neighbouring village together with other schoolgirls, so that they could join in the lessons – with flag-raising and roll-call every morning – of a class from a Bielefeld school that had been evacuated there.

A fragment of a letter from their time in Horn has been preserved – a few lines of a letter from Ernst that Paula later carefully cut out. On 11 February 1945, my father's birthday, Ernst wrote, 'Pass on Daddy's best wishes to E. now he is six. Tell him the Extern Stones are watching to see that he becomes a decent chap.' What could a six-year-old make of birthday greetings like this from his far-away father, of its mixture of delight in his children and the stern demand that he become a 'decent chap'? And what significance did the reference to the

Extern Stones, the site of an old Teutonic shrine near Horn, have for my grandparents?

Paula also later kept only a fragment of what was presumably the last letter from her husband that she received there. From a small town in Thuringia on 20 March 1945 he sent her his best wishes for her 'big' birthday – on the 29th she would be forty – including the wish that 'the dark clouds might finally lift'. He himself, he said, had left Berlin at 10.10 a.m. in the charcoal-gasifier car with all its 'little moods', and 'we arrived here at 6.30 p.m. in golden evening sunshine. I thought to myself: take a deep breath, make yourself at home, it's like the first evening on a holiday. The very picture of peace . . .' The rest of the letter is missing. I would love to know what my grandmother discarded and why. The time the journey took gives an idea of the difficulty of driving anywhere on official business in those days, repeatedly held up by air-raids, damaged roads, refugees. My grandfather clearly shared the Himmler habit of keeping his head above water in that kind of chaotic situation by sticking steadfastly to precise record-keeping. He was, he continued, in an area where they had been 'in November 1938, and [again at] the beginning of 1941 on our second honeymoon'. After he had finished the letter, he said, he was going 'to take an evening stroll round the little town and think of you as we went for a walk along the beautiful but now so sorry Rhine at Bacharach. But they can't take our happy memories away from us, we will not let the colours inside us fade.' With it he sent her a card with a bouquet of tulips: 'To my darling Gertraud-maiden, my good wife, the dear mother of my four nice children for her birthday on 29 March 1945, by the Irmensul, from her Ernst.'

The Irmensul was another old Teutonic sacred place. According to one legend, it was Yggdrasill, the 'world tree', the crown of which supported the firmament. The Irmensul was, in fact, somewhat further west from where Ernst was, but clearly he and Paula must have found something comforting in his closeness to the old site of ritual worship at a time when the world seemed to be collapsing around their ears.

As the shellfire came closer, Paula continued fleeing with her children, this time not from the Russians but from the British. In the course of their flight my grand-mother was to discover for the first time what it was like not to enjoy a privileged position, but to have to fend for herself. My father remembers that she and the children were forced to get off the truck that was to carry them to safety – apparently they had been recognized. Paula objected loudly, she felt abandoned with her four small children in those chaotic conditions.

She then managed to fight her way back to Berlin by train. By this time the city was a raging inferno; fires were burning day and night, the provision of supplies for the civilian population had almost completely collapsed. Ernst was still working for the Radio, but since the beginning of April he had been detailed to the Volks-sturm. Even at home, my aunt told me, they kept talking about the Führer's 'wonder weapons', still to be deployed. I can hardly believe that even my grandparents believed in that propaganda myth.

On 25 April Berlin was encircled by the Russians, but

during the next few days there were still a few escape routes left. At the last moment, on the 26th, Paula and the children left the city once more. My aunt told me that this time her father said farewell to her, his 'big girl', with the words, 'Look after Mummy.' Only later did she find out that he had given her mother poison capsules, one each for Paula and the children. Why? Were they panicking at the idea that they might fall into the hands of the Russians? Were they going to commit suicide if that should happen? Did the collapse of Nazi Germany mean the collapse of their hopes for a future that was worth living? In *Inside Hitler's Bunker: The Last Days of the Third Reich* Joachim C. Fest describes how in the last months of the Reich thousands committed suicide in Berlin, numerous fathers killing themselves together with their families as the Russian Army drew menacingly closer. The sense of an approaching apocalypse was widespread among the inhabitants. Anyone who still believed in the future, or simply possessed the will to survive, had long since fled Berlin.

It must have been on that same day, or during the night, that Paula and the children arrived at Professor Gebhardt's clinic in Hohenlychen. Again it was Heinrich who had organized a car and a place of refuge for them. By now Gebhardt's clinic had been turned into an SS field hospital. Paula knew that her brother-in-law had set up his headquarters in Hohenlychen; Ernst had probably told her to go to Heinrich as soon as she arrived and ask for further help. But he was unavailable. Paula had the feeling she had suddenly been left in the lurch by this powerful man, whose help she had been relying on all the time. She did not know that by then Heinrich had moved to new quarters further west, near Schwerin, where he was involved in the secret negotiations that he conducted during the last few weeks to try and save his own skin.

Only after long hesitation had Heinrich Himmler let himself be persuaded by his personal physician, Felix Kersten, and Walter Schellenberg, the head of the foreign section of the SS Security Service, to dissociate himself from Hitler and the lost war and offer the Western powers a partial peace. Schellenberg was determined not to go down with the bankrupt system, but to secure a new career for himself under the new rulers. It was his oath of loyalty to Hitler that made Himmler hesitate for so long. Finally, however, he came to believe he was the only person capable of succeeding the Führer.

On 19 February, 2 April and 22 April 1945 he met Count Bernadotte in Hohenlychen. At their meeting on the 22nd he told the Swedish diplomat – according to Schellenberg – 'We Germans must declare ourselves defeated by the Western powers. To capitulate to the Russians, however, is impossible for us Germans, especially for me. We will continue to fight against them until the German front is replaced by that of the Western powers.' He would, he said, never hand himself over alive to the 'Bolshevists', against whom he had fought a life-and-death struggle. They met for one last time during the night of 23 April, in the vicinity of Lübeck. The negotiations came to nothing; Himmler drove back to his quarters near Schwerin, where on 27 April he received the news from Count Bernadotte that his offer of a partial peace had been rejected by the Western powers.

When the Russians were only a few kilometres from Hohenlychen, Heinrich once more supplied a car that took Paula and the children to Schleswig-Holstein. As my aunt recalls, they were in a column of cars, probably with the last departing members of the Reichsführer SS's Personal Staff. Some of the top Nazis had already fled to Schleswig-Holstein because they hoped to be treated more leniently by the British occupying forces than they would be by the Russians. During the night Paula reached Timmendorf, on the Baltic coast, where Gebhard was waiting for her; he had been evacuated from Berlin a few days previously with his reserve unit of the Waffen SS. He gave his sister-in-law some money, then returned to his company, which was heading further north. From now on Paula had to fend for herself again.

Ernst was the only one of the three brothers to stay behind in Berlin. He probably went in great fear of the Red Army, not only because of his surname, but also because of the years of radio propaganda about 'subhuman Bolshevists'. The gun that was pressed on him as a member of the Volkssturm would not have changed that – he had never been a soldier. Why did Heinrich not help his brother get out of Berlin, when he usually looked after all the members of the family? Ernst had contacted Gebhard by field telephone and told him he had to stay there for the moment, since his reserve unit had not yet received orders to evacuate the city.

Although resistance had long been pointless, the broadcasting building was to be defended to the end – without consideration for the women, children and old people who had taken refuge in the air-raid shelter there. Reich Radio's 'garrison' consisted of the thirty-man strong permanent SS guard, twelve anti-aircraft personnel, thirty Hitler Youth anti-aircraft auxiliaries and

Volkssturm Battalion 505, set up in December 1944 under the command of SS Obersturmbannführer (Lieutenant Colonel) Werner Naumann, in civilian life Secretary of State in the Ministry of Propaganda. The 4th Company of this battalion, commanded by Reserve Lieutenant Oskar Haaf, consisted of staff from the broadcasting building and soldiers of the Propaganda Company. On 23 April, having received orders to march to the Ministry of Propaganda in Wilhelmstrasse, Haaf withdrew with part of the Company. That left roughly four hundred and fifty Volkssturm men in the building, who also had the technical and office work to do; one of them was my grandfather Ernst.

On 28 April the Exhibition Centre on the other side of Masurenallee was already under fire from Russian artillery, and Naumann, in a final special broadcast from the Reich Radio building, called on all the men, women and children in 'Fortress Berlin' to hold out to their last breath. On the afternoon of 1 May the newly appointed commandant of the city, General Helmuth Weidling, telephoned through the order to evacuate the building, which was still almost entirely undamaged, and destroy the technical installations. The latter order was not carried out; only a few pieces of equipment were destroyed just so as to make it look as if it had been. As night fell on 1 May, the last German soldiers left, only civilians remaining in the air-raid shelter.

Adolf Hitler and Eva Braun had already committed suicide on the afternoon of 30 April, though the news was announced to the population only on 1 May, in a broadcast at 10.26 p.m. It was the last propaganda lie from Reich Radio that Ernst Himmler and his colleagues transmitted.

The announcement said that that afternoon Hitler had met his end 'in his command post in the Reich Chancellery, fighting to his last breath against Bolshevism'.

Then broadcasting ceased. That very same night Ernst must have tried, together with an unknown companion, presumably a colleague, to get out of the burning city – a crazy thing to attempt. They must have known they were likely to be arrested or simply shot at any moment. Was there any chance that he might have been able to make his way through to his family on the Baltic coast? To escape the Russians and reach the Americans or the British? Like many leading figures in the Nazi state, Ernst carried a poison capsule in his mouth. Heinrich would kill himself with one a few weeks later, when he was captured by the British and unmasked.

In 1952 the family received the news of Ernst's death. As Gebhard's eldest daughter recalls, an old acquaintance visited them, 'Tüpferl' ('Dot') – that is, Joseph Tiefenbacher, the man on the Reichsführer SS's Personal Staff who had been responsible for Heinrich's personal security. During his internment, he said, he had heard the story of Ernst's attempt to escape Berlin from a man who had been with him. The two had reached Staaken, on the western edge of the city, when Ernst had either stumbled or been hit by a bullet and had bitten on the poison capsule in his mouth 'by mistake'. Most likely, we will never be able to ascertain whether it was a tragic accident or suicide.

At 9.50 on the morning of 2 May, by which time Ernst was probably already dead, the Russians occupied the premises of the Broadcasting Company. Their commander, Major Popov, knew the place well, having worked there himself as an engineer from 1931 to 1933. Under his direction, the first news bulletins and appeals to the population were sent out, in which, as in the news placards that had been posted everywhere, all public service organizations were called on to resume work. The prime interest of the Soviet military authorities was to get things back to normal again.

During the night of 1 May Paula had had a vision. She woke up in the morning, her daughter recalls, and said, 'Daddy died last night. He came to everyone's bedside to say goodbye.' Then she told the eldest to take the other three children and find something to eat. 'We spent hours wandering around, it was terrible.'

The next day there was another event that the children found disturbing. On 3 May English planes sank the *Cap Arcona* and the *Thielbeck*, two ships with more than 7,500 prisoners from German concentration camps on board, off Neustadt in Lübeck Bay. Both my aunt and my father can remember 'bloated corpses being washed up on the beach for days afterwards'. But those were not the only terrible sights the children were confronted with during those days. They saw the corpses of children who had starved to death, traumatized refugees, the wounded and the maimed. There, too, people were committing suicide all the time – 'We kept hearing that someone else had jumped from the landing stage or hanged himself in the garden.'

Their mother did what she could to bring order to this chaos. The two eldest children were given lessons by two former leaders of the German Girls' League with whom she had made friends. Like most of the refugees, Paula and the children were living in one room in which there was little more than a bed which, during the cold time of the year, they left only to go to the soup kitchen to fetch food in a set of dixies: turnips three times a week, cabbage once and groats twice, one of the times cooked with jam.

The eldest had to go to the harbour regularly to exchange her mother's cigarette coupons for fish or some other food. Paula was in despair and close to suicide. There had been no more signs of life from Ernst. In a letter of March 1946 she wrote to her sister:

> Everything's so terribly difficult, you have to struggle your way through on your own to get anything, and your good friends won't help you any more. I still can't believe Ernst is dead. You keep hoping from one month to the next, but no news comes. Then you start brooding about the meaning of life and what has become of us. And how will it turn out? You mustn't think about things, just drift along mindlessly. If I didn't have the four children, I wouldn't care at all. And the starvation diet. My greatest wish is for an atom bomb in the area, then my troubles would be over.

I can well understand that my grandmother had lost the will to live in her predicament at that time. But how horrible to wish that an atom bomb would fall on them. However much Paula's thoughts were dominated by these ideas, how could she imagine her own death as part of a collective end, accept it, condone it?

But the children needed her; the youngest was only three and a half, had the measles and had lost a lot of weight. Members of the British forces were billeted in the house next to theirs and the women there gave the little child, who until then had had almost no toys at all, a doll they had sewn themselves. 'And during the night we stole coal from their courtyard,' my aunt said shamefacedly.

But sometime towards the end of February the fishing boats came back with such a large catch that they over-flowed. 'The whole bay was full of fish. We stood up to our bellies in the ice-cold water, Mother and I, and scooped up the fish. Those fish saved our lives.' Hundreds of people were doing the same, fishing out the fish with buckets and hooks. Paula stayed in the icy water for an hour, in flurries of snow and a temperature of minus two, 'wet through to my vest, the waves often came up so high, and half frozen stiff with the cold. I felt like rebelling against it, but at least we had herrings to eat.' A man who had been disabled in the war smoked the fish in an oven he had built himself, so that the supply would have supplemented their meagre diet for quite some time.

Somehow or other Paula had heard that Gebhard, after his capture in Kappeln in north-east Schleswig-Holstein, had been sent to the internment camp at Neu-münster-Gadeland, due east of Timmendorf. At the beginning of March 1946 she went there to hand in a parcel with a cake for him. It is a mystery to me how she managed to get hold of the ingredients for a cake when her children scarcely had enough to eat. It cannot have been easy, either, to make the forty-mile trip (65 km) between Timmendorf and Neumünster there and back in one day, especially since she had no money and had to rely on lifts, probably from British Army lorries. After-wards she wrote to her sister about the visit: '1 large

factory building with 11,000 men in it, 1,000 in each
section. Surrounded by 5-metre [16-foot]-high barbed-
wire fences. Watchtowers every 30 metres with 2 Tom-
mies. From far-off you can see the men in there walking
round as if in a cage. It gives you some idea of what
freedom means. How happy I would be if I knew Ernst
was in an Eng. camp.' She must have known beforehand
that she would not have the opportunity to see her
brother-in-law, for she had concealed a letter to him in a
small glass tube inside the cake. She received an answer
from Gebhard only a few days later, for she wrote, again
to her sister, 'I had a long letter from Gebh. yesterday.
He gives a lot of lectures and seems quite happy. I have
also been in contact with Hilde, who is still living in
Tegernsee. They all write and tell me I shouldn't despair,
Ernst is still alive.'

After that she lost contact with Gebhard for a while,
as he was transferred to Fallingbostel on Lüneburg Heath
and later to other camps. He spent three years in seven or
eight different internment camps, his daughter recalls.
And in all of them he met men he knew. From his period
of internment he kept six notebooks containing poems,
by himself and others, songs he had written and sketches
of camp life he had drawn. In 1946 he organized a
Christmas Party in Fallingbostel for the Bavarian prisoners. The previous year he had written a poem for
Christmas in which he himself appeared in the camp as
an angel expressing his amazement:

> *Whatever can your misdeed be*
> *To languish under lock and key?*
> *At home they grieve, while you poor men*

Are kept imprisoned in a pen
Of wire with barbs so sharply clad.
Was what you did so very bad?

Many of Gebhard's poems reveal how little he, and with him presumably the majority of his contemporaries, were prepared to come to terms with the past and their crimes. He saw himself, as another poem puts it, as someone who had been 'led astray'.

In the summer of 1946 he was taken to Nuremberg where, on 28 July, he submitted a written character appraisal of his brother Heinrich for the trial of the main war criminals. Heinrich Himmler's biographer, Joseph Ackermann, quotes from this affidavit in which Gebhard describes his brother as a 'tireless seeker after truth in the political field . . . incorruptible and matter-of-fact, but passionate at heart'. He had eventually found his way in Hitler's ideas and had followed them, 'in full recognition of the approaching abyss', all the way to the 'tragic end', at the dictate of a loyalty that he had raised to 'mythical heights'. While the true extent of the Nazis' crimes was gradually being revealed to a horrified world at Nuremberg, and Heinrich Himmler and his SS were becoming synonyms for terror and mass murder, Gebhard had nothing to say about his brother's responsibility for all that; instead, in overblown, bombastic words, he praised his single-minded determination, his incorruptibility and his idealism.

At the end of his internment the eldest of the Himmler brothers was in the Ungerstrasse camp in Munich, where his family finally managed to make contact with him again. On 29 July 1948 he celebrated his fiftieth birthday, still in Ungerstrasse, but by then he had already been informed that he was to be released. His eldest daughter and her fiancé were waiting at the camp gate when he came out. She had met her future husband soon after the end of the war; unlike her, he came from a Social Democratic working-class family. They had been together to Ungerstrasse several times to visit Gebhard. In the first passport photos he had taken after his release, he looks as if he had aged by years.

Hilde and her three daughters had had very mixed feelings about the liberation by American troops in Gmund. Her eldest daughter still feels outraged when she remembers how the Americans came to their house to make an inventory of all their possessions, confiscating some and just throwing the rest in a pile after having made a meticulous list. All their crockery was broken, she said, and most of their bed linen and underwear dirtied or torn.

Gebhard's wife and children had managed to survive, though only with difficulty. While her mother sewed blouses, the eldest daughter had to leave school six months before she would have taken her *Abitur*. She found a job in a factory in Munich, initially as a factory-floor worker, but then, through an old acquaintance of her father's, was taken on to the clerical staff and became the main earner in the family. With her surname, the second daughter had great difficulty finding a place as an apprentice. After many unsuccessful attempts, she finally managed to find a dressmaker in Berlin who was prepared to take her.

Perhaps this was why Paula stayed in Timmendorf for so long. It was easier to remain incognito there. After the war, probably when she arrived in Timmendorf, she had gone back to her maiden name of Melters. But in May 1946, after a year on the Baltic coast, she decided to return to her home town of Dinslaken, although it must have been obvious to her that she would not be very welcome there. After all, everyone in Dinslaken knew that Heinrich Himmler had been her brother-in-law. My father remembers being teased and mocked, sometimes even attacked. Adults treated the family either with hatred and contempt, or else nodding approval for what Heinrich Himmler had done. In a pompous ceremony in June 1934 Hermann Göring had been made a freeman of Dinslaken; during Kristallnacht in 1938, almost all the male Jews there had been arrested and taken to Dachau.

Word quickly got round the small town that Paula had returned, and soon after her arrival she was several times summoned for questioning by the British occupation authorities. 'They showed her films of the concentration camps,' my father remembers. Since it was the British zone of occupation, it is very likely that she was shown the documentary film *Memory of the Camps* that the British made in the summer of 1945. It shows horrifying pictures from various camps after the liberation, and was used by the Allies as part of their re-education programme. They would certainly also have asked Paula what she thought of Heinrich Himmler, but her denazification questionnaire does not record a statement on that. The witness attesting to the accuracy of her information was one of her sisters.

Her application to be allowed to open a millinery shop was rejected by the Investigating Committee on 1 February 1947 on the grounds that she was not a suitable person to run her own business. The Committee classified her as an 'offender' (the second-highest category), because, as the sister-in-law of the Reichsführer SS, she had received preferential treatment in acquiring a house from the German Labour Front.

Paula and the children lived then in what had been her father's workshop. 'It was bloody cold and the earth closet in the yard outside stank,' her children recall. 'If you sat still in the evening you could see the mice scuttling around.' They shared a bedroom in her parents' house. That was all the room there was because, apart from Paula's mother and one sister, there were several lodgers living there; Paula's mother was dependent on the rent they paid, since her father had died in 1940. Paula's relationship with her mother was strained; she thought her daughter had married the wrong man, and said so.

As early as 1946 Paula probably made a clandestine trip with a group of people across the zonal border to Berlin so as to find out whether there were still things in the house in Ruhleben and, as she wrote to her sister, to assert her claim to the house, although the family had been officially registered as no longer living there since July 1945. She asked her sister for her identity card, because she was afraid she might have problems with the Russians on account of her surname. New lodgers had long since moved into the house. Paula found many of her things in the neighbours' houses. The new owners had tried to obliterate the traces of the previous ones, she would later recall, tearing pages with dedications out of books and sometimes writing in new names. But her fight to recover her possessions was so successful that she had to arrange a small lorry to take them back to Dinslaken.

The furniture, books, kitchen- and tableware she now had made life slightly more bearable, but they did nothing to quell the pangs of hunger. At night they went out into the fields to steal cabbages. Paula and her second daughter would cut them, while the eldest kept watch. In general they were out a lot, gathering things to eat – elderberries for a fruit soup and beechnuts in the autumn; once they had laboriously collected a sackful, they could exchange them for oil at the nearby oil mill.

On 11 June 1947 Paula applied again to the Dinslaken Denazification Tribunal to be allowed to open a millinery shop, this time making her application through the Wesel District Craft Association. It was once more rejected, with the curt note that it was impossible to ascertain whether anything was known against her or not.

The constant hunger, her ignorance of what had happened to Ernst and the apparent hopelessness of her situation gave rise to thoughts of suicide again. One day she told her eldest daughter she thought it would be best if they died together. She still had the poison capsules, she told her, and they would put an end to their misery. Her daughter, who was twelve or thirteen at the time, managed to persuade her to give up the idea. 'I wanted to live! But for a long time after I was afraid she might think of it again.'

How exhausted Paula must have been, how tired of life! And what was she asking of her daughter, whose life had only just begun! Later she and the children received regular parcels from a former admirer of Paula's who had emigrated to the United States many years earlier and become rich. He had even divorced his wife, my father told me, in order to propose marriage to his old sweetheart,

which she rejected. Presumably she did so out of love for
Ernst – though perhaps by this time she had become too
accustomed to her freedom and independence to give them
up again.

Heinrich's end is well-known. After the Western powers
had refused to negotiate with him, Hitler had heard of the
treachery of his loyal subordinate from an Allied broadcast
and removed him from all his offices, naming Admiral
Dönitz as his replacement.

On 30 April 1945 Heinrich Himmler made one more
attempt to negotiate with Dönitz about participating in a
new administration, but the latter had been evasive. After
that Himmler was completely exhausted and for the first
time, according to Schellenberg, talked of retiring from
politics, possibly even by suicide. During the days that
followed he tried to maintain contact with Dönitz, following him and the members of his government from Plön to
Flensburg. On 6 May Dönitz formally dismissed him from
all his offices, but Himmler maintained the façade of his
power, driving round in his Mercedes accompanied by his
SS escort in their cars and lorries 'like a medieval condot-
tiere'. He rejected the suggestion of Joseph Kiermaier, his
longstanding security specialist, that they use the plane
they still had at their disposal to fly to Bavaria so that they
might at least see their wives again; at such times as these,
he said, no one should follow his personal wishes. He
similarly shrank from taking the advice to hand himself in
and publicly accept his responsibility for what he and the
SS had done. With a few loyal comrades, forged papers
and an eye-patch he made a last hopeless attempt to

escape. On 23 May he was arrested by the British in the vicinity of Fallingbostel, south-west of Lüneburg, and after he had disclosed his identity committed suicide with a cyanide capsule during a body search.

Marga Himmler and her daughter Gudrun (Püppi) had been arrested by American troops on 13 May in Bolzano in the South Tyrol, close to the villa of SS General Karl Wolff, and spent eighteen months interned in various camps, at first in Italy and France, then in Germany. The two of them can be seen in an old film from their time in the camps: Marga very much aged, Gudrun much too childish for her age, incredibly thin, pale and disturbed. In October 1946 they were brought to Nuremberg, to testify at the trials. In her cell Gudrun made greeting cards for the accused whose names she had read on the cell doors as she passed by them. Did Gebhard know that his seventeen-year-old niece was in a nearby cell in the section reserved for witnesses? After the trial they were sent back to Ludwigsburg internment camp, from which they were released in the November. They found refuge at Bethel, Pastor Bodelschwingh's sanatorium near Bielefeld. During the next few years that they spent there they corresponded with my grandmother Paula. Gebhard's eldest daughter said Gudrun only learnt about her half-sister and brother after the war. She tried to make contact with them, but Hedwig Potthast refused.

At the end of the war Hedwig and her children were no longer at their home, either, but staying by the Achensee in the Tyrol. After the news of Heinrich Himmler's death was broadcast on 23 May 1945, she went into hiding on Eleonore Pohl's farm near Rosenheim in Bavaria. According to the journalist Peter-Ferdinand Koch, it was not until a few weeks later that she was discovered there by the Americans and interrogated over several weeks in Munich.

Shortly after the end of the war Hedwig Potthast turned up at Hilde Himmler's house in Gmund. Gebhard's eldest daughter and her husband say that 'Häschen' seemed very strange to them, talking all the time of 'King Heinrich', meaning the father of her two children. But Hilde, Heinrich's sister-in-law, must also have clung on to his memory for a long time. Gebhard's youngest daughter remembers one of her late Uncle Heinrich's birthdays in the early postwar years. Her mother Hilde, she said, spent a long time sitting looking at a photo of him and was annoyed at her eldest daughter's lack of respect in preferring to spend the day taking a steamer trip on the Tegernsee with her fiancé.

That Hedwig became close friends with Gebhard's family after the war is clear from two letters she wrote to them on 22 October and on the fourth Sunday in Advent 1949. 'To all my dear friends in Gmund,' she wrote, asking solicitously how they were getting on; her children sent a picture they had painted themselves and she concluded the letter with 'your Häschen'. She hardly had contact with anyone, she said, apart from them and 'Wölffchen' (Karl Wolff), who had just paid her a surprise visit. She presumed that he had gone on to visit Gebhard's family in Gmund.

At that time Hedwig was fighting, together with Gebhard and Wolff, for an 'appropriate' portrayal of Heinrich Himmler in a planned publication by a Frau Wiedemann. This was presumably Melitta Wiedemann, a journalist, born in St Petersburg, who during the Third

Reich had edited a magazine called *Die Aktion. Kampf-blatt für das neue Europa* (Action: A Campaign Journal for a New Europe) and written several letters to Heinrich Himmler strongly urging him to bring about a change of approach to the 'Russian people'. Together with them, she said, they should wage a 'war of liberation' against the 'international evil of Bolshevism' and against the 'Jewish domination of the world'. It appears that Melitta Wiedemann had questioned various 'authentic' witnesses such as Hedwig, Gebhard and Marga for a planned series of articles on the SS and they had readily responded with information. Now Hedwig, at least, strongly regretted her cooperation because she was 'horrified' at the way Heinrich Himmler was presented. She felt her trust had been abused and sensed that behind it was Marga, who, she claimed, hoped to make money from the publication.

Hedwig Potthast withdrew more and more from the outside world, suspecting that she would 'gradually become completely unsuitable for society in every sense', – which, in fact, she felt was best. In the fifties, after a final visit by Gebhard's family to Hedwig in Theissendorf, near Traunstein in south-eastern Bavaria, all contact between the families ceased.

At the beginning of the eighties Peter-Ferdinand Koch traced Hedwig Potthast in Baden-Baden. She told him that she had got married there, but that her husband had died soon after. By marrying she had acquired a new name, which helped to protect her from the curiosity of those around her. Her son, in poor health throughout his life according to Koch, had stayed with his mother, and her daughter had become a doctor. To Koch, Hedwig

Potthast claimed to have been the one who had persuaded Himmler to negotiate with the Allies. She had nothing at all to say about her former lover's crimes or his guilt. What can she have told her children about the father they had scarcely known? She died in 1997.

16

'A Victim of His Brother':
After 1945 – the New Beginning

On 20 July 1948, the day of the currency reform, the Deutschmark was introduced in the western occupied zones. And suddenly all the things appeared for sale in the shops that until then had been obtainable only on the black market – though at prices beyond the reach of most Germans.

After a further application, Paula was finally granted a trade licence. On 23 September she registered with the trade guild as a time-served milliner. One of Ernst's friends came from south Germany to help renovate and set up the workshop, and the milliner under whom she had served her apprenticeship in Cologne sent materials and tools to help her start up. On 1 October she opened her workshop, which had a sales area attached, and could finally start looking for a place of her own to live.

It was her eldest daughter who paid the price for Paula's return to work. She was doing well at school but now, at the age of fourteen, had to leave. In farewell her classmates sang 'We are young, the world lies before us.' For the next year she ran the household and looked after the younger children on her own, since her mother was busy in her workshop the whole day. At the time she didn't really understand what it would mean for her future life, my aunt told me. She only rebelled when, the year after, her sister left school and started an apprenticeship as a milliner with her mother. 'Later on she'd be properly qualified, while I'd have nothing.'

Soon afterwards the eldest daughter started work with a firm belonging to the H.s, 'old Nazis' her mother had got to know during the holidays at the health spa in Sobernheim. She was only a trainee; typing, shorthand and bookkeeping skills she had to acquire herself at evening classes. She worked for the H.s for six years, tirelessly attending the classes so as to add to her qualifications. Eventually she was doing all of the bookkeeping for the business – until she had had enough of working for people who were proud to be employing Heinrich Himmler's niece.

Now she wanted to emigrate to the USA. One of 'SS Berger's' relatives, whom she had got to know when he was steward of Gottlob Berger's farm in the Warthegau, had since emigrated to the USA and offered to help. But he was unable, or unwilling, to vouch for her, so her dream of emigration was shattered. Eventually, through a friend, my aunt went to England in 1958 as an au pair, where she started to grapple with Germany's past in lively and argumentative discussions in the students' union at the University of Birmingham. For the first time she read books about the Third Reich – *The Diary of Anne Frank* was a crucial experience for her. When she came back she had a very different view of Germany and the Germans. She did not want to return to the small town of Dinslaken and found a position as secretary with a large firm near Hamburg.

In 1946 and 1947 the Nuremberg Trials took place, which were followed with close attention throughout the world. While the initial trials dealt with the major war criminals, there were several subsequent ones to ascertain the guilt of commanders of the *Einsatzgruppen* (special units of the Security Service – death squads), concentration camp guards, doctors and nursing staff.

Paula, too, followed these trials, above all because in 1947 an old acquaintance was one of the accused: Oswald Pohl, whom she had first met in 1941 at the Jungborn spa in Eckertal in the Harz Mountains. At that time Pohl was still director of SS Production Enterprises. Head of the SS Business Administration Department from 1942 onwards, he was now being held to account for the ruthless exploitation of the slave labour in the concentration camps and for the total utilization of the bodies and belongings of those murdered. He had no sense of personal guilt; everyone, he claimed, knew what was going on. 'As far as the textiles and the handing over of valuables was concerned – along the line of command down to the lowest clerk – they must all have known what was happening in the concentration camps.' At that time, he said, there were different laws in force. He accused the Nuremberg Tribunal of not trying to establish the truth but of being solely interested in 'exterminating as many opponents as possible' – because 'the prosecuting authorities, clearly driven by the thirst for revenge, were dominated by Jewish representatives'. The judges he described as 'gangsters'.

Pohl was sentenced to death on 3 November 1947 and transferred with other war criminals to Landsberg. During the next few years the Landsberg prisoners, among them twenty *Einsatzgruppenführer* who had been responsible for the murder of tens of thousands, presented themselves as sacrificial victims who were being kept as hostages in place of others. The solidarity of large parts of the population made them feel their attitude was justified. Even the President, Theodor Heuss, remembered them in his New Year's speech of 1950.

On 31 January 1951 the American High Commissioner McCloy amnestied all those who had been sentenced to less than fifteen years at Nuremberg. Ten death sentences were commuted to life imprisonment, but five were upheld, among them Oswald Pohl's. Subsequently McCloy was bombarded with petitions, most of them concerning Oswald Pohl. On 9 January even a delegation of the Federal Parliament had demanded he be amnestied.

My grandmother, too, felt solidarity with this prominent prisoner. She had written him a letter in the autumn of 1950 and sent a parcel at Christmas. Pohl, touched by her sympathy and support, sent his thanks by return of post. He wrote on 26 December:

Dear Frau Melters,
    I am very grateful for the understanding you show for my situation. Despite the fact that I was unable to reply to your kind letter of 12 November, you did not let that deter you from sending precious gifts to cheer

up my Christmas. Now I am able to thank you for
both by a somewhat circuitous route. [I am]
inordinately pleased. I have often thought how
strange people's paths through life sometimes are.
A chance encounter at my never-forgotten spa brings,
years on, these delicious fruits of selfless charity.
And it is the fruits of like-mindedness that I value the
most. For that, dear Frau Melters, I would like to
thank you most particularly.

How did my grandmother come to be sending
Christmas parcels to this man, of all men? She who at the
time had almost nothing herself. Was it sympathy for a
man condemned to death whom she had known in better
days? I doubt it. Paula would presumably have indicated
how similar their ideas were. What other interpretation
can one put on Pohl's thanks for her 'fruits of like-
mindedness'? Most likely, what she told him was also in
accordance with Ernst's views. For in fact both she and
Ernst had known Pohl better than his remark about a
'chance encounter' suggests. Evidence of this is, amongst
other things, a postcard Heinrich sent to Ernst in 1941,
with warm greetings from Pohl.

Pohl's letter was smuggled out of prison and taken to
his wife Eleonore in Halfing, who sent it on to 'Paula
Melters, Dinslaken' from Munich on 12 January 1951.
Two months later, after the death sentence on her husband had been upheld, Eleonore Pohl sent out a circular
letter from her husband, to my grandmother among
others. In it he gave thanks for the 'comforting sympathy
of the German people'. He had received 'well over 100
letters & telegrams'; even the Pope had sent a telegram
with his greetings and blessing. 'The Archbishop of

Regensburg sent me his pectoral cross. Many unknown women & men offered to die in my place.'

Despite all the protests and petitions, the five men – Oswald Pohl, Otto Ohlendorf, former head of internal affairs in the SS Security Service and commander of Einsatzgruppe D, Paul Blobel, commander of several special units, Erich Naumann, former leader of Einsatzgruppe B, and Werner Braune, who had commanded a special unit under Ohlendorf – were executed in Landsberg on 7 June 1951. According to the writer Jörg Friedrich, the deaths of these men who had caused so much suffering to others 'got under the skin of the nation'. Pohl, who had received more parcels, letters and declarations of solidarity than anyone before or since, seems to have been particularly well suited to the role of the martyr 'who sacrificed himself for the sins of a whole nation'. He had left the Protestant Church in 1936 and was accepted into the Catholic Church at the beginning of 1950. In prison he wrote a book about his conversion to Christianity with the title, *Credo. Mein Weg zu Gott* (Credo: My Road to God). There was a copy on my grandmother's bookshelf.

Did Paula perhaps feel solidarity with him because of the harassment she and her children had to put up with in Dinslaken? Did she hold on to their like-minded views out of defiance? Or did she feel an obligation towards her husband's 'legacy', did she feel she must take Ernst's place and stick to the old political convictions? Another letter from the postwar period suggests the latter.

On 12 October 1952 'Mariandl', Marianne von Lützelburg, who was living in Weilheim again after her husband had died in 1948, wrote a long letter of condolence to 'Dear, kind Paula'; she had learnt of Ernst's death when Heinrich's and Gebhard's daughters paid her a visit together. 'He was taken from us by the workings of a tragic fate, a victim of his brother,' she wrote – this woman who, while Heinrich was still alive, had set great store by her connection with one of the most powerful men in the Nazi state. 'But that is better,' she went on, 'than living a wretched life of misery as a slave in the hands of the Russians.' That my grandmother also – after the end of the Third Reich – saw Ernst as a victim of his brother is suggested by the legend current in the family that it was only through Heinrich that Ernst had become a convinced Nazi.

Was Paula happier that Ernst was dead rather than held by the Russians? Marianne would scarcely have written something like that unless she was pretty sure Paula would agree with her. During his negotiations with Count Bernadotte Heinrich, too, had made it clear that he would never hand himself over to the 'Bolshevists'. Marianne mentioned Heinrich's former foster-son, Gerhard von der Ahé, who, she wrote, had been 'banished to the Urals for twenty-five years'. Where did she get that story from? Presumably it came not least from her deep-seated fear of the Russians. Marga Himmler maintains in her diaries that her foster-son, after having to leave the National Political Educational Institute in Berlin because of unsatisfactory results, joined the SS in Brno at the beginning of 1945 and shortly afterwards went 'into battle'. At that time he was just sixteen. Presumably he was captured by the Russians. But he must have returned, since in 1966 Gebhard told the journalist Heinz Höhne that he later lived in north Germany.

Marianne reminded Paula of the idyllic Sunday afternoons she and her husband used to spend in Ruhleben and of the marvellous way Ernst had with the children. 'Now, for all the sorrow that fills your heart, you must stand tall and be brave and continue the ideal task of motherhood. You can be proud of what you have achieved, & your Ernst in the world beyond is proud of the magnificent wife he possessed and who has kept up his legacy with such heroic courage.' Marianne's letter, imbued with her unbroken Nazi conviction, seems to have been a comforting if sad memory of better times for Paula; it is one of the few letters she carefully kept for the rest of her life.

Meanwhile life went on. Paula's hat business was a commercial success; her second daughter completed her apprenticeship, qualified as a master craftsman and stayed in her mother's business, which by then was employing several women at various stages of training. She was, my father recalls, a cheerful person, the 'life and soul' of the firm; she got on well with everyone. Mother and daughter shared the instruction of the apprentices, looked after sales, obtained material from the wholesalers and tried to keep up with fashion by attending trade fairs. But even in the fifties the decline of the industry was becoming apparent. In vain German hatmakers tried to counter the hatless lifestyle of the postwar years – for instance, with an advertising brochure that said, 'People whose intellectual capacity is low, such as the negroes in the jungle, need no headgear, but even among those primitive people, chieftains and medicine men wear hats to indicate their intellectual superiority.'

When he was still quite young my father joined a

Catholic youth group, with which he went away every summer; even today his eyes light up as he talks of camping and walking in the Alps. In 1955 he became leader of a youth group himself and took them to see Alain Resnais's film *Nuit et Brouillard* (Night and Fog), which is largely based on films made at various concentration camps after the liberation. He was deeply shocked by the images he saw. Only then, he said, 'did I understand all the remarks, the hints I had been hearing for years about Heinrich Himmler and the SS'. And he started to ask his mother about the extent of his father's guilt. At this she became agitated and had palpitations, so that he quickly gave up. He was the only one of Paula's children to go to university and for years felt guilty about it towards his elder sisters. Paula's youngest daughter was not an enthusiastic pupil and refused to stay on for the *Abitur*. She trained as a nursery school teacher, then became a secretary like her eldest sister and spent several years in the USA.

Throughout these years Paula remained in loose contact with Ernst's family, with Gebhard and Hilde as well as with Marga and her daughter. After the war, though, she rarely saw her Munich relatives. There had been differences, my father and his sister said, because Gebhard asked his sister-in-law to share the costs of his parents' grave in Munich, which Paula indignantly refused. When Gebhard asked Paula for a *Persilschein* – a 'Persil certificate', [based on the slogan 'Persil washes whiter'] – for his denazification procedure, attesting that he had not been a Nazi, again she refused. It is strange that their relationship deteriorated to such an extent; after all, she had been concerned for him while he was interned, even

making the difficult journey from Timmendorf to Neumünster to give him the cake.

Her children, however, who for a long time had felt
resentful towards their uncle because he had done nothing
after the war to support them and their mother, had
known nothing about Gebhard's long period of internment until I started my researches. Nor had they known
that during the immediate postwar years his family had
lived on welfare, just as they themselves had, and that the
Denazification Tribunal had placed Gebhard in the second category of guilt, as an 'offender'. In the first years
after his release he had to take a poorly paid job in a
factory making condensers. Only at the beginning of the
fifties, when he was in his mid-fifties, did he find work
at the European–Afghan Cultural Institute, though his
income remained modest.

Gebhard probably found that position through a former colleague in the Ministry. The Institute was very
small, with only three employees. Gebhard's task was to
organize training places for Afghan students and apprentices. This gave him the opportunity to renew contacts
from his time as a vocational-school teacher and as
principal of the Senior Technical College. He would have
preferred to teach again, his daughter said, but as an
'offender' he was not allowed to work as a teacher (or as
any kind of state official) for several years at least. And
he lost his pension rights. For years Gebhard fought to
have these restored. His youngest daughter remembers
constant discussions on that topic at home in the fifties.
The past, the time of the Third Reich, on the other hand,
was never discussed. In 1959 Gebhard was finally successful in getting his claim accepted. Now he could afford a

few little luxuries again, and he and his wife went to Italy every year.

Marga's daughter Gudrun (Püppi) did a dressmaking apprenticeship in Bielefeld and went back to Munich in 1952. Finding work was difficult, since many of the formerly enthusiastic supporters of the Nazis now self-righteously distanced themselves from the families of the major offenders. Anyone called Himmler had difficulty finding work. When she was thirty she gave an interview to the journalist Norbert Lebert, which, together with other contributions, was published for the first time in 2000 by his son Stefan Lebert in a book called *My Father's Keeper: Children of Nazi Leaders*. In the interview she talked about trying to rehabilitate her father; she intended to do research in the archives and publish a book that would show him in his true light. Gebhard, who looked after her as far as possible during the postwar years, gave her, presumably for that project, the only copy of his sixteen-page character portrayal of Heinrich that he had written in 1956. She never wrote the biography of her father.

As a young woman she must have hung on to her name defiantly. Thus she was forced to change her job again and again, working as a dressmaker's cutter, a pieceworker, a clerical assistant and, finally, as a secretary. Later on she married, eventually becoming a housewife and mother of two children. At the same time she seems to have sought refuge and support in circles that remained true to the National Socialist ideology and played down or denied the terrible deeds of her father.

*

Richard Wendler had been captured by the Americans sometime after 8 May 1945, under the name of Kurt Kummermehr. He had assumed the name because he was afraid of being handed over to Poland and sentenced to death there. On 3 August 1948 the Americans discovered his true identity and Wendler was transferred to the internment camp at Ludwigsburg, near Stuttgart. In November that year he wrote to Gebhard and Hilde that since his internment he had felt freer within himself 'because it weighed on me to be running around at liberty while comrades who had not done anything wrong either were behind barbed wire. Now I am with the others.'

On 20 December 1948 he was classified by the North Württemberg Denazification Tribunal as a 'major offender' and condemned to imprisonment in a labour camp. The reason the Tribunal gave for its decision was that the accused had always been a convinced Nazi and had loyally served the regime. Witnesses had testified that he had not unreservedly approved of all the violent measures taken, but as commissioner in Kielce, as city commissioner for Czestochowa and as Governor of Cracow and Lublin he had to be counted as a member of the leadership group of the Nazi terror regime.

Richard Wendler immediately appealed against the sentence. But he wrote to Gebhard in March 1949 that he did not have great hopes of a more lenient sentence since no good could be expected of the Stuttgart Denazification Tribunal. The assessors were scum, he said, members of the Communist Party and of the *Verband Verfolgter des Naziregimes* (Association of those Persecuted by the Nazi Regime), and their judgements 'indescribable'. 'Rogues and mostly that kind of people' were making the most of the 'liberation from Nazism and militarism'. On 28 April the Central Denazification Tribunal upheld his classification as a 'major offender', since the position of governor of a district could only be occupied by leading Nazis or supporters of the Nazi tyranny. However, Wendler was released as early as 20 December that year and returned to Rosenheim, where his wife was working in a clinic while completing her degree in medicine. Soon afterwards they moved to nearby Prien on the Chiemsee.

Wendler's ceaseless efforts to get himself rehabilitated eventually led to a new appeal being heard by the Württemberg-Baden Central Denazification Tribunal, which resulted in his classification being reduced, by a decision of 12 September 1952, to the category of 'offender'. This meant that the confiscation of his property 'in atonement' was largely reversed. In the six-page document setting out the reasons for their decision, the Tribunal said that 'with the best will in the world they found it impossible to believe the appellant's claim' that he had carried out his duties in Poland not as a National Socialist but merely as an official, and had no idea what the Party intended to do with the Jews and the Poles, even less what was going on in the Government-General. The court also regarded his contention that he had found it impossible to get round Himmler's expectation that he join the SS, but that he had never been on active service for that organization, as lacking credibility. Wendler had, after all, been promoted to the rank of SS Gruppenführer and awarded countless decorations such as the Dagger of Honour, the

Sword of Honour and the Party Badge in Gold. However, even the Polish prosecution service had not been able to prove any direct involvement in criminal acts of violence.

The Tribunal rejected, though, Wendler's further request that he be classified as a 'follower':

> To equate a man who has risen through the SS to the rank of general [*Obergruppenführer*; Wendler's actual rank corresponded to that of lieutenant general, K.H.], a man who from the very beginning until the collapse occupied such a leading position in the administration of a former occupied territory that suffered what must have been the worst of the tyranny and of the brutal destruction carried out by the National Socialists – to equate such a man with a harmless follower would be to make a mockery of the process of purging political life.

Now, at least, Wendler could look for work. He eventually found a place as a clerical assistant in a lawyer's office in Munich; during the week he stayed with his eldest niece and her family. He was not satisfied with this status, however; he wanted to be fully rehabilitated and to practise as a lawyer again. He submitted a plea for clemency, which he was granted in late 1955, even before Gebhard. However incredible it may seem today, from 1 November 1955 he was classified as a 'follower', which meant that he was completely rehabilitated and could indeed practise as a lawyer once more.

In the spring of 1959, the Federal Archives in Koblenz approached him indirectly to assist in building up their Eastern Europe documentation with an account of what he could remember. In a leaflet produced in 1957 the

Federal Archives had emphasized that they were independent of any political party, that their concern was neither to condemn nor to gloss over the past, but to provide an objective appraisal of the historical events. This, they claimed, was in the interests of the whole of the German nation, not least as a prerequisite 'for clearing away the serious obstacles to good relations between Germany and the Slav countries, without which peace in Europe is impossible'.

This request was passed on to Wendler by an old friend and former colleague, Friedrich Siebert, who had been sentenced in 1948 in Cracow to twelve years' imprisonment but had been released in 1956, and by this time once more held the respected position of Bürgermeister – of Prien on the Chiemsee. But Wendler must have had reservations about collaborating with the Federal Archives, which were for him an unknown quantity. Then, in 1970, preliminary proceedings were instituted against him by the district court in Munich 'on suspicion of having been involved in the deportation of Jews in Cracow in the years 1942 and 1943'. The proceedings were abandoned on 7 October.

Early in 1971 charges were once more brought against him. To represent him he appointed the Munich attorney Dr Alfred Seidl. Seidl had qualified in Munich in 1937, then worked as an assistant lecturer at the university; he joined the Party that year. After 1945, at the Nuremberg Trials, he had defended not only Wendler's former boss Hans Frank but also Rudolf Hess, and at the Nuremberg doctors' trial the notorious SS senior physician from Hohenlychen, Professor Karl Gebhardt, as well as Dr Fritz Fischer and Dr Herta Oberheuser, all three of whom had been responsible for cruel medical experiments on prisoners in Ravensbrück. Seidl had also defended Oswald Pohl. In the 1970s he had for two years been chairman of the Christian Social Union Party in the Bavarian Parliament, and in 1977–8 Bavarian Minister of the Interior and thus responsible for the surveillance of the activities of extreme right-wing groups.

Seidl was a master of specious arguments. He contended that the suspicion that the accused had committed a punishable offence did not stand up because it could not be proved that, as Governor of Cracow(!), he had actually been aware of the existence of a ghetto. One also had to take into account, he went on, 'that the concept of a "ghetto" is extremely vague, individual blocks of flats frequently being referred to as ghettos'. At the same time he made application for his client to be declared unfit to stand trial. According to the doctor's certificate, Richard Wendler had suffered a serious heart attack; vascular and cerebral sclerosis meant that his 'powers of concentration and memory were considerably weakened'. The proceedings were 'temporarily suspended' on 14 August 1971. One year later, on 24 August 1972, Richard Wendler died in Prien on the Chiemsee.

'Wölffchen', Karl Wolff, who maintained contact with Hedwig Potthast and Gebhard Himmler for a long time, had also retained Dr Alfred Seidl when charges were brought against him in January 1961 for being accessory to the murder of hundreds of thousands. During the trial Wolff, a respectable, elegant figure, presented himself – in tune with the Cold War times – as an anti-Bolshevist who had joined the SS in 1931 for that reason and whose offer, as Senior SS and Police Commander, of capitulation to the Western Allies from Italy in 1945 was an expression of that same belief. Early in 1947 he had testified at Nuremberg for his friend Oswald Pohl, the former SS Obergruppenführer and head of the SS Business Administration Department. Wolff's praise of Pohl as an excellent business manager had worked more to the latter's disadvantage. He was condemned to death and executed.

At his own trial Wolff got a bad press. He was portrayed as a vain, garrulous man whose protestations that he had known nothing of the murder of the Jews sounded less and less credible. On 30 September 1964 he was sentenced to fifteen years in prison for being an accessory to at least three hundred thousand cases of murder (the deportation of Jews to Treblinka); he was released on health grounds at the end of August 1969. After that he made a living from selling militaria and from interviews and lectures on his glorious past. He spent the last years of his life in Prien on the Chiemsee, a place that clearly held great attraction for old Nazis. He died on 15 July 1984 in Rosenheim hospital.

In the fifties and sixties Gebhard gave interviews to several people writing biographies of Heinrich Himmler. He was happy to give them information on Heinrich's childhood and youth, but refrained almost entirely from any judgement of his brother's political career. Heinrich, he said, had been a soft-hearted, sensitive man who had always maintained good personal contact with his brothers and had never forced any of his relatives to join the SS.

As early as 1956 he had written notes on Heinrich in which he defended him and played down his murderous deeds, as he had in his testimony at Nuremberg ten years earlier. Heinrich's 'greatest sorrow', he writes there, was that his work had always been concerned with 'the negative side of humanity'. This corresponds to the accounts of Heinrich by the head of the foreign section of the SS Security Service, Walter Schellenberg, and by his personal physician Felix Kersten. Both were close to Himmler and both record almost identical remarks by the Reichsführer SS in their memoirs. Does this mean that the greatest mass murderer of all times suffered from having to do the dirty work, when in fact what he really longed to do was to contribute, like others, to the building of an ideal society? It is true that Heinrich Himmler put little energy into the running of the various Central Offices he was in charge of, largely leaving it to his deputies; he saw himself first and foremost as an 'educator' who had to preserve the ideological and political uniformity of his empire, which was growing at ever-increasing speed. Consequently he devoted most of his time to supervising and fostering the ideological development of the SS personnel. He doubtless saw his 'sacrifice' for the people and his Führer as an honour, the task entrusted to him as a special distinction. His daughter Gudrun seems to have been aware of that. It was only to the most loyal of his followers, she said with disarming honesty to Himmler's biographer Joseph Ackermann, that Hitler could entrust the task of 'dealing with the Reich's garbage'.

At one point Gebhard described Heinrich as a 'dangerous romantic'. Once, shortly before the end, he told his daughter, he had taken Heinrich to task for not turning his back on Hitler sooner – surely he must have seen the catastrophe coming. To which Heinrich had replied helplessly, 'You try breaking an oath of loyalty.'

Despite distancing himself from Heinrich politically, one purpose of which was to exonerate himself, Gebhard constantly attempted to defend this brother of his whom posterity would see as the incarnation of evil. He presented Heinrich as a selfless, self-sacrificing servant of the regime whose only fault had been not to realize in time that he had been serving the wrong man – and he himself, as his big brother, had already put that criticism to him.

In his retirement Gebhard spent a lot of time arranging the family documents and creating chronological family albums, in which he carefully stuck photos of Heinrich at state receptions and other official functions. In a similar way, he also liked to see himself in uniform; in all the photos from the war years he is posing proudly with his accumulated insignia and decorations. In the seventies he wrote the 'Reminiscences' for his children that I have quoted from above. In them he portrayed his own career during the Nazi period as if it had had nothing to do with the system. He mentioned neither joining the Party nor being a member of the SS, and glossed over his own membership of the Waffen SS as well as the fact that the Central Office for Technology was a Party organization. His activity between 1933 and 1945 thus appeared as that of a non-political civil servant who had merely done his patriotic duty, both as an official and as a soldier, and whose punishment after the war with internment, being debarred from his profession and the loss of his pension rights had been disproportionately harsh.

Part of all this was his portrayal of himself as a man

who, in contrast to his brother Heinrich, had not suc-
cumbed to the idolatry surrounding the Führer and had
therefore always been on the right side. Hitler does not
appear in his memoirs; it is as if he had never existed,
even though during his internment he expressed his outrage at the man who had led the German nation astray.
But very quickly after 1945 the Germans' idolization of
the Führer and their faith in him had turned into silence
– and, above all, silence about their own enthusiasm,
which no one was willing to admit to any more.

Epilogue: Family Stories

I had known Dani, a Jewish Israeli, for a long time, but had lost sight of him for some years. In the autumn of 1997, a few months after I had started looking at my grandfather's files, we went to Cracow for a few days, a journey to a country where his family had had its roots. Our fathers had both been born in 1939, one as a Polish Jew who survived the war in occupied Warsaw as a child provided with 'Aryan' papers, the other as a nephew and godchild of Heinrich Himmler who always received a present from the Reichsführer SS on his birthday and at Christmas.

In the romantic old town of Cracow, with its ancient houses, squares and alleys, there were expensively renovated art nouveau cafés; right beside them were establishments exuding, unchanged, all the charm of the Socialist era. We strolled past buildings with commemorative plaques recalling earlier periods when the town had flourished culturally. A few yards further on pop music boomed out of brightly lit restaurants offering the same fast food as everywhere else in the world. In a side street we found a tiny bakery selling cheesecake cut in huge squares straight from the baking tray. Dani beamed all over his face – the cake tasted just the same as the ones his Warsaw grandmother used to bake.

The quiet in Kazimierz, the former Jewish quarter of Cracow, was eerie. Before the war there had been some fifteen thousand Jews living in the city. In 1941 they were forced into a tiny ghetto, as were Dani's parents in Warsaw. A year later the Germans started deporting them to extermination camps, where only a few survived. Dani's grandfather, who was a doctor, managed to escape deportation – a colleague helped him get out through the back door of the hospital on the square that was the assembly point in the Warsaw ghetto. Shortly afterwards Dani's father, three years old at the time, also managed to escape deportation. With false names and false papers, he and his parents were taken in by the non-Jewish brother-in-law of Dani's grandmother. Until the end of the war she lived with a false 'Aryan' husband and a genuine Jewish one, who had to hide in the wardrobe whenever danger threatened.

Steven Spielberg's famous film, *Schindler's List*, was made in the main square in Kazimierz. Oskar Schindler was a businessman who managed to save some Cracow Jews from deportation. Was it filmed here because the district still looks so authentic? Or did it only look authentic because it had been restored to serve as a set for the film? The deserted square was surrounded by grey, dilapidated houses; cars were parked in the middle of it. Only two buildings stood out: restaurants where expensive food accompanied by klezmer music was served to Jewish Americans stopping off there before going on to Auschwitz or Majdanek. While Dani found the deserted district depressing, I had the weird feeling that time had stood still, the inhabitants had only just been deported. Auschwitz is only sixty kilometres (about 37 miles) away.

Halfway between the old town and Kazimierz is the Wawel, the old royal castle. It was from here between 1939 and 1945 that Hans Frank, for whom Richard Wendler 'did his duty', ruled western Poland as Governor-General. When Frank fell into disfavour with Himmler he was still supported by Hitler, since he was clearly carrying out to the Führer's full satisfaction the task of turning the Government-General's terrain 'into a heap of rubble'. It made me think of the book by Frank's son Niklas, which caused such outrage when it appeared in 1987 because in it he dealt so ruthlessly with his father. I read later that Norman, Hans Frank's eldest son, did not want to have children; he wanted the name of Frank to disappear from the world.

When I was young I also wished I could get rid of my name. After the war all sorts of difficulties had been put in the way of Paula and her children in their home town because of it. My father remembers it well. At some point or other he came to terms with his name, but when my parents went to Israel for the first time to visit Dani's parents, he was very relieved when he had got through passport control without any fuss having been made. Years later Dani's father told me that he, too, had been concerned about what might happen when my parents entered the country. His concern had only gone away when, on a sudden impulse, he had checked the Tel Aviv telephone directory and found that there was actually someone with the name of Himmler in it. As a child I had often comforted myself with the thought of how lucky it was that my sister and I were girls – later on we could marry and get rid of the terrible name, thus freeing the whole family from the stigma, since there were no male descendants. At some point or other I came to accept my name. My son has been spared it.

Almost a year after our trip to Poland together, Dani came to live with me in Berlin. We spent a lot of time walking around the city. Together we searched for traces of the Nazi period and of my grandparents' generation who had lived there. First of all we went to the broadcasting building in Masurenallee, where Ernst had worked for twelve years. I would have liked to go in, but did not know what explanation I could give should the doorman ask me. So we turned back at the main entrance. Dani wanted to see the Olympic Stadium that Hitler had had built for the 'national mission' of the Games in 1936. As we stood in the immense empty structure, we saw very different images in our mind's eye: Dani saw the Führer standing on the rostrum, I tried to imagine my grandparents among the spectators. They lived close to the Olympic Park.

After such searches for traces of the past we would spend hours talking about our family histories. As teenagers we had both been given reading material on National Socialism by our fathers, and we had probably been more interested in the subject than most others of our age. Dani was above all well informed about the military history of the Second World War. When he was younger he had been keen on building models of German Stukas, Heinkel 111s and Messerschmitt 109s from the 1940s, which he had carefully adorned with swastikas. For my part, I had always been interested in the history of the victims and their struggle for survival. Each of us had chosen the easier way to deal with the oppressive burden of our family histories by turning to the history of the other side, borrowing a different identity from them, so to speak. Later on, at a discussion circle for the descendants of Nazi criminals and of their victims, I was taken aback to discover that the function of the children of those who had been persecuted and had suffered was to provide relief for the children of the war criminals. They were the ones to comfort the offspring of the oppressors, give them a shoulder to cry on and then grant them absolution. I was horrified when I realized that.

If it was, indeed, a secret wish for reconciliation between the side of the oppressors and that of the victims that had brought Dani and me together, there was no sense of this in our daily life. During that summer there were also fierce battles between us, in which our different family heritages were more deeply involved than we would have liked to admit.

It seemed to be 'no problem' at all for Dani that he was living in the former capital of the Third Reich with a great-niece of Heinrich Himmler. Sometimes, however, he could suddenly feel the whole environment had become hostile, even threatening, especially when confronted with official checks, with the Germans' pigheaded insistence on correct procedure – at such times even an unfriendly bus driver could turn into a 'Nazi'. At first I found it amusing; eventually, however, it made me furious. Perhaps it was the power of the emotions released that frightened me. In such moments a gulf of incomprehension opened up between us. We kept on coming upon situations, emotive words and images that set off violent reactions in both of us.

Once, when we had got into another argument because Dani had called someone a 'bloody Nazi' under his breath and I demanded that he should be less sweeping in his judgement of others, he replied angrily, 'The main thing for you is always to behave properly!' I just couldn't take that remark; the word 'properly' had horrendous connotations for me. It reminded me of my great-uncle's notorious Poznan speech, in which he praised himself and his SS Gruppenführer for the 'proper' way in which they had carried out their murderous activities. Immediately Dani was overcome with remorse, but I found it impossible to separate such words from their historical connotations. Situations like that made us aware how close below the surface the past was still lurking. Under normal conditions we felt we were comfortable in dealing with it. When conflict arose, though, we were suddenly reduced to being the offspring of oppressors and victims, a German and a Jew.

Much has already been written about the extent to which the experiences of the Nazi period have dominated the families of the oppressors as well as those of the victims. The victims are mostly haunted by nightmares throughout their lives, tormented not only by their memories but also by shame – shame at the degradation they suffered, but also shame that they were the ones to survive. Even their children and grandchildren still have dreams of fear and persecution, Dani too. He often dreamt of unknown people pursuing and killing him. I can only remember such dreams from childhood, dreams in which I was chased and at the same time paralysed with terror. Since then I have much more often had dreams in which I do violence to others.

After the war, before she emigrated to Israel, Dani's grandmother set down the family history in a document. One can only guess at the horror of her experiences at the time, the ever-present fear of death behind the matter-of-fact style, as for example when she describes the countless times the family had to find a new hiding place, how often they only just escaped being arrested and delivered up to the Gestapo because someone had informed on them – and that despite their forged papers and the hush money they were constantly paying out. Only late on did Dani's father realize how much his traumatic childhood experiences had left their imprint on his later life. It was only a year ago that he found the courage to read his mother's record and to have it translated for us and his grandchild.

My grandmother Paula's documents also lay for decades buried among other papers in my father's house, without him ever looking at them. It was only the research on this book that brought them to my family's notice.

The Israeli psychologist Dan Bar-On has spoken of the 'wall of silence' that has been erected over many years and that weighs heavily on the families of the victims and of their oppressors. It is almost impossible to break down because the descendants, the second and even the third generations, continue to hand on the myths current in the family, thus becoming 'accomplices' of the older generation. In such circumstances a reconstruction of the past that corresponds as far as possible to the truth is unlikely. Not only because after so many years the tangle is almost impossible to unravel; not only because so much time has elapsed; not only because in the course of a person's life memories are repeatedly 'overwritten' and are therefore anything but reliable. But also because every member of the family has developed his or her own version of the past. The same past suddenly has many 'truths'. It was something I came across myself while working on this book.

I have probably undertaken this search for the past under the most favourable conditions imaginable when investigating the history of one's own family – namely, with the agreement of my close relatives. No obstacles were put in my way, no one refused to talk to me, no documents were kept from me. On the contrary, my relatives would quite unexpectedly hand over to me important private documents I had until then had no idea existed. Yet despite all that, progress was often painfully slow and laborious. I kept having the feeling I was fighting against some invisible resistance.

It was as if I were making my way through a thick fog consisting of vague facts half understood, glossed over, reinterpreted or even falsified. This fog had its attractions; in the end it made everyone to a greater or lesser extent complicit in maintaining the family myths.

Despite my determination to clear things up, I took a long time to free myself from those myths. When one is investigating the history of one's own family, it is difficult to overcome the blind spots caused by the closeness to one's subject. It is an uncomfortable process, constantly accompanied by fears of the loss it might bring. It is difficult to confront one's own father with research results that threaten to bring back to the surface things that have long been repressed. It is difficult to look at family photos together when until then all that has been seen in them are unspoilt childhood scenes or a happy bride and groom, not the Party badges, swastika armbands or the oak-leaf and death's-head insignia of the SS.

Perhaps I was able to ask more uninhibited and critical questions than had been possible for my parents and aunts, although at times I myself broke off the conversations with my relatives, changed the subject or simply asked no further questions at the precise moment when something truly revealing was in danger of coming out. And I often found it difficult to carry on with my research, since some of the things I came across in the files so numbed my mind that I could not continue for weeks, even months. It was only slowly that I became aware that the long breaks, even the apparently aimless burying myself in trivial details, made sense when looked at in retrospect, since they freed me from the mental block that invariably occurred when I confronted the 'important' documents directly.

Not infrequently I got the feeling I had bitten off more than I could chew, was afraid I had too little personal distance from the subject, wondered, after expending much energy following another trail that had led nowhere, why I was going to all this trouble anyway. And why me, why not my sister or one of my cousins? What was it that had driven me to look into the history of my family?

Two years after my father's telephone call, which was the starting point for this book, Dani's and my son was born. I am still afraid of the moment when he will learn that one side of his family made every effort to wipe out the other. The only thing that makes it easier for me to contemplate that moment is that it will be possible for me to answer his questions and give him clear information on the extent of the guilt and responsibility of my forebears.

Abbreviations

BA (Bundesarchiv)	Federal Archives
BA-B	Federal Archives, Berlin
BA-DH	Federal Archives, temporary holdings Dahlwitz-Hoppegarten
N 1126	Himmler Papers, Federal Archives, Koblenz
NS	National Socialist files, Federal Archives
REM	Reich Education Ministry
SSO	SS Officers

Notes

My sources for personal information on the Himmler family, apart from the extensive Himmler papers (N 1126) in the Federal Archives in Koblenz, are countless documents, letters, certificates and photos belonging to individual members of my family, for which detailed references are not given here. Much of the information also comes from Gebhard Himmler's 'Reminiscences', which he wrote for his children in the 1970s, as well as from conversations I had in the last few years with Gebhard's eldest and youngest daughters, with my father and his eldest sister and with a cousin of my grandmother.

1. I Never Called Him 'Grandfather'

BA-B (formerly Berlin Document Center), SSO file: Ernst Himmler, b. 23 Dec. 1905, Film 98-A as well as PK (Party Correspondence) Ernst Himmler; various films in NS 19/17.01 FC (formerly *Bestandsergänzungsfilme* – films to supplement holdings) and BA-DH, ZM 213, A 14.

2. A Perfectly Ordinary Family

Alfred Andersch: *The Father of a Murderer*, tr. Leila Venne-
witz, New York, 1994; readers' letters in the *Süddeutsche
Zeitung* of 9/10 Aug. 1980 and Dr Otto Gritschneder in the
Süddeutsche Zeitung of 7 Aug. 1980.

On Hans Himmler, b. 19 May 1915, see his SS file, Film
98-A, and Eugen Kogon: *The Theory and Practice of Hell:
The German Concentration Camps and the System behind
Them*, New York, 1950 (p. 32).

On conditions at university and student fraternities see
e.g. Konrad H. Jarausch: *Deutsche Studenten 1800–1970*,
Frankfurt am Main, 1984.

On the history of Germans in St Petersburg see Natalija
Juchneva: *Die deutschen in einer polyethnischen Stadt. Petersburg vom Beginn des 18. Jahrhunderts bis 1914*, Hamburg,
1994; Stefan Kestler: *Betrachtungen zur kaiserlich-deutschen
Russlandpolitik. Ihre Bedeutung für die Herausbildung des
deutsch-russischen Antagonismus zwischen Reichsgründung
und Ausbruch des Ersten Weltkrieges*, Hamburg, 2002;
Andreas Keller: *Das deutsche Theater und die Entwicklung
der deutschen Gesellschaft in St Petersburg im 18. und 19.
Jahrhundert*, MA thesis, Freiburg, 2001.

On Freiherr von Lamezan see *Der Oberpfälzer*, no. 60,
n.d. [1936].

Family trees of the Himmler, Heyder and Kien families
drawn up by Gebhard Himmler senior in N 1126, vol. 35.

For the Himmler family history see also the very detailed
research by Bradley F. Smith in *Heinrich Himmler: A Nazi
in the Making, 1900–1926*, Stanford, 1971; Roger Manvell
and Heinrich Fraenkel: *Heinrich Himmler*, London, 1965;
Joseph Ackermann: *Heinrich Himmler als Ideologe*, Göttingen, 1970.

Notes

3. 'Bring Up the Children to be German-minded'

On Germany's entry into the war see Gerhard Hirschfeld et al.: *Enzyklopädie Erster Weltkrieg*, Paderborn, 2003.

On the subject of the 'east' as 'chaos' and the equating of people and vermin, see Sarah Jansen: *'Schädlinge'. Geschichte eines wissenschaftlichen und politischen Konstrukts 1840–1920*, Frankfurt am Main, 2003; Wolfgang Mommsen in *Enzyklopädie Erster Weltkrieg*, Paderborn, 2003.

4. 'Just One Shell Hole after Another'

On children and young people on active service in the war see Michael Wildt: *Generation des Unbedingten*, Hamburg, 2003; on the cadet corps see Gudrun Fiedler: *Jugend im Krieg*, Cologne, 1989; Walter Z. Laqueur: *Young Germany: A History of the German Youth Movement*, London, 1962.

War memoirs and experiences in the front line: Carl Zuckmayer: *A Part of Myself*, tr. Richard and Clara Winston, London, 1970; Erich Maria Remarque: *All Quiet on the Western Front*, tr. Brian Murdoch, London, 1994 (pp. 14–15); Ernst Toller: *I Was a German*, tr. Edwin Crankshaw, London, 1981.

For the war as experienced by the generation who were schoolchildren see Sebastian Haffner: *Defying Hitler: A Memoir*, tr. Oliver Pretzel, New York, London, 2002 (pp. 12–14).

For the discussion of war guilt and the 'stab in the back' after the First World War see Karl-Dietrich Bracher et al.: *Die Weimarer Republik 1918–1933*, Bonn, 1987, among others the article by Ulrich Heinemann: 'Die Last der Vergangenheit. Zur politischen Bedeutung der Kriegsschuld- und Dolchstoss-

Notes

diskussion'; Michael Jeismann: 'Propaganda', in *Enzyklopä-
die Erster Weltkrieg*, Paderborn, 2003 (pp. 198ff.); Sebastian
Haffner: *Die sieben Todsünden des Deutschen Reiches im
Ersten Weltkrieg*, Bergisch-Gladbach, 1981.

5. 'On Friday We're Going Shooting'

For the situation in Munich after the First World War see
Wilfried Rudloff: 'Zwischen Revolution und Gegenrevolu-
tion: München 1918 bis 1920', in Richard Bauer et al. (eds):
München – 'Hauptstadt der Bewegung', catalogue of exhi-
bition at Munich City Museum, 2002; Ian Kershaw: *Hitler:
A Profile in Power*, London, 1991.

For Kurt Eisner's role in Munich see Amos Elon: *The Pity
of It All: A History of the Jews in Germany 1743–1933*,
New York, 2002.

Heinrich, Gebhard and Lu joining the 14th Volunteer
Company, Rifle Brigade 21, on 4 Nov. 1919, in N 1126, vol.
1; receipt for rifle, pistol and ammunition, issued by Epp to
Heinrich Himmler on 16 May 1920, ibid.

For a general survey of Citizens' Guards in Bavaria, the
Freikorps Epp and its successor organization Rifle Brigade 21,
see Wilfried Rudloff in Bauer et al.: op. cit.; Erwin Könnemann: *Einwohnerwehren und Zeitfreiwilligenverbände*, East
Berlin, 1969.

For the history of the Freikorps see Hagen Schulze, *Freikorps und Republik 1918–1920*, Boppard am Rhein, 1969.

Gebhard's first diploma: personal papers in the archives
of the Technical University, Munich.

6. 'They All Went Wild with Excitement'

On friends and acquaintances of the Himmler family, see Heinrich's diaries from 1910 onwards; Professor Rauschmeyer was a colleague of Gebhard Himmler senior in Landshut, and the families remained friends; Mariele Rauschmeyer, who was studying medicine, was one of the circle that met at the Pension Loritz; she also often met Heinrich at the fraternities' drinking evenings (N 1126, vol. 17), and regularly went out walking with Ernst.

For Ernst's training as a short-term volunteer see SSO file Ernst Himmler, Film 98-A, as well as Könnemann: op. cit.

For Hitler's speeches in Munich before the Putsch and at the rallies of the *Vaterländische Verbände Bayerns* see Bauer et al.: op. cit.; Kershaw: op. cit.

For the hyperinflation of 1922–3 see Kershaw: op. cit.; Sebastian Haffner: op. cit.; Stefan Zweig: *The World of Yesterday*, London, 1943.

On Ernst Röhm see Bauer et al.: op. cit.; Kershaw: op. cit.; Ernst Klee: *Das Personenlexikon zum Dritten Reich*, Frankfurt am Main, 2003.

For the Hitler Putsch see Kershaw: op. cit.; Bauer et al.: op. cit.

For the situation in Munich after the failed Putsch and the percentage of votes won by the right-wing nationalist parties at the elections in June and December 1924 see Kershaw: op. cit.

7. Service and Sacrifice

For Hitler's trial see Kershaw: op. cit.; in addition, Otto Gritschneder: 'Besonderheiten des "Hitler-Prozesses"' in Bauer et al.: op. cit.

Heinrich Himmler's reading list, N 1126, vol. 9.

For the *Bund der Artamanen* see Smith: op. cit. and Ackermann: op. cit.

For Dr Wilhelm Patin, b. 25 June 1879, see his SSO file, Film 365-A; Wolfgang Dierker: *Himmlers Glaubenskrieger*, Paderborn, 2002; Heinz Höhne's record of a conversation with Gebhard Himmler of January 1966.

For Paula Stölzle see N 1126, vol. 13.

Ernst Himmler's matriculation at the Technical University, Munich: registration form in the university archives.

For Marianne Nässl see letter of 8 Sept. 1926 in N 1126, vol. 17; her membership card is in the Federal Archives, MF (microfiche) card index of local Party groups, Film N 0080.

Bradley F. Smith comes to the conclusion that the price Heinrich Himmler paid for being a Party member in Landshut after 1924 was 'the sacrifice of many of the friendships of his student years and the evaporation of most of the closeness which he had enjoyed with relatives'; after 1924 his parents had regarded him as the 'proverbial lost son . . . in their eyes he was a failure', and he could only bear this loss because he gained 'his emotional satisfaction from his Party work' (Smith, op. cit., p. 164). Given the regular contact with his family even after he had left Munich, however, and given the wealth of encouragement Heinrich received from his family as well as from friends and other relatives for his commitment to the National Socialist cause and the nationalist cause generally, I come to the opposite conclusion – namely, that Heinrich did not lose his most important social ties. In particular Mariele Rauschmeyer did not criticize him for his fanaticism, as Smith thinks (pp. 140–1), but assured him she shared the same convictions. Smith does not mention Marianne Nässl's fervent agreement with his ideas, emphasizing instead Heinrich's parents' exhortations, mentioned in her letter (p. 164); he also refers to Emil Wäckerle's letter to

Heinrich without mentioning the enthusiasm he expresses for his friend's work.

Joseph Ackermann also claims Heinrich Himmler's Party work left him in a financial and social dead end 'because he put his whole being in the service of the great cause' (op. cit., p. 27). This is a quotation from the above-mentioned letter from Wäckerle, but it refers not to Himmler, as Ackermann thinks, but to a mutual friend.

For Gebhard taking up his post at the Deroystrasse Technical College see BA, REM file on Gebhard Himmler.

On Gregor Strasser see Kershaw: op. cit.

8. 'We Must Be Happy'

All letters from Marga to Heinrich quoted here are in N 1126, vol. 14.

Marriage certificate of Heinrich and Marga Himmler in Berlin-Schöneberg Registry Office, Münchener Strasse 49 (now Tempelhof-Schöneberg). For the birth of Gudrun see Heinrich Himmler's pocket diary.

For the increasing electoral success of the Nazi Party after 1929/30 see Kershaw: op. cit.; Martin Broszat: *The Hitler State: The Foundation and Development of the Internal Structure of the Third Reich*, tr. John W. Hiden, London, New York, 1981; Bracher et al.: op. cit.

For the beginnings of the SS and its Security Service see Wildt: op. cit.; George C. Browder: *Hitler's Enforcers: The Gestapo and the SS Security Service in the Nazi Revolution*, New York, 1996; Shlomo Aronson: *The Beginnings of the Gestapo System*, Jerusalem, 1969.

For the history of the *Verein für das Deutschtum im Ausland*, see Gerhard Weidenfelder: *Verein für das Deutschtum im Ausland 1881–1918. Ein Beitrag zur Geschichte des deutschen Nationalismus im Kaiserreich*, Frankfurt am Main, 1976; for the history of the *Verein* in the Nazi state see Rudolf Luther: *Blau oder Braun? Der Volksbund für das Deutschtum im Ausland im NS-Staat 1933–1937*, Neumünster, 1999.

For Philipp von Lützelburg see BA-B SSO Film 283-A, MF card index of local Party groups, Film N 0080, and Michael Kater: *Das 'Ahnenerbe' der SS 1935–1945*, Stuttgart, 1974.

For the history of Siemens & Halske and the development of electrical engineering see P. Noll: *Nachrichtentechnik an der TH/TU Berlin – Geschichte, Stand und Ausblick*, Berlin, 2001.

For the distribution of the Nazi Party votes up to 1933 see Broszat: *Hitler State.*

9. 'Finally Got a Foothold in the Fortress'

For the political and economic situation during the last years of the Weimar Republic and for the seizure of power, see Broszat: *Hitler State*; Kershaw: op. cit.; Bracher et al.: op. cit.

Heinrich's correspondence with his parents between 1933 and 1937 is in N 1126, vol. 13.

For the building up of the Bavarian Political Police by Himmler after 10 March 1933 see Broszat: *Hitler State*; Bauer et al.: op. cit.

A. Dennhardt and E. H. Himmler: *Leitfaden der Rundfunkentstörung*, Berlin, 1935.

SSO file for Dr Alfred Dennhardt, Film 143.

For Dr Klaus Hubmann see his SSO file, Film 119-A, and Heinrich Himmler's diary for November 1921.

For the beginning of Nazi broadcasting see Heinz Pohle: *Der Rundfunk als Instrument der Politik*, Hamburg, 1955;

Notes

Hans-Joachim Weinbrenner (ed.): *Handbuch des deutschen Rundfunks*, Heidelberg, 1938; Peter Reichel: *Der schöne Schein des Dritten Reiches. Faszination und Gewalt des Faschismus*, Munich, 1991; Joseph Goebbels: *Nationalsozialistischer Rundfunk*, Munich, 1935; various files in R (Reich Ministry for Public Enlightenment and Propaganda) 55 and R (Reich Broadcasting Company) 78.

For Walter Melters see BA, SM (SS NCOs and men) file, Film M 0030; Heinrich Himmler's appointments book, entries for 16 and 17 Sept. 1941; Himmler's correspondence with his parents in N 1126, vol. 13.

For Himmler's taking command of the police in the separate states up to 1934 and for the Röhm putsch see Wildt: op. cit.; Broszat: *Hitler State*; and Kershaw: op. cit.

10. 'National Socialist Reliability'

For the history of the trade union estate of Ruhleben see file 259 of the Building Control Department, Berlin-Charlottenburg. For the change in the estate's population structure see Berlin address books and telephone directories 1933–45.

For Gebhard's application to have his Party membership backdated see his NSLB (National Socialist Teachers' Association) file in the Federal Archives.

Postcards to Heinrich from his parents in N 1126, vol. 13.

Marga Himmler's diaries are archived in the US Holocaust Memorial Museum (1999.A.0092).

For the Party rallies in general and the 1935 rally in particular see Kershaw: op. cit.; Reichel: op. cit.

For the training courses of the NS Teachers' Association see Karlheinz König: *Die Schulung der Lehrer im Nationalsozialistischen Lehrerbund – eine Massnahme zur Profession-*

alisierung der Lehrerschaft im Dritten Reich?, Bad Heilbrunn, 1999.

For King Henry I and the ceremony for the thousandth anniversary of his death see Karl-Heinz Janssen: 'Himmlers Heinrich. Wie ein König des frühen Mittelalters zum Patron der deutschen Vernichtungspolitik im Osten wurde', in *Die Zeit*, 43, 19 Oct. 2000; Ackermann: op. cit.; Gebhard Himmler senior's cuttings book in N 1126, vol. 34.

In her denazification file Marga claimed to have been resident in Berlin during 1934–40.

For the 1936 Olympics see Stiftung Topographie des Terrors (ed.): *Die Olympischen Spiele und der NS*, Berlin, 1996.

For the history of German television and the role of the Reich Postal Service and the Reich Broadcasting Company in its development, see Gerd Ueberschär: 'Die deutsche Reichspost im Zweiten Weltkrieg', in *Deutsche Postgeschichte*, ed. Wolfgang Lotz, Berlin, 1989; William Uricchio (ed.): *Die Anfänge des deutschen Fernsehens. Kritische Annäherungen an die Entwicklung bis 1945*, Tübingen, 1991; Joseph Hoppe: 'Fernsehen als Waffe. Militär und Fernsehen in Deutschland 1935–1950', in *'Ich diente nur der Technik'*, Schriftenreihe des deutschen Technik-Museums Berlin, vol. 13, 1995.

11. Educating People to Make Sacrifices for the Community

For the trip to Norway on the *Robert Ley* see Reichel: op. cit.

For the Central Office for Technology of the Nazi Party and for Fritz Todt see Karl-Heinz Ludwig: *Technik und Ingenieure im Dritten Reich*, Düsseldorf, 1974; Franz W. Seidler: *Fritz Todt. Baumeister des Dritten Reiches*, Munich, 1986; Klee: op. cit.

Gebhard Himmler: 'Aufgaben und Berufsethos des deutschen Ingenieurs', in *Reich und Geist*, Oct./Nov. 1942, supplement to magazine *Der Altherrenbund*.

For the correspondence of Gebhard Himmler as official in charge of professional matters for the Association for German Technology from 1938 to 1945 see BA, NS 14.

For the colonial ambitions of the engineers working for Todt see Ludwig: op. cit.

For the policies pursued by the Association for Germans Abroad between 1933 and 1937 and for its demise see Luther: op. cit.

For Germany's war against Poland and Gebhard's regiment see Autorenkollektiv unter der Leitung von (Team of writers headed by) Wolfgang Schumann and Gerhart Hass: *Deutschland im Zweiten Weltkrieg*, Berlin, 1975; Georg Tessin: *Verbände und Truppen der deutschen Wehrmacht und Waffen-SS im Zweiten Weltkrieg 1939–1945*, vols 1–17, Osnabrück, 1977–2002.

For the departments of the Ministry of Education as well as Gebhard's position in the Ministry see *Findbuch REM* in the BA; Warnack (ed.): *Taschenbuch für Verwaltungsbeamte*, 1943.

I would like to thank Michael Wildt for a suggestion regarding the assessment of Gebhard's activity as an inspector of the Waffen-SS.

12. 'Keep Marching. Keep Fighting. Keep Working.'

For Hermann Behrends see his SSO file, Film 52; Browder: op. cit.; Valdis O. Lumans: *Himmler's Auxiliaries. The Volksdeutsche Mittelstelle and the German National Minorities of Europe 1933–1945*, Chapel Hill and London, 1993; Dierker: op. cit.; Brett Exton at www.islandfarm.fsnet.co.uk

For Hubmann's dismissal and his employment up to 1945 see BA-DH, ZA (temporary archive) IV 842.

For Dr Heinrich Glasmeier see his SSO file, Film 15-A and Weinbrenner: op. cit.

For Gottlob Berger see Klee: op. cit.

Minutes of the programming meetings in the broadcasting building on Masurenallee between 21 June 1944 and 7 Mar. 1945 in BA, R 55/556.

Reports on the mood of the population towards broadcasting by the Central Security Department of the Reich in BA, R 55/531; see also Heinz Boberach (ed.): *Meldungen aus dem Reich 1938–1945*, Herrsching, 1984.

Letter from Ernst Himmler to Heinrich, May 1944, in Ernst Himmler's SSO file.

For Heinrich Himmler's interest in weapons technology see Hubert Faensen: *Hightech für Hitler. Die Hakeburg – vom Forschungszentrum zur Kaderschmiede*, Berlin, 2001; Ludwig: op. cit.

13. 'Ever Your Faithful Richard'

For personal details on Richard Wendler and his role in the civil administration of the Government General see his SSO file, Film 235-B; Werner Präg and Wolfgang Jacobmeyer: *Das Diensttagebuch des deutschen Generalgouverneurs in Polen 1939–1945*, Stuttgart, 1974; Bogdan Musial: *Deutsche Zivilverwaltung und Judenverfolgung im Generalgouvernement. Eine Fallstudie zum Distrikt Lublin 1939–1944*, Wiesbaden, 1999; Israel Gutman, Eberhard Jäckel, Peter Longerich, Julius H. Schoeps (eds): *The Encyclopedia of the Holocaust*, New York, 1990.

For German policy towards Poland 1939–45 see Martin Broszat: *Nationalsozialistische Polenpolitik 1939–1945,*

Stuttgart, 1961; Wildt: op. cit.; Peter Witte et al.: *Der Dienst-kalender Heinrich Himmlers 1941/42*, Hamburg, 1999.

For Richard Wendler's denazification as well as various preliminary proceedings against him see private documents, some held at the Central Office of the State Justice Administration in Ludwigsburg.

For civil servants urging the acceleration of the final solution see Wildt: op. cit.; Musial: op. cit.

For Heinrich Himmler's speech to SS leaders in Kharkov on 24 Apr. 1943 see the transcription in *Judenverfolgung und jüdisches Leben unter den Bedingungen des NS*, vol. 1, *Tondokumente und Rundfunksendungen 1930–1946*.

For Richard Wendler's conflict with Globocnik and his relationship with Heinrich Himmler see correspondence between them in July/Aug. 1943 in SSO file Odilo Globocnik, b. 21 Apr. 1904.

14. 'Do Not Forget Me. Your X'

For Hedwig Potthast and second wives in general in the SS see N 1126, vols 37 and 38; Peter Ferdinand Koch: *Himmlers graue Eminenz – Oswald Pohl*, Hamburg, 1988; Gudrun Schwarz: *Eine Frau an seiner Seite. Ehefrauen in der 'SS-Sippengemeinschaft'*, Hamburg, 1997; record of Hedwig Potthast's interrogation.

Felix Kersten: *Totenkopf und Treue. Heinrich Himmler ohne Uniform*, Hamburg, 1952.

For Marga Himmler and her daughter in Gmund see Matthäus: op. cit.; letters from Marga to Heinrich up to 1941 in N 1126, vol. 14; 'Töchter und Väter' in *Der Stern*, no. 2, 6 Jan. 1983, pp. 60ff. (extracts from Gudrun [Püppi] Himmler's diary); extracts from Gudrun Himmler's diary in private ownership.

Notes

For Hedwig Potthast at Schneewinkellehen see Heinz Höhne: *The Order of the Death's Head: The Story of Hitler's SS*, tr. Richard Barry, London, 1969; H. R. Trevor-Roper: *The Bormann Letters*, London, 1954; Norbert and Stefan Lebert: *My Father's Keeper: Children of Nazi Leaders – An Intimate History of Damage and Denial*, London, 2001.

15. 'They Can't Take Our Happy Memories away from Us.'

Memories of Anne-Margarete von K. in Detlev Mittag (ed.): *Kriegskinder '45. Zehn Überlebensgeschichten*, Berlin, 1995.

For Heinrich Himmler's secret negotiations with the Western Allies see Wildt: op. cit.; Kersten: op. cit.; Walter Schellenberg: *The Schellenberg Memoirs – A Record of the Nazi Secret Service*, London, 1956.

On the broadcasting building in the last days before the end of the war see Fritz L. Büttner: *Das Haus des Rundfunks in Berlin*, Berlin, 1965.

For Berlin during the last days of the Third Reich see Joachim Fest: *Inside Hitler's Bunker: The Last Days of the Third Reich*, tr. Margot Bettauer Bembo, New York, 2004.

For Berlin under Soviet military administration see Winfried Ranke et al.: *Kultur, Pajoks und Care-Pakete. Eine Berliner Chronik 1945–1949*, Berlin, 1990.

For Paula Himmler's denazification see file in the Main State Archives, Düsseldorf.

For Dinslaken under the Nazis see Dinslaken Town Archives (ed.): *Dinslaken in der NS-Zeit. Vergessene Geschichte 1933–1945*, Dinslaken, 1983; Anselm Faust: *Die 'Kristallnacht' im Rheinland. Dokumente zum Judenpogrom im November 1938*, Düsseldorf, 1987, including Yitzhak Sophoni Herz on Dinslaken; for further information I thank Anne Prior.

On Heinrich Himmler's end see Fraenkel and Manvell: op. cit.

On Marga and Gudrun Himmler's internment see Lebert and Lebert: op. cit.

16. 'A Victim of His Brother'

Documents on Paula's setting-up of her business in Dinslaken Town Archives.

For the Nuremberg Trials and Oswald Pohl as accused see Jörg Friedrich: *Die kalte Amnestie. NS-Täter in der Bundesrepublik*, Munich, 1994; Norbert Frei: *Adenauer's Germany and the Nazi Past: The Politics of Amnesty and Integration*, tr. Joel Golb, New York, 2002.

Advertising leaflet of *Gemeinschaftswerbung Herrenhut* from the 1950s in a review of an exhibition in H-SOZ-U-KULT (H-NET).

For Gudrun Himmler after the war see Lebert and Lebert: op. cit.; Oliver Schröm and Andrea Röpke: *Stille Hilfe für braune Kameraden. Das geheime Netzwerk der Alt- und Neonazis. Ein Inside-Report*, Berlin, 2001.

For Karl Wolff see Jochen von Lang: *Top Nazi: Karl Wolff: The Man between Hitler and Himmler*, New York, 2005.

For Hedwig Potthast after the war see Koch: op. cit., and *Geheim-Depot Schweiz: Wie Banken am Holocaust verdienen*, Munich, 1997.

Epilogue: Family Stories

For the history of Cracow see Thomas Urban: *Von Krakau bis Danzig. Eine Reise durch die deutsch-polnische Geschichte*,

Notes

Munich, 2000; Katarzyna Jone and Christiane Rahn: *Warschau/Krakau*, Bielefeld, 1997; Folkert Lenz: 'Nachkolorierte Erinnerungen', *taz* 22/23 Aug. 1998.

Niklas Frank: *In the Shadow of the Reich*, tr. Q. S. Wensinger with Carole Clew-Hoey, New York, 1991.

Martin S. Bergmann, Milton E. Jucovy (eds): *Generations of the Holocaust*, New York, 1982.

Christian Staffa, Katherine Klinger (eds): *Die Gegenwart der Geschichte des Holocaust. Intergenerationelle Tradierung und Kommunikation der Nachkommen*, Berlin, 1998, including Kurt Grünberg: 'Schweigen und Ver-Schweigen. Zur Differenz der Bearbeitungsformen in Opfer- und Täterzusammenhängen'.

Bibliography

Ackermann, Joseph, *Heinrich Himmler als Ideologe*, Göttingen, 1970

Bauer, Richard, et al. (eds), *München – 'Hauptstadt der Bewegung'*, catalogue of exhibition at Munich City Museum, 2002

Bracher, Karl-Dietrich, et al., *Die Weimarer Republik 1918–1933*, Bonn, 1987

Broszat, Martin, *Nationalsozialistische Polenpolitik 1939–1945*, Stuttgart, 1961

——*The Hitler State: The Foundation and Development of the Internal Structure of the Third Reich*, tr. John W. Hiden, London, New York, 1981

Browder, George C., *Hitler's Enforcers: The Gestapo and the SS Security Service in the Nazi Revolution*, New York, 1996

Dierker, Wolfgang, *Himmlers Glaubenskrieger*, Paderborn, 2002

Haffner, Sebastian, *Defying Hitler: A Memoir*, tr. Oliver Pretzel, London, New York, 2002

Kershaw, Ian, *Hitler: A Profile in Power*, London, 1991

Kersten, Felix, *Totenkopf und Treue. Heinrich Himmler ohne Uniform*, Hamburg, 1952

Bibliography

Klee, Ernst, *Das Personenlexikon zum Dritten Reich*, Frankfurt am Main, 2003

Koch, Peter Ferdinand, *Himmlers graue Eminenz – Oswald Pohl*, Hamburg, 1988

——, *Geheim-Depot Schweiz: Wie Banken am Holocaust verdienen*, Munich, 1997

Könnemann, Erwin, *Einwohnerwehren und Zeitfreiwilligenverbände*, East Berlin, 1969

Lebert, Norbert and Stefan, *My Father's Keeper: Children of Nazi Leaders – An Intimate History of Damage and Denial*, London 2001

Ludwig, Karl-Heinz, *Technik und Ingenieure im Dritten Reich*, Düsseldorf, 1974

Luther, Rudolf, *Blau oder Braun? Der Volksbund für das Deutschtum im Ausland im NS-Staat 1933–1937*, Neumünster, 1999

Manvell, Roger and Fraenkel, Heinrich, *Heinrich Himmler*, London, 1965

Musial, Bogdan, *Deutsche Zivilverwaltung und Judenvervolgung im Generalgouvernement. Eine Fallstudie zum Distrikt Lublin 1939–1944*, Wiesbaden, 1999

Reichel, Peter, *Der schöne Schein des Dritten Reiches. Faszination und Gewalt des Faschismus*, Munich, 1991

Smith, Bradley F., *Heinrich Himmler: A Nazi in the Making, 1900–1926*, Stanford, 1971

Weinbrenner, Hans-Joachim, (ed.) *Handbuch des deutschen Rundfunks 1938*, Heidelberg, 1938

Wildt, Michael, *Generation des Unbedingten*, Hamburg, 2003

Sources

US Holocaust Memorial Museum

Marga Himmler's Diaries (1999.A.0092).

US National Archives

Minutes of the interrogation of Hedwig Potthast on 22 May
1945, in IRR, Himmler files, XE-00632.

Federal Archives

NS 6 Akten der Partei-Kanzlei der NSDAP (files of the
Chancellery of the NSDAP)
NS 12 Akten des NS Lehrerbundes (files of the NS Teachers'
Association)
NS 14 Akten des Hauptamtes für Technik – Reichswaltung
des NS-Bundes deutscher Technik (files of the Central
Office for Technology – Reich administration of the NS
Association for German Technology)
NS 19 Persönlicher Stab Reichsführer SS (Personal Staff of
the Reichsführer SS)

Sources

NS 26 Hauptarchiv der NSDAP (main archive of the NSDAP)

R 55 Reichsministerium für Volksaufklärung und Propaganda (Reich Ministry for Public Enlightenment and Propaganda)

R 58 Reichssicherheitshauptamt (Central Security Department of the Reich)

R 78 Reichsrundfunkgesellschaft (Reich Broadcasting Company)

Bestand SSO, SM and RHSA-Personalakten (personal files on SS officers and men, and of the Central Security Department)

Bestand REM Reichserziehungsministerium: Personalakte Gebhard Himmler (holdings of the Reich Education Ministry, Gebhard Himmler's personal file)

O.238 Sammelordner Heinrich Himmler, Allgemeines, Persönliches, Reden (box file: Heinrich Himmler – general, personal material, speeches)

O.280 Sammelordner Technik (box file: technology)

O.427 Sammelordner SS-Hauptamt/SS-Führerpersonalhauptamt (box file: SS Central Office, SS Personnel Department, leaders)

O.429 Sammelordner SS-Führerlisten (box file: SS lists of leaders)

N 1126 Nachlass Himmler (Himmler's papers)

Zwischenarchiv Dahlwitz-Hoppegarten

ZM 213 (Sammelakte – collective file) and A 14 (Ernst Himmler)

ZA IV (Dr Klaus Hubmann)

Sources

Landesarchiv Berlin

Berliner Einwohnermeldekartei (card index of residents' registration), Ernst Himmler

State Archives, Düsseldorf

Entnazifierungsakten (denazification files), Paula Himmler und Marga Himmler

Historisches Archiv der TU, Munich

Personalakten Gebhard und Ernst Himmler (Gebhard and Ernst Himmler's personal files)

Town Archives, Dinslaken

Personaldokumente Familie Melters (personal documents on the Melters family)

Standesamt Berlin-Schöneberg/Tempelhof

Heiratsurkunde Heinrich Himmler und Marga Boden (Heinrich Himmler and Marga Boden's marriage certificate)

Sources

Bezirksamt Charlottenburg/Wilmersdorf, Abteilung Bauwesen

Akte 259 der Städtischen Baupolizei (Haus Brombeerweg)
(file 259 of the City Building Control Department – the
Brombeerweg house)

SS Ranks

Reichsführer SS	Heinrich Himmler
Obergruppenführer	general
Gruppenführer	lieutenant general
Brigadeführer	major general
Oberführer	brigadier
Standartenführer	colonel
Obersturmbannführer	lieutenant colonel
Sturmbannführer	major
Obersturmführer	lieutenant
Untersturmführer	2nd lieutenant
Oberscharführer	quartermaster sergeant
Scharführer	staff sergeant
Unterscharführer	sergeant
Sturmmann	lance corporal
Mann	private